GUN DI

Buyers Guide to
Assault Weapons

Phillip Peterson

© 2008 By Krause Publications
Published by

Gun Digest® Books

An imprint of F+W Publications
700 East State Street • Iola, WI 54990-0001
715-445-2214 • 888-457-2873
www.gundigestbooks.com

Our toll-free number to place an order or obtain
a free catalog is (800) 258-0929.

Library of Congress Control Number: 2008925112

ISBN-13: 978-0-89689-680-2

ISBN-10: 0-89689-680-3

Designed by Marilyn McGrane

Edited by Dan Shideler

Printed in the United States of America

Contents

FOREWORD

Gun Digest Buyers Guide to Assault Weapons includes a variety of firearms that might be categorized as an "assault weapon" by those that have knowledge or interest in firearms.

The main criteria for inclusion in this guide are that the firearm be semi-automatic and accept detachable magazines that hold more than ten rounds of ammunition. A few, such as the Barrett M-82 and SVD Draganov sniper rifle, have ten-round magazines but due to their design they are still included. While military type features such as a pistol grip, flash hider, bayonet mount or folding stock are found on many rifles, there are some guns found herein that have a more traditional "sporting" appearance. Some of this is due to legislation that dictates legality based on the appearance of the firearm.

The Classics

Many semi-automatic AW designs manufactured over the last forty years are based on existing select-fire models being used in actual military service. Some are made by the original manufacturer while others are copies made by commercial companies wishing to cash in on the U.S. civilian arms market. The "original manufacturer-built" firearms are what I refer to as classics.

During research for this book I was surprised to find out how many of the makers of the world's true assault weapons have offered semi-automatic versions on the U.S. market. This began in 1964 with the introduction of the Colt AR-15. This legendary rifle is still made in a cosmetically altered form by its original manufacturer today (and by many, many others).

Most of the other classic designs were made in other countries. The FN-FAL, HK G-3, CETME, Valmet, Galil, Steyr AUG, FAMAS, SIG AMT and more were legally imported to the U.S. in the 1960s and '70s. When these models were first on the open market they were not great sellers. Most were too expensive to appeal to the average shooter. Some of these classic models were imported in limited quantities; in some cases only 100 or so ever came to the U.S.

In addition to the classics, there were several independent designs that were manufactured by small companies. Many of there were designed by fans of the classics and incorporated desirable features in new models. Guns that might fit in this category include the Ruger Mini-14, Bushmaster ARM pistol, Holloway HAC-7, Wilkinson Arms Terry carbine and Leader Mk5. Some of these were made in small quantities and the companies folded quietly without much notice. Others, such as the Ruger Mini-14, continue to be popular models.

In the mid 1980s the demand for these military lookalike firearms began to grow faster than it had in the previous twenty years. This might be attributed to a new generation of shooters coming of age, one whose members had grown up viewing these type firearms on the news and in movies. The generation of WWII-era shooters had mostly favored traditional steel and walnut firearms. The younger group of enthusiasts was more accepting of the alloy and stamped construction with synthetic stocks. The American firearm press and industry began using the term "assault weapon" to identify this evolving class of firearms.

Unfortunately, the 1980s saw a growth in the criminal misuse of firearms. When a criminal used a semi-automatic UZI carbine to murder twenty people in a fast food restaurant in San Ysidro, California, in 1984, the national media focused much negative attention to the type of firearms used. Other mass shootings followed. Despite the fact that few of this type of firearm were ever used in everyday street crime, the media and antigun politicians jumped on the band wagon to demonize this class of firearms and those who owned them.

Subsequently, California passed a ban on the sale of or import into the state of new semi-automatic assault weapons. Those who had them could register and keep them but no new ones could be brought into the state. This California legislation was the first large-scale effort to ban guns by model name and physical characteristics.

The big change occurred in 1989 when the Reagan administration banned the import of firearms that did not meet a "sporting use" criteria set forth in Federal law. The sporting-use rules had been on the books since the Gun Control Act of 1968 but the definition was revised to ban import of firearms previously deemed acceptable. See the legal chapter for the text of the sporting use criteria and banned features.

The import ban affected foreign firearms but domestic production continued as before. Unfortunately, in 1989 there were not that many domestic designs on the market. Prices for the pre-ban imported guns shot through the roof. The period from 1989 to 1994 saw an increased demand for many models that had been slow sellers before the ban. Ever eager to fulfill the wants of American buyers, some U.S. manufacturers had begun building new firearms using American made receivers with imported parts. The government moved to close this "loophole" by imposing the parts count rules listed in Federal regulation 922r.

As they observed with horror the growing demand for assault weapons among American shooters, the anti-gun forces were relieved when a like-minded president was elected in 1992. The Clinton administration joined with members of congress to push through the infamous Assault Weapon ban of 1994. This law was one of the least effective pieces of firearm legislation ever passed. First, it "grandfathered" all existing firearms and allowed them to be freely owned and transferred as before. Next, it defined "Assault Weapon" by the external characteristics of the firearm, listing several features that were found on pre-ban models: pistol grip, flash hider, folding stock, etc. See the Legal section for a copy of this law. A firearm could be legal if it had any one of these characteristics. If it had two or more it was banned. Finally, in order to get the legislation past some pro-gun factions they added a ten-year sunset provision. This meant that unless congress voted to renew the law, it would expire after ten years.

So from 1994-2004, the American firearms industry built guns that complied with the definitions set forth by the law. This resulted in oddities such as AR-15s with pinned collapsible stocks, permanent recoil compensators and American-made AKs without bayonet lug and flash hider. Of course, many of the anti-gun congressmen who fought for the law complained that these things were violating the "spirit" of the law. Some small manufacturers that had begun business in the late 1980's grew rapidly when they began shipping new ban-compliant versions. But tell an American shooter he can't have a gun today that he could have had yesterday, and that shooter will suddenly desire the gun he previously didn't want. People used their ban-compliant firearms for a decade, all the while nursing their desire for pre-ban models.

While much of America saw that the ban was meaningless and ineffective, many gun owners were quietly waiting for the ban to expire.

The Dam Breaks

When the assault weapons ban sunset in September of 2004, there were many manufacturers and retailers waiting to begin supplying the models they had been unable to sell for a decade, and there was an unprecedented demand for this type of gun that had been building for a decade. 2004 was the dawn of a new age for the American firearms industry.

While other facets of the firearm market were static or slowly shrinking, the demand for assault weapons is expanding to this day. Much can be attributed to the fact that the anti-gun forces continue to fight for a renewal of the assault weapons ban – but this time without a sunset clause. Additionally, they want to close any loopholes that allowed any configuration of the banned firearms to remain legal to manufacture. Thus, manufacturers and their customers feel that "the clock is ticking," and this naturally fuels a huge demand for this type of firearm.

As of early 2008 there are several new manufacturers filling demand in the assault weapons market. There are currently more than twenty companies that make versions of the AR-15. The only difference in these lies in the quality of the parts used and a few proprietary features that some are offering. Most makers of AR-style weapons are filling orders as fast as they can ship them. With some, production is three months or more behind. The same is true for AK-47/AKM series. There are at least a dozen U.S. manufactures that build new Kalashnikov rifles using new American receivers along with domestic and imported parts.

Heavy Iron

Another growing segment of the market is the semi-automatic versions of true machine guns and submachine guns. The U.S. Browning Model 1919 belt fed was one of the first models to be offered. They have been available for over a decade from a few small manufacturers. After 2004 there have been several new models added to the list. If you want a new semi automatic German MG-34, British Bren, Russian RPD, DP-28, PPSH, U.S. M-60, 1918 BAR and several others, all you need do is fork over the cash. These firearms are built with new semi-automatic receivers along with some original parts that have been modified to function only in semi-automatic mode.

Home Gunsmithing

Finally, I must mention another significant trend that started back in the 1990s. I call it "rolling your own." This is when a new receiver is purchased by the end user, who builds a functional firearm around it using new custom or used surplus parts.

There have been AR-15 lower receivers available on the market since the late 1970s but since 2004 the number of models being assembled by the end user has grown. One can currently purchase finished semi-automatic receivers for the CETME, G-3, FN FAL, M-14, AK Series, U.S. M-1 carbine, M 1917mg, M-2 .50 mg, and others. Due to the fact that each non-factory firearm is unique, this book does not list pricing for these "kit" guns.

When examining an unfamiliar "home built" firearm it is important to consider the skills of the builder and the quality of the parts used. This is especially true for the countless AR-15 type firearms out there on the market. With all the major companies selling their lower receivers and any combination of upper assemblies it is impossible to know for sure which guns are factory assembled and tested or one assembled by a hobbyist in his garage. There are also small companies that buy receivers and assemble custom guns for resale.

Be careful when buying, and enjoy your assault rifle responsibly.

Phillip Peterson
Albion, Indiana

Introduction: What's in a Name?

Assault Weapon.

Those words, on the cover of this book, are probably what drew you to pick it up. "Assault weapon" is a term that causes arguments within the pro-gun community. Any use of the terms "assault weapon" or "assault rifle" by media or politicians is attacked by some pro-gun writers, organizations and many firearm owners. Long wordy debates take place on internet message boards arguing the definitions and usage of terms.

Why is that?

The main reason seems to be that the term has gained use by the anti-gun movement and media. Whenever a crime is committed with a semi-automatic military pattern firearm, the mainstream media will quickly jump in with headlines like "assault weapon used in killing spree" or "drug sweep nets assault weapons." The only time many in the non-gun owning public are exposed to this class of firearms is through negative media exposure.

If you use the historically applied terminology, an assault weapon must be capable of full-automatic fire, i.e., a machine gun. The term assault rifle had its beginning with the Germans during WWII and was applied to a new class of firearm: the "SturmGewehr," or storm rifle, properly known as the MP-44.

This is generally considered to be the first true assault rifle. It was a select-fire rifle that used an intermediate-sized rifle cartridge called the 8x33mm Kurz (short).

The intermediate cartridge concept helps define an assault rifle in military circles. The intermediate cartridge is smaller than the rifle cartridges used in belt-fed machine guns and larger than the pistol cartridges used in submachine guns. Intermediate cartridges are what many semi-automatic assault weapons chamber. These include the 5.56mm (.223), 7.62x51mm (.308), 7.62x39mm, and 5.54x39mm.

What is an assault weapon? If one were to use a strict definition, it could be ANY object that is used against another individual to cause bodily harm. That can be a firearm, a rock or a feather poked in the eye. The military definition was discussed in the last paragraph. In the context of this book, however, "assault weapon" refers to a semi-automatic firearm that accepts high capacity magazines (10+ rounds) and is patterned after military issue select-fire weapons. This can mean an exact copy of an existing design, minus the components that allow full-automatic fire. Or it can be a new design that utilizes similar characeristics.

The popularly-held idea that the term "assault weapon" originated with anti-gun activists, media or politicians is wrong. The term was first adopted by the manufacturers, wholesalers, importers and dealers in the American firearms industry to stimulate sales of certain firearms that did not have an appearance that was familiar to many firearm owners. The manufacturers and gun writers of the day needed a catchy name to identify this new type of gun.

The fact that some of the semi-automatic versions of the military-style firearms retained their bayonet lugs, extended pistol grips, high capacity magazines, folding stocks and even threading for muzzle brakes and grenade launchers has been used to erroneously define "assault weapons." But these design features were part of the attraction to this kind of firearm. All of these features are merely cosmetic and there is little if any evidence that their inclusion on a gun has been essential to some specific criminal use.

Look in many 1980s-era editions of *Gun Digest* and you will find listings of several makes and models of guns that were categorized as assault rifles or assault pistols. There were also some issues of a magazine called *The Complete Book of Assault Rifles* published in the 1980s. *Guns & Ammo* magazine published at least one issue of a magazine with the title *Assault Rifles: The New Breed of Sporting Arm*. And the truth is that many gun owners have used and still use the term in everyday conversations about firearms.

Some alternate monikers suggested by the never-call-them-assault-weapons crowd include paramilitary firearms, military pattern semi-automatics, homeland defense rifles, tactical firearms, sports utility rifles, EBRs (Evil Black Rifles), or simply firearms. I tend to favor the term neat guns, but that could be just about any gun. There needs to be a commonly understood name for this type of firearm that does not require a drawn out definition. It really should not be that complicated.

Whatever arguments can be made about what terminology to use, the name assault weapon has been defined by law with the passage of several state and local AW laws and by the Federal Assault Weapon Ban, also known as the Crime Control and Law Enforcement Act of 1994. This law, and most of the others, regulate these firearms by model name and characteristics. (See the chapter on legal issues to read the exact wording of the currently expired Federal AW law.) By using the term "assault weapon" throughout the text of the law, they have forever added this name to the American dictionary.

HOW TO USE THIS BOOK

The firearm entries in this book are listed in alphabetical order. Most entries are listed by manufacturer. Some foreign firearms are listed under an importer's name if that name is more commonly associated with the model that the actual company that manufactured it. A few are listed by model name if the gun is usually known by that. We also try to include cross references for some obscure items, in case the reader knows the model name but the actual manufacturer, or if the importer is not apparent.

Condition Ratings

This guide uses five condition categories: MSRP, NIB, Excellent, Very Good, and Good.

MSRP (Manufacturer Suggested Retail Price)

If a manufacturer lists a suggested retail price in their catalogs or on a web site that price is included here. The price listed is for the base model firearm as described in company sources. Please remember that many current production firearms are offered with a variety of options that can change the actual price to be paid. While the price of a few of these add-on options might be mentioned, it is not possible to list every feature in this book.

Another thing to bear in mind when reading a MSRP is that guns rarely sell at MSRP. The retail markup in the firearms business varies by seller. With a lot of wholesale pricing available to the public, few retailers can expect to charge full MSRP. There is a great deal of competition among retailers and any who insist on charging full MSRP may be sitting on inventory for a while. However, with the nature of supply and demand, some hard to get models may actually bring more than MSRP, especially if there is any legislation pending that could ban or limit future manufacture.

NIB (New in Box)

This term refers to unfired, pristine-condition currently-manufactured merchandise that is not advertised with a MSRP. The NIB price reflects the trend in price at retailer outlets. We have decided not to list out-of-production items with a NIB price. The reason is that there are too many variables in pricing this way that can ot be reflected in this sort of guide. For instance, consider a 30-year-old FN FAL that is unfired in the box, along with all the items that originally were shipped with the rifle. These items would likely add $250-$1000 to the price for a collector who wants the best possible example of this model. But what about lightly used but still in the box? What is a box worth? On the FAL, it would still add quite a bit to the price with some buyers. With a Norinco AK-47/s, maybe not so much. One must also consider what items originally were included in the box with the firearm. How much to subtract from a price for missing magazines, cleaning kits or instruction manuals? That's a tough question, and one that depends entirely on the buyer.

Excellent

Collector quality firearms in this condition are highly desirable. The firearm must retain at least 98 percent of the factory original finish. Synthetic stocks, forearms and pistol grips should have no appreciable wear or scratches. The firearm must also be in 100 percent original factory condition without refinishing, repair, alterations, or additions of any kind. Sights must be factory original as well. The price listed includes one standard capacity original magazine. Prices for extra magazines and add-ons such as optics are not included in pricing.

Very Good

Firearms in this category are also sought afte,r both by the collector and the shooter. Firearms must be in working order and retain approximately 90 percent metal and wood finish. Synthetic stocks, forearms and pistol grips can have minor cosmetic scratches and surface wear. It must be 100 percent factory original, but may have some small repairs, alterations, or non-factory additions. No refinishing is permitted in this category. The bore should remain bright and shiney with no sign of wear or corrosion.

Good

Firearms must retain at least 80 percent metal and wood finish. Synthetic stocks, forearms and pistol grips might have obvious surface wear or scratches. They should not have cracks or pieces chipped off. Small repairs, alterations, or non-factory additions are sometimes encountered in this class. Factory replacement parts are permitted. The overall working condition of the firearm must be good as well as safe. The bore may exhibit wear or some corrosion.

Semi-automatic assault weapons are rarely found in a condition that rates below good. The oldest of these firearms is just over 40 years old and most were made for the civilian market and have not seen much actual use.

The Romance of Retail Pricing

The firearms prices listed in this book are RETAIL PRICES. Any firearm can bring more or less depending on many variables. If you choose to sell your gun to a dealer, you will not receive the retail price but instead a wholesale price based on the markup that particular dealer needs to operate.

Also, in certain cases there will be no price indicated under a particular condition but rather the notation "N/A" or the symbol "—". This indicates that there is no known price available for that gun in that condition or the sales for that particular model are so few that a reliable price cannot be given. This will usually be encountered only with very rare guns, and with newly introduced firearms.

The prices listed here come from a variety of sources: retail stores, gun shows, individual collectors, and auction houses. Due to the nature of business, one will usually pay higher prices at a retail store than at a gun show. In some cases, internet auctions will produce excellent buys or extravagant prices, depending on any given situation.

In recent years, internet sales of semi-automatic assault weapons firearms has become a major factor in this market. Auction sites such as www.GunBroker.com or www.AuctionArms.com have over taken storefront or gun show purchases for many buyers.

In my own business, I find that the auction sites bring me more buyers with more money than I ever had from traditional venues. I usually set up at gun shows to buy merchandise and then sell it online so as to reach more buyers. The better quality firearms I find rarely get displayed on my gun show table, they sell on line first, frequently for more than they will bring locally. The downside of this for those not participating in the internet revolution is that they are missing out on a lot of interesting firearms that will never be offered in any other venue. This internet selling has levelled out the market. Any pricing found online is going to reflect a nationwide trend.

In the "old days" one could find seasonal and regional differences in the prices of firearms. A small gun or pawn shop in the middle of farm country might have had a Poly Tech Legend AK-47 priced at $650 sit on the shelf for years. The local buyers purchase their firearms for hunting, not casual shooting or collecting. Now these local dealers need only offer these slow selling guns on the internet and they suddenly have the entire country as potential customers. Throw that Poly Tech up on an internet auction and it would easily bring $1200-1800.

Collectors will sometimes pay higher prices for a firearm that they need to fill out their collection, when in other circumstances they will not be willing to pay market price if they don't have to have the gun. Then there is also a number of persons or companies that buy up of assault weapons in speculation that future legislation will drive the prices up. Their primary goal is to make a large profit in times of panic buying. The point here is that prices paid for firearms is an ever-changing affair based on a large number of variables. The prices in this book are a GENERAL GUIDE as to what a willing buyer and willing seller might agree on. You may find the item for less, and then again you may have to pay more depending on the variables of a particular situation. There is a saying among collectors that goes "I didn't pay too much for this gun, I bought it too soon." This reflects a solid trend with firearms that the prices continue to rise with each year. This is especially true with semi automatic assault weapons. With the likelihood that future Federal, State or Local leglislation will restrict or completely stop the manufacture or import of these type of firearms the prices can rapidly fluctuate. If news of any significant change in the status of these guns reaches the public watch out for a buying panic that will drive prices through the roof. It has happened before and will undoubtedly occur again in the future.

In the final analysis, the prices listed here are given to assist the shooter and collector in pursuing their hobby with a better understanding of what is going on in the marketplace. If this book can expand one's knowledge, then it will have fulfilled its purpose.

MANUFACTURER'S LISTINGS

AMERICAN INDUSTRIES
Cleveland, Ohio

(dba Calico Light Weapons System of Sparks, Nevada)

■ CALICO M-100

A .22LR semi-automatic carbine. It has a 16-1/8 inch barrel that ends in a flash hider. Synthetic hand guards. Folding steel stock. The Calico firearms utilize a unique high capacity helical magazine that holds 100 rounds. Manufactured 1989-98. Re-introduced in 2004, after expiration of the assault weapon ban.

MSRP	EXC.	V.G.	GOOD
637	550	475	400

Note: *add $100-150 for each functional 100 round magazine.*

■ MODEL 100P/M-110

A pistol version of the M-100. It has a 6 inch barrel that ends with a muzzle brake. No shoulder stock.

MSRP	EXC.	V.G.	GOOD
688	500	425	375

CALICO MODEL 100P

■ MODEL 100S SPORTER/M-105

A Model 100 carbine with solid walnut stock and forearm.

EXC.	V.G.	GOOD
600	525	450

CALICO MODEL 100S SPORTER

■ MODEL 101 SOLID STOCK CARBINE

Introduced shortly after passage of the 1994 assault weapon ban, this is a Model 100 with a fixed stock made from synthetic material.

EXC.	V.G.	GOOD
500	425	350

■ MODEL 900 / LIBERTY 1

A 9mm semi-automatic carbine. It uses a unique retarded blowback method of operation. 16 inch barrel. Fixed rear sight. Adjustable front sight. Collapsible shoulder stock. 50 or 100 round helical magazine. Manufactured 1989-90 and 1992-93. Re-introduced after 2004 as the Liberty series. Top photo shows 50 round version; bottom shows 100 round.

MSRP	EXC.	V.G.	GOOD
875	700	625	550

■ MODEL 900-S / LIBERTY II

As above with a fixed synthetic shoulder stock.

MSRP	EXC.	V.G.	GOOD
875	650	575	500

■ MODEL 950 PISTOL / LIBERTY III PISTOL

A handgun version of the model 900. It has a 6 inch barrel. Shipped with a 50 round magazine.

MSRP	EXC.	V.G.	GOOD
872	600	525	450

■ MODEL 951T TACTICAL RIFLE

A Model 950 with the addition of a muzzle brake and a hand grip on the forearm. Manufactured 1990-94.

EXC.	V.G.	GOOD
750	675	600

Note: *There are .40 S&W caliber versions of Calico products slated for introduction in 2008.*

AMERICAN TACTICAL IMPORTS
Rochester, New York

Imports a rifle made by German Sports Guns.

■ GSG-5

A .22LR semi-automatic carbine patterned after the Heckler and Koch MP-5 sub-machine gun. 16-1/4 inch barrel covered with an outer tube to simulate a suppressor. Total length 33-1/2 inches. Fixed stock, 22 round magazine. The first shipment cleared BATF approval in January, 2008.

MSRP	EXC.	V.G.	GOOD
500	475	425	375

ARMALITE
Costa Mesa, California

In business 1959 through the 1970's.

■ AR-180

5.56mm/.223 semi-automatic. 18-1/4 inch barrel. Side folding stock. Originally designed to be a low cost alternative to the M-16, the fully automatic AR-18 used steel stampings for major components instead of machined parts. No major military contracts were placed for the select fire version but the semi-automatic AR-180 found some success on the civilian market. It was manufactured by three makers under the Armalite name.

ARMALITE AR-180

▶ **Armalite 1969-72**

EXC.	V.G.	GOOD
1500	1200	900

▶ **Howa, Japan 1972-74**

EXC.	V.G.	GOOD
1400	1100	800

▶ **Sterling, England 1976-1979**

EXC.	V.G.	GOOD
1100	900	750

ARMALITE, INC.
Geneseo, Ill.

Current manufacturer. Formed in 1995, after Eagle Arms purchased the old Armalite name.

■ 7.62X51MM/.308 RIFLES

▶ AR-10A2

The 7.62mm equivalent of the famed M16A2. 20 inch chrome lined double lapped barrel. A2 style upper receiver. Weight 9.8lbs. The AR-10 series uses modified M-14 20 round magazines.

MSRP	EXC.	V.G.	GOOD
1506	1250	1100	950

ARMALITE AR-10A2

▶ AR-10A2 Carbine

The AR-10 A2 Carbine is the compact companion to the Infantry Model, with the convenient 16 inch long barrel. The handy intermediate length handguards provide more flexibility in hand position than the shorty handguards and the 12 inch intermediate gas tube improves reliability over the shorter gas tube.

MSRP	EXC.	V.G.	GOOD
1506	1250	1100	950

**ARMALITE
AR-10A2 CARBINE**

▶ AR-10A4 SPR

Combining the tactical build of the AR-10 A2 rifle with the MIL STD 1913 (Picatinny rail) receiver and gas block of the AR-10(T) rifle, the AR-10 A4 model provides the tactical flexibility of removable conventional sights with ArmaLite's sturdy telescopic sight mounts. The barrel is a double-lapped barrel to retain better accuracy and chrome lined to provide corrosion resistance. At home, on the range or in the field, the AR-10 A4 model is a serious rifle for tactical or sport purposes.

MSRP	EXC.	V.G.	GOOD
1506	1250	1100	950

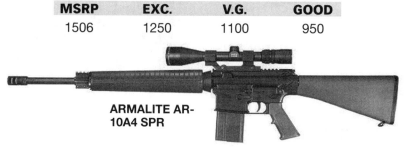

ARMALITE AR-10A4 SPR

The AR-10A4 Carbine offers the same sighting choices as the AR-10A4 SPR in a handy compact format. Hard hitting and rugged, at home, on the range or in the field. All our AR-10A4 and AR-10(T) rifles feature our clamping gas block, allowing the removable front sight to be rotated to zero. This assures that the rear sight is centered and full left and right windage movement is available when shooting in strong winds. Post-ban model available.

MSRP	EXC.	V.G.	GOOD
1506	1250	1100	950

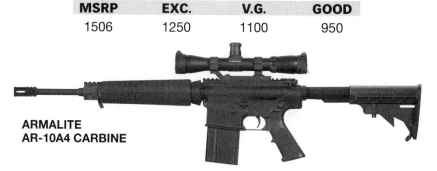

**ARMALITE
AR-10A4 CARBINE**

▶ AR-10B

The .308 caliber AR-10B is the perfect rifle for those collectors who could only wish for an ArmaLite in its early days. The AR-10B represents ArmaLite's return to some of the early features that captured the imagination of millions. A closer copy of the original AR-10 produced in the 1960's. The AR-10B features the unique charging handle in the carry handle of the first AR-10 rifles, brown Sudanese style furniture, elevation scale window, and the famed ArmaLite Pegasus Logo. 20 inch barrel.

MSRP	EXC.	V.G.	GOOD
1699	1500	1300	1100

ARMALITE AR-10B

▶ AR-10 Super SASS Rifle

The Latest Evolution in the Era of AR Innovation, the Armalite AR-10 SuperSASS is the ultimate suppressed, long range rifle system available. Engineering innovations include the adjustable gas system to optimize rifle function with suppressor as well as the AR designed enhancements that our engineers have made standard on every Armalite AR-10; improved reliability of feeding, extraction and ejection.

MSRP	EXC.	V.G.	GOOD
2999	2500	2100	1700

ARMALITE AR-10
SUPER SASS RIFLE

▶ AR-10 (T) Rifle

The AR-10(T)TM offers outstanding accuracy and reliability for both competition and tactical use. The triple lapped stainless steel barrel floats within a rugged fiberglass handguard. The Mil Standard sight base (Picatinny rail) on the upper receiver and the gas block allow for rapid and repeatable interchange of removable iron or scope sights.

Featuring the famed ArmaLite machined, tool-steel National Match two stage trigger group, the AR-10(T) is Armalite's top of the line rifle.

MSRP	EXC.	V.G.	GOOD
2126	1800	1600	1400

ARMALITE
AR-10 (T) RIFLE

■ 5.56MM/.223 RIFLES

▶ M14A4

Carbine with M203 Step Down Barrel The same model carried by the Illinois State Police is now commercially available. 16 inch barrel. Flat top receiver with picatinny rail and removable carrying handle.

MSRP	EXC.	V.G.	GOOD
1040	900	750	600

ARMALITE M14A4

▶ M14A4 Carbine with A4 Front Sight

The 15A4CBA2 combines the flexibility of the MIL STD 1913 upper receiver with the strength of the fixed A2 front sights, and ArmaLite's exclusive mid-length handguards provide the handiness of a 16 inch barrel, flexibility in grip position and optimal gas pulse to power the operating system.

MSRP	EXC.	V.G.	GOOD
1040	900	750	600

▶ M15A2 Rifle Service Model

The M-15A2 Rifle is ArmaLite's semi-automatic civilian version of the famed M-16A2 service rifle. Durable and reliable for long field service, its superb accuracy is based on the 20 inch double-lapped and chrome lined barrel. Includes ArmaLite's front sight base with bayonet lug and flash suppressor.

MSRP	EXC.	V.G.	GOOD
1100	900	750	600

▶ M15A2 Carbine

The carbine version of the M-15A2 rifle, the .223 caliber twin to the popular AR-10A2 Carbine, featuring ArmaLite's exclusive mid-length handguards provide the handiness of a 16 inch barrel, flexibility in grip position and an optimal gas pulse to power the operating system.

MSRP	EXC.	V.G.	GOOD
1100	900	750	600

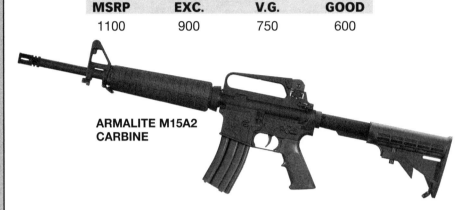

ARMALITE M15A2
CARBINE

▶ M15A2 National Match

ArmaLite's National Match rifles are specifically designed to meet the requirements of CMP (formerly DCM) sanctioned competition. More national-level military shooters have chosen ArmaLite rifles than any other brand. The M-15 A2 National Match rifles feature a special, triple-lapped barrel, National Match 1/4 windage - 1/2 elevation sights with clear digits and the strongest floating barrel sleeve in the industry.

MSRP	EXC.	V.G.	GOOD
1472	1200	1000	800

ARMALITE M15A2
NATIONAL MATCH

▶ M15A4 SPR Rifle

The M-15 A4 model offers the flexibility of the Picatinny rail applied to a standard grade .223 caliber rifle. Light recoiling and accurate, this is a fine, flexible rifle for Law Enforcement. All of ArmaLite's flat-top models accept ArmaLite's removable front sights and carry handles, and other devices conforming to MIL STD 1913 (Picatinny) rail.

MSRP	EXC.	V.G.	GOOD
1100	900	750	600

**ARMALITE M15A4
SPR RIFLE**

▶ **M15A4 Carbine**

Handy and good looking, this rifle is compact, lightweight and maneuverable. This is the .223 caliber model comparative to the famed AR-10A4 Carbine. The M-15A4 carbine provides the benefits of ArmaLite's economical flat-top flexibility in a short barreled, light recoiling format.

MSRP	EXC.	V.G.	GOOD
1100	900	750	600

**ARMALITE M15A4
CARBINE**

▶ **M15A4 SPR II National Match Rifle**

ArmaLite's National Match Rifles are unsurpassed. More national-leve military shooters have chosen ArmaLite rifles than any other brand. National Match rifles feature a special, triple-lapped stainless steel barrel, and the strongest floating barrel sleeve in the industry. The ArmaLite A4 National Match rifle allows for additional sight system flexibility by featuring a forged flattop receiver while still remaining competitive by including a removable carry handle with National Match sights.

MSRP	EXC.	V.G.	GOOD
1472	1200	1000	800

**M15A4 SPR II
NATIONAL MATCH RIFLE**

▶ M15A4 (T) Rifle

The M-15A4(T) Rifle offers outstanding accuracy and reliability for both competition and tactical use, and features the same configuration as the famed AR-10(T) Rifle in .308 but in the accurate, light recoiling smaller .223 caliber. The 24 inch triple-lapped stainless steel barrel floats within a rugged fiberglass handguard and the Military Standard sight base (Picatinny rail) on the upper receiver and gas block allow rapid and repeatable interchange of removable iron or scope sights. The M-15A4(T) features the Armalite National Match two-stage trigger.

MSRP	EXC.	V.G.	GOOD
1504	1250	1050	850

M15A4 (T) RIFLE

▶ AR-180B Rifle

With the best features of the .223 caliber M-15 and the 1st Generation AR-180 rifles, the lower on the new ArmaLite AR-180B is made of a high strength polymer and features the trigger group and magazine well of the AR-15 so that magazines and repair parts are readily available. The AR-180B upper is formed sheet metal like the 1st Generation AR-180 and features the AR-180 gas system to keep operating gasses outside the receiver. The chrome moly barrel features an integral muzzle brake and our exclusive adjustable front sight base. The new AR-180B upper and lower receiver groups are interchangeable with those of the 1st Generation AR-180, so earlier models may now be repaired by replacing the upper or lower half.

MSRP	EXC.	V.G.	GOOD
750	700	650	600

AR-180B RIFLE

ARMI JAGER
Milano, Italy

Manufacturer of a series of .22LR rifles copied from famous assault rifles. They have been imported by Bingham Ltd., Mitchell Arms and others.

■ AP-74 /M-16

A copy of the U.S. M-16 rifle. Upper and lower receivers are made from cast alloy. The early models have triangular hand guards. The newer versions have round hand guards. 15 round magazine.

EXC.	V.G.	GOOD
325	250	200

Note: There was a 7.65mm/.32 automatic version of this rifle. A few were imported, although sales were slow because of the price of ammunition. 10 round magazine. Values are as follows:

EXC.	V.G.	GOOD
400	350	300

■ AK-22

A .22-caliber copy of the Soviet AK-47. The receiver is made from cast alloy. Sheet steel top cover. 15 and 30 round magazines.

EXC.	V.G.	GOOD
400	350	300

■ GALIL-22

A .22-caliber copy of the Israeli Galil. It uses the same action as the AK-22 with a different bolt handle and rear sight. 15 and 30 round magazines.

EXC.	V.G.	GOOD
400	350	300

■ MAS-22

A .22-caliber copy of the French FAMAS rifle. Bull pup design. Same action as the AK-22. 15 and 30 round magazines.

EXC.	V.G.	GOOD
500	425	350

ARMI JAGER MAS-22

■ PPS-50

A .22-caliber copy of the Russian WWII PPSH sub-machine gun. 16 inch barrel within a perforated barrel jacket. 30 round stick or 50 round drum magazine. Price for rifle with one 30 round stick magazine. Add $100-200 for each functional drum magazine.

EXC.	V.G.	GOOD
400	350	300

ARMI JAGER PPS-50

ARMITAGE INTERNATIONAL
Seneca, South Carolina

■ SCARAB SKORPION PISTOL

A 9mm semi-automatic based on the Czech Model 61 Skorpion machine pistol. It has a 4-5/8 inch barrel with threaded muzzle. Black finish. Magazines hold 12 or 30 rounds. Approximately 600 were manufactured 1989-90. This model was recently put back in production by Leinad.

EXC.	V.G.	GOOD
550	475	400

ARMITAGE INTERNATIONAL SCARAB SKORPION PISTOL

ARMSCOR
Marikina City, Philippines

Manufacturer based in the Philippines. Maker of a line of low cost .22LR rifles that resemble the M-16 and AK. Has been imported under several names over the years, including Armscor Precision, KBI and Squires Bingham.

■ MODEL 1600

A copy of the U.S. M-16 rifle with an 18 inch barrel. Plastic stock. 10 or 15 round magazine.

EXC.	V.G.	GOOD
200	150	125

■ MODEL 1600R

As above with collapsible wire stock.

EXC.	V.G.	GOOD
225	170	140

■ MODEL 1600W

As above with mahogany stock.

EXC.	V.G.	GOOD
200	150	125

■ MODEL AK22

A .22LR copy of the Soviet AK-47. 18 inch barrel. 10 or 15 round magazines. Mahogany stock.

EXC.	V.G.	GOOD
225	190	150

■ MODEL AK22F

As above with folding wire stock.

EXC.	V.G.	GOOD
250	200	175

ARMSCORP OF AMERICA
Baltimore, Maryland

Manufacturer and importer 1982-94. They have offered custom built M-14 rifles assembled to customer specifications. Since each one is a unique item it is not practical to list all variations in this guide.

■ M-14 R RIFLE

7.62mm/.308 Excellent condition USGI M-14 parts set assembled on a new U.S. made semi-automatic receiver. Introduced 1986.

EXC.	V.G.	GOOD
1400	1000	800

■ M-14 BEGINNING NATIONAL MATCH

Built with excellent condition USGI parts and an air gauged premium barrel. Made 1993-96.

EXC.	V.G.	GOOD
1500	1100	950

■ M-14 NM (NATIONAL MATCH)

Offered with three barrel weights, NM sights, op rod and other parts. Introduced 1987.

EXC.	V.G.	GOOD
1600	1250	1000

■ M-21 MATCH RIFLE

NM rear lugged receiver. Custom barrel, stock and sights.

EXC.	V.G.	GOOD
2000	1750	1500

■ T-48 FAL ISRAELI PATTERN RIFLE

7.62mm/.308 manufactured with U.S.-made receiver and Israeli parts in original metric dimensions. Parts are interchangeable with FN Belgium made parts. Offered 1990-92

EXC.	V.G.	GOOD
1250	1000	800

■ T-48 FAL L1A1 PATTERN

Copy of English L1A1. Add $200 for wood furniture.

EXC.	V.G.	GOOD
1200	900	750

■ T-48 BUSH MODEL

Similar to Israeli pattern but with 18 inch barrel.

EXC.	V.G.	GOOD
1250	1000	800

■ FRHB

Assembled with Israeli parts. Heavy barrel with bi-pod. Offered 1990 only.

EXC.	V.G.	GOOD
1800	1500	1100

■ FAL

New Armscorp manufactured receiver with Argentine made parts. 21 inch barrel. Offered 1987-90

EXC.	V.G.	GOOD
1250	1000	800

■ FAL BUSH MODEL

As above with 18 inch barrel with flash hider. Offered 1989 only.

EXC.	V.G.	GOOD
1400	1100	900

■ FAL PARATROOPER MODEL

A Bush Model with side folding metal stock. Offered 1989 only.

EXC.	V.G.	GOOD
1900	1600	1250

■ M36 SNIPER MODEL

A 7.62mm/.308 bullpup type rifle that used a M-14 receiver. 22 inch free floating barrel with integral flash hider. Folding bipod. Copied from an Israeli design. According to some sources only 10 pieces were made in 1989.

EXC.	V.G.	GOOD
5000	4500	4000

ARSENAL, INC.
Las Vegas, Nevada

This is the current importer for AK type rifles made in Bulgaria. Several ban era variations have been discontinued. Not every variation is listed here. Pricing is in the same range as those listed.

■ 7.62X39MM RIFLES

▶ SLR-107F

Stamped receiver. 7.62x39 with a 16-1/4 inch barrel. Black or desert tan synthetic stocks. Left-side folding butt stock. Total length is 36-7/8 inches with stock open or 27-3/8 with stock folded. Flash hider, bayonet lug, accessory lug, stainless steel heat shield, 2 stage trigger, and Russian type scope rail on the Left side. Also available as a "ban" model without muzzle threads and bayonet mount. New for 2008.

MSRP	EXC.	V.G.	GOOD
879	750	700	650

ARSENAL SLR-107F

▶ SLR 107CF

Stamped receiver, 7.62x39 with a 16-1/4 inch barrel. Front sight block / gas block combination, 500m rear sight, cleaning rod. Stainless steel heat shield. Black or desert tan polymer stocks. Left-side folding butt stock, Total length is 34-1/2 inches with stock open or 25 inches with stock folded. 2 stage trigger and scope rail.

MSRP	EXC.	V.G.	GOOD
979	850	775	700

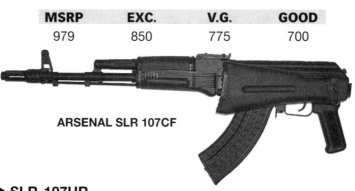

ARSENAL SLR 107CF

▶ SLR-107UR
Stamped receiver, 7.62x39 caliber, short gas system, front sight block / gas block combination, cleaning rod, black polymer furniture, stainless steel heat shield, left-side folding polymer stock, 2 stage trigger and scope rail.

MSRP	EXC.	V.G.	GOOD
979	850	775	700

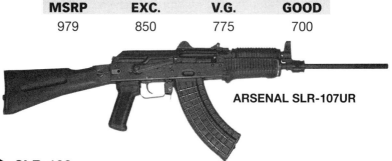

ARSENAL SLR-107UR

▶ SLR-108
Stamped receiver. Standard AK type rifle in 7.62x39mm. 16-1/4 inch barrel. Slant muzzle compensator. Fixed black polymer stock.

MSRP	EXC.	V.G.	GOOD
650	600	550	500

▶ SA M-7R
A milled receiver AK rifle in 7.62x39. Black polymer fixed stock. Available with or without threaded muzzle and bayonet lug.

MSRP	EXC.	V.G.	GOOD
970	850	775	700

▶ SA M-7 Classic
As above fitted with blond wood furniture. Discontinued.

EXC.	V.G.	GOOD
875	800	725

▶ SAS M-7

Milled receiver, front sight block with bayonet lug. 16 1/4 inch barrel with flash hider. Black polymer furniture, with collapsible underfolding buttstock. New in 2008.

MSRP	EXC	V.G.	GOOD
1250	1000	900	800

▶ SAS M-7 Classic

As above made with blond wood forearm and pistol grip.

MSRP	EXC	V.G.	GOOD
1275	1000	900	800

▶ SLR-101/SLR-96

A assault weapon ban era AK rifle with polymer thumb hole stock. Caliber 7.62x39mm. Milled receiver. Pinned muzzle break. Discontinued.

EXC.	V.G.	GOOD
650	550	450

▶ SA RPK-7

US made milled receiver. Caliber 7.62x39mm. 21 inch RPK heavy barrel, 14mm muzzle threads, muzzle nut, folding bipod, cleaning rod inside bipod, no bayonet lug, blond wood furniture, paddle style butt stock. Limited production. No pricing information available.

■ 5.56MM/.223 RIFLES

▶ SLR-106F

Stamped receiver, 5.56 NATO caliber, Left side folding polymer stock. 16-1/4 inch barrel with muzzle brake, bayonet lug, accessory lug, stainless steel heat shield and 2-stage trigger.

MSRP	EXC.	V.G.	GOOD
799	700	625	550

ARSENAL SLR-106F

▶ SLR-106F With Metal Stock

Stamped receiver, 5.56 NATO caliber, original metal left-side folding stock, 16-1/4 inch barrel with muzzle brake, bayonet lug, accessory lug, stainless steel heat shield and 2 stage trigger.

MSRP	EXC	V.G.	GOOD
749	675	600	525

▶ SLR-106UR

Stamped receiver. Cal. 5.56mm NATO. 16-1/4 inch barrel. Short gas system. Black polymer furniture. Left side folding stock. Replica dummy suppressor.

MSRP	EXC.	V.G.	GOOD
1179	1000	N/A	N/A

ARSENAL SLR-106UR

▶ SA M-5

US made milled receiver. Caliber 5.56mm Nato. 16-1/4 inch barrel. Muzzle brake, cleaning rod, bayonet lug, black polymer furniture. NATO pact buttstock. Discontinued

EXC.	V.G.	GOOD
800	700	600

▶ SA RPK-5

US made milled receiver. 21 inch RPK heavy barrel, cal 5.56mm. Folding bipod, cleaning rod inside bipod, no bayonet lug, blond wood furniture, paddle style buttstock. Limited production. No pricing information available.

AUTO ORDNANCE
West Hurley, New York

A manufacturer of the Thompson submachine guns through 1986, they also made several semi-automatic versions of the classic sub gun. Became a division of Kahr Arms in 1999. Add 20% for pre-Kahr Arms/AOC West Hurley, NY production.

Note: *Kahr Arms offers variants of its Thompson M1 and 1927 models in "SB" (short barrel) variations modeled after the original 10.5 inch, full-auto Thompson submachine guns. These short-barreled rifles are subject to the same ownership restrictions as submachineguns. See www.tommy-gun.com for more information.*

■ THOMPSON 1927A-1 STANDARD CAL. 45 ACP

16 inch plain barrel. Horizontal forearm. Shipped with a 30-rd stick magazine. Discontinued.

EXC.	V.G.	GOOD
950	850	700

■ THOMPSON 1927A-1 DELUXE

All the classic details of the time honored original 1928 are reproduced in this semi-auto Thompson. The frame and receiver are machined from solid steel. The wood is genuine American walnut. Pistol grip forearm. This .45 caliber carbine features a 16-1/2 inch finned barrel, compensator and is available with a blued steel receiver.

MSRP	EXC.	V.G.	GOOD
1221	1100	950	850

**KAHR/AUTO-ORDNANCE
THOMPSON 1927A-1 DELUXE**

■ THOMPSON 1927 A-1 DELUXE WITH DETACHABLE BUTTSTOCK

As above but has a detachable buttstock similar to that on the 1928 SMG. Introduced in 2007.

MSRP	EXC.	V.G.	GOOD
1675	1400	1200	1000

KAHR/AUTO-ORDNANCE THOMPSON 1927A-1 DELUXE WITH DETACHABLE STOCK AND 50 ROUND DRUM (TOP); "SB" (SHORT BARREL) MODEL BELOW.

■ THOMPSON 1927 A-1C LIGHTWEIGHT DELUXE

Same as the deluxe model but with an aluminum alloy receiver.

MSRP	EXC.	V.G.	GOOD
986	850	750	600

■ THOMPSON 1927 A-1 COMMANDO

A replacement for the standard model. Horizontal forearm. 16-1/2 inch finned barrel with compensator. Has a parkerized finish on the steel and a black finish on the stocks. Introduced in 1998.

MSRP	EXC.	V.G.	GOOD
1200	950	800	700

KAHR/AUTO-ORDNANCE THOMPSON 1927A-1 COMMANDO

■ THOMPSON 1927 A-4

Pistol version made with an alloy receiver, 13 inch barrel, pistol grip fore-arm. No provision for mounting a stock. Discontinued in 1994. Reintro-duced with 10.5 inch barrel as Model T5 by Kahr Arms in 2008.

EXC.	V.G.	GOOD
1500	1250	900

Note: Add $300 for 50 round drum magazine or $100 for 39 round drum XL magazine that accompanied many Thompson 1927 models. For 100 round drum add $300.

■ THOMPSON M-1

A semi-automatic version of the WWII era M-1 A-1 sub-machine gun. 16 inch barrel, horizontal forearm. Cocking knob is on the right side of the receiver instead of on top as the 1927 models. Does not accept the drum magazines.

MSRP	EXC.	V.G.	GOOD
1148	950	800	700

KAHR/AUTO-ORDNANCE THOMPSON M1 STANDARD (TOP); "SB" (SHORT BARREL) VARIANT BELOW.

■ THOMPSON 1927-A3 .22 CAL.

Has a 16 inch finned barrel with compensator. Alloy frame and receiver. Walnut stock. Pistol grip forearm. 30 round curved magazine. Discontinued 1994.

EXC.	V.G.	GOOD
1250	1100	950

■ AUTO-ORDNANCE M-1 CARBINE

A close copy of the classic U.S. Carbine Cal. .30 M-1. New manufacture. Has walnut or synthetic stock.

MSRP	EXC.	V.G.	GOOD
777	600	450	350

AUTO-ORDNANCE M-1 CARBINE WALNUT STOCK (TOP); FOLDING SYNTHETIC STOCK (BOTTOM)

BARRETT F.A. MFG CO.
Murfeesboro, Tennessee

■ MODEL 82 RIFLE

A .50 Browning semi-automatic rifle. 37 inch barrel with a muzzle compensator. 11 round detachable magazine. Parkerized finish. Approx weight 35 lbs. Manufactured 1985-87.

EXC.	V.G.	GOOD
7000	6000	5000

■ MODEL 82A1 /M107

Updated version of the Model 82. Offered with 29 or 20 inch barrel. Weight approx 30 lbs. Currently issued to the U.S. military as the M107.

MSRP	EXC.	V.G.	GOOD
8050	7500	7000	6500

BERETTA, PIETRO
Gardonne, Italy

■ AR-70

A 5.56mm/.223 semi-automatic rifle. 17.7 inch barrel. Black epoxy finish with a black plastic stock. Sold with 8 and 30 rd magazines. Weight 8-1/2 lbs. Mfg in Italy by Beretta. Imported by the Berben Corp. NY, NY. Importation discontinued in 1989.

EXC.	V.G.	GOOD
2000	1750	1500

AR-70

■ BM-59

A 7.62mm/.308 version of the M-1 Garand that takes detachable 20 round magazines. A few were imported by Springfield Armory in the 1980s. Springfield Armory also manufactured their own version of this model. (Bottom illustration shows receiver markings.)

EXC.	V.G.	GOOD
2300	2000	1700

BERETTA BM-59 RECEIVER MARKINGS (RIGHT); RIFLE (ABOVE)

BERETTA U.S.A.
Accokeek, Maryland

■ CX4 STORM

A semi-automatic carbine with a 16-5/8 inch barrel. Offered in 9mm, .40S&W or .45ACP. Uses the same magazines from Beretta handguns in these calibers. Synthetic stock. Introduced in 2003.

MSRP	EXC.	V.G.	GOOD
775	700	625	500

BERETTA CX4 STORM

BUSHMASTER FIREARMS
Portland/Bangor, Maine

■ BUSHMASTER ARMS PISTOL

A 5.56mm semi-automatic pistol built in a bull pup configuration. 11-1/2 inch barrel. Alloy or steel frame. Operating handle is on top, later changed to the side. Pistol grip housing can be adjusted sideways to allow for left or right hand operation. Parkerized finish. Uses AR-15/M-16 magazines. Discontinued in 1988.

EXC.	V.G.	GOOD
900	800	700

BUSHMASTER ARMS PISTOL

■ BUSHMASTER RIFLE

A rifle built with the same operating mechanism as above, but not a bull pup. 18-1/2 inch barrel. Side folding stock. Fixed wood stock was available as an option. Discontinued.

EXC.	V.G.	GOOD
800	700	600

BUSHMASTER FIREARMS
Windham, Maine

This company was formed in 1986 when Quality Parts Co. bought the old Bushmaster trade mark. They currently manufacture a variety of AR-15 type rifles. Bushmaster recently purchased Professional Ordnance and has added the Carbon 15 series of firearms to their offerings. Owned by Cerberus Capital, which also owns Remington and Marlin.

■ BUSHMASTER O.R.C.

(Optics Ready Carbine) This top quality Bushmaster Carbine was developed for the shooter who intends to immediately add optics (scope, red dot or holographic sight) to the rifle - as it is shipped without iron sights. Various add-on rear iron sights can be easily attached to the flat-top upper receiver, and Bushmaster's BMAS front flip-up sight for V Match rifles (Part # YHM-9360K) can be mounted over the milled gas block. The premium 16 inch M4 profile barrel is chrome lined in both bore and chamber to provide Bushmaster accuracy, durability and maintenance ease.

MSRP	EXC.	V.G.	GOOD
1085	950	825	700

BUSHMASTER O.R.C.

■ BUSHMASTER MODULAR CARBINE

The B.M.A.S. Modular Carbine incorporates a number of Bushmaster's popular Bushmaster Modular Accessories into a unique, lightweight, feature packed carbine that will stand out at any range. Features popular Bushmaster modular accessories such as B.M.A.S. four rail tubular forend which free-floats the barrel from the barrel nut forward to avoid any possibility of barrel deflection or accuracy degradation. Molded rubber Sure-Grip rail covers snap over the rail sections on the handguard to add ergonomic comfort and rail protection. The rear sight is a detachable dual aperture B.M.A.S. Rear Flipup unit with windage calibrated to 1/2 M.o.A.The front sight is our B.M.A.S. clamp-on designed to fit directly over the milled front gas block. It folds down with the touch of a button to allow scope use, and incorporates an elevation adjustable M16A2 front sight post. The ergonomic pistol grip is an ambidextrous design, molded of urethane with a stipple finish to provide a solid non-slip grip and firm control. The 5.56 mm/.223 Rem. Chrome-lined 16 inch chrome-moly vanadium steel barrel is fluted for lighter weight and enhanced cooling capabilities, and includes the A2 "birdcage" flash suppressor. The modular carbine is available with either a lightweight skeleton stock or a six-position telescoping stock.

MSRP	EXC.	V.G.	GOOD
1745	1400	1250	1000

BUSHMASTER MODULAR CARBINE

■ BUSHMASTER CARBON 15 9MM CARBINE

The Bushmaster Carbon 15 9mm Carbine combines durable carbon fiber receivers, the familiarity of AR15 type operating controls, a six-position telestock and a receiver length picatinny optics rail into a light weight, powerful, and compact firearm ideal for law enforcement or personal protection.

MSRP	EXC.	V.G.	GOOD
1050	950	850	750

BUSHMASTER CARBON 15 9MM CARBINE

■ BUSHMASTER CARBON 15 TOP LOADING CARBINE

The unique Carbon 15 "top loading" model has been developed specifically for the California market (and other states with similar restrictions). It offers traditional AR-15 type features, rugged carbon fiber composite molded receivers for light weight and durability, and a 10 round internal magazine - loaded by simply pushing in the receiver takedown pin and then pivoting open the receivers. This exposes the internal magazine components – which are permanently fixed in position within the lower receiver. Cartridges can then be inserted into the magazine feed lips in the same manner as any removable AR-15 type magazine. Shipped in Bushmaster's lockable hard case with black web sling, safety block, sighting in target, operation and safety manual - one year warranty. To comply with California state statutes, and for other states with similar restrictions, the Carbon 15 top loading rifle has a 10 round internal magazine that is loaded by simply pushing in the receiver takedown pin and then pivoting open the upper and lower receivers. This exposes the internal magazine components – which are permanently fixed in position within the lower receiver. Then cartridges can be inserted into the magazine feed lips in the same manner as any removable AR-15 type magazine. Internal magazine capacity is limited to 10 rounds, and the bottom of the magazine well is sealed.

MSRP	EXC	V.G.	GOOD
1070	950	850 7	50

■ BUSHMASTER CARBON 15 M4 FLAT TOP CARBINE

The Bushmaster C15 M4 type carbines are a unique hybridization of traditional AR-15 type features with space-age carbon 15 composite molded receivers for light weight and rugged durability. Lightweight carbon 15 composite receivers, 40% stronger and 40% lighter than comparable aircraft aluminum receivers, unaffected by moisture, will not corrode. Matte black throughout (no surface finish to wear off). Upper receiver includes anodized aluminum picatinny rail for unlimited sight, scope or optics mounting. 16 inch M4 profile barrel chambered for 5.56mm NATO/.223 Rem. Caliber, – chrome-lined in both bore and chamber for long wear and ease of maintenance – standard threaded muzzle. Fitted with izzy flash suppressor. Barrel finish is mil-spec manganese phosphate for protection against corrosion and rust. Front sight is AR type base with post – adjustable for elevation. Rear sight is a B.M.A.S. dual aperture flip-up, adjustable for windage. Six-position telestock offers light weight, carrying ease and quick handling. Carbine length handguards have internal aluminum shields to protect against heat build-up in rapid fire sequences.

MSRP	EXC.	V.G.	GOOD
1155	1000	900	800

■ BUSHMASTER "AK" CARBINES

Bushmaster AK carbines offer compact size, balanced swing weight, and great accuracy from their chrome-lined, chrome-moly vanadium steel barrels. Bushmaster forged aluminum receivers, six position telestocks, and carbine length handguards complete the shared features of these versatile carbines. Chrome-moly vanadium steel barrels in various lengths as indicated - all manganese phosphate finished to insure protection against corrosion or rust. The 16 inch heavy barrel has a threaded "birdcage" flash suppressor. AK47 type muzzle brake and 5.5 inch suppressors are permanently pinned and welded onto barrels to achieve legal length barrel units. Dual aperture rear sights on A2 models have 1 MOA elevation adjustments and 1/2 MOA windage adjustments with a 300-800 meter range. The A3 type carbines (removable carry handle included) have 1/2 MOA adjustments for both elevation and windage with a 300-600 meter range. The A3 upper has a picatinny rail for the attachment of sights, scopes, or night vision optics. A2 front post type sights are adjustable for elevation. Six position telescoping stocks are fitted to all models - other stocks are available as optional installations.

MSRP	EXC.	V.G.	GOOD
1180	1000	875	750

■ BUSHMASTER CARBON 15 R97S RIFLE

With many parts molded of Carbon 15 Composite, these rifles are the lightest in the Bushmaster lineup.

MSRP	EXC.	V.G.	GOOD
1265	1050	900	775

■ BUSHMASTER CARBON 15 R4 RIFLE

The Bushmaster C15 Model 4 Carbines are a unique hybridization of traditional AR-15 type features with space-age Carbon 15 composite molded receivers for light weight and rugged durability. Upper and lower receivers are molded of durable, water resistant Carbon 15 composite with operational controls same as any AR15 type firearm. Color-coded safety lever markings on both sides of receiver for quick visual check of firing condition. 14.5 inch M4 profile barrel – chrome lined chrome-moly steel – includes an "izzy" flash suppressor pinned and welded in place to achieve 16 inch overall barrel length. Barrel and other critical steel parts are manganese phosphate finished for corrosion and rust protection. Upper receiver includes a receiver length raised picatinny optics rail with integral dual aperture rear sight (windage adjustable). Front sight is standard A2 post type gas block adjustable for elevation. Six position tele-stock reduces overall length by 4 inch when retracted.

MSRP	EXC.	V.G.	GOOD
1155	1000	875	750

BUSHMASTER CARBON 15 R4 RIFLE

■ BUSHMASTER CARBON 15 R21 RIFLE

With many parts molded of Carbon 15 Composite, these rifles are among the lightest in the Bushmaster lineup.

MSRP	EXC.	V.G.	GOOD
990	850	775	700

BUSHMASTER CARBON 15 R21 RIFLE

■ BUSHMASTER SUPERLIGHT CARBINES

Bushmaster SuperLights feature a 16 inch barrel design adapted from the original G.I. "pencil barrel" profile. When combined with a six-position telestock or a "stubby stock," it is Bushmaster's lightest aluminum carbine ever.

MSRP	EXC.	V.G.	GOOD
1250	1100	950	800

Bushmaster Tech Sheet

BUSHMASTER SUPERLIGHT CARBINES

Bushmaster SuperLights feature a 16" barrel design adapted from the original G.I. "pencil barrel" profile. When combined with a 6 Position Telestock or a "Stubby Stock", it makes our lightest aluminum Carbine ever.

A2 SuperLight Carbine with Telestock (Part # BCWA2F 16SL)
also available with Stubby Stock (Part # BCWA2Y 16SL)

A3 SuperLight Carbine with Stubby Stock (Part # BCWA3Y 16SL)
also available with Telestock (Part # BCWA3F 16SL)

A3 "Flat-top" Models include the
A3 Type Removable Carry Handle

Feature	Specification [Metric in brackets]
Caliber	5.56mm or .223 Rem.
Operation	Gas Operated / Semi-Automatic
Magazine Capacity	30 Rounds (accepts all M16 / AR15 type)
Overall Length - Telestock	34.5" [87.63 cm]
Overall Length - Stubby	31.25" [79.38 cm]
Barrel Length	16" [40.6 cm]
Rifling	1 turn in 9" [22.8 cm] R.H. Twist / 6 grooves & lands
Weight w/o Mag. A2 Tele	6.25 lbs. [2.84 kg]
Weight w/o Mag. A2 Stubby	5.8 lbs. [2.63 kg]
Weight of empty Magazine	.25 lbs. [.11 kg]
Weight of loaded Magazine	1.0 lbs. [.45 kg]

- 16" Superlight Slim Profile Barrel is Chrome lined in both Bore and Chamber for excellent accuracy and long life. Dimensions are .670" to .565" diameter under the sight base, and .570" diameter out to the muzzle. The ChromeMoly Steel Barrel, and other exposed steel parts of the weapon are Manganese Phosphate finished to insure protection against corrosion or rust.

- Upper Receivers available in A2 or A3 Configurations – A2 Upper Receiver has a 300 – 800 meter rear sight system (with 1 M.o.A. Elevation and ½ M.o.A. Windage adjustments). A3 Upper Receiver has a 300 – 600 meter rear sight system (with ½ M.o.A. Elevation and Windage adjustments). The A3 Upper Receiver incorporates a Picatinny configuration mounting rail allowing easy attachment of most accessory sights, scopes, or optic devices.

- Available Buttstocks include either the 6 Position Telestock or the "Stubby" sized Buttstock (7.25" long).

- Shipped in a Lockable, Hard Plastic Case with Operator's Safety Manual, 30 Round Magazine, Orange Safety Block and Black Web Sling

- One Year Bushmaster Warranty

NOTE: Some States have regulations against certain components of these firearms (such as bayonet lugs, flash suppressors, high capacity magazines, telestocks). For sales in those States, Bushmaster offers configurations of these rifles without those features. Contact Bushmaster's Sales Department for details.

For Quotations and Information, contact...

Bushmaster Firearms International, LLC
P.O. Box 1479 • 999 Roosevelt Trail, Windham, Maine 04062 • U.S.A.
24 Hr. Toll Free Order Line: 1 800 998 7928 • Customer Service: 1 800 883 6229
Tel.: 207 892 3594 • Fax: 207 892 8068 • www.bushmaster.com • E-mail: info@bushmaster.com

Made with Pride
In the U.S.A.

© 7/2006 Bushmaster Firearms International, LLC

BUSHMASTER SUPERLIGHT CARBINES

■ BUSHMASTER DISSIPATOR CARBINE

This versatile carbine has features that are unique to the AR-15 Type fire-arm including a carbine length barrel, full length handguards and the sight radius of the original rifle design.

MSRP	EXC.	V.G.	GOOD
1205	1050	875	750

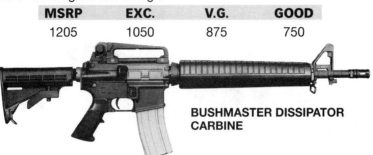

BUSHMASTER DISSIPATOR CARBINE

■ BUSHMASTER M4 TYPE "POST BAN" CARBINE

This model offers features that make it legal for sale in states where re-strictions similar to the Assault Weapons Ban of 1994 are still in place. A 14.5 inch chrome lined M4 type barrel with a permanently attached "izzy" brake yields a 16 inch overall length (BATF legal) barrel. The buttstock is a fixed length "tele-style" unit, but it is not collapsible in order to conform with those regulations. Magazine capacity is limited to 10 rounds, and the bayonet lug is milled off on this "Post-Ban" model.

MSRP	EXC.	V.G.	GOOD
1265	1100	950	800

■ PREDATOR

Built as a result of numerous requests by the hunters who wanted a slightly shorter barrel and lighter swing weight in a carry rifle for predator hunting/calling, this 20 inch barreled version of the Varminter will deliver all the accuracy you've come to expect from a Bushmaster. The New "Camo" version features "RealTree© Max1" camouflage, and the finish is applied over almost the whole rifle (excepting barrel and a few small metal parts - ejection port cover, etc.).

MSRP	EXC.	V.G.	GOOD
1310	1100	950	800

BUSHMASTER PREDATOR

■ STAINLESS VARMINT SPECIAL

Similar to the Predator but with a 24 inch stainless steel barrel and lacking the camo finish.

MSRP	EXC.	V.G.	GOOD
1325	1100	950	800

BUSHMASTER STAINLESS VARMINT SPECIAL

■ CARBON 15 .22 LR RIMFIRE

Designed for the indoor range and the youth shooter, this Carbon15 .22 LR rim fire is a lightweight AR style rifle.

MSRP	EXC.	V.G.	GOOD
790	700	625	550

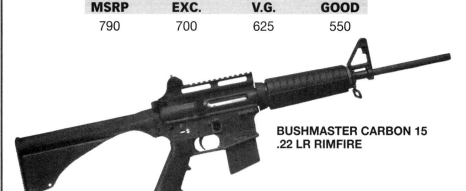

BUSHMASTER CARBON 15 .22 LR RIMFIRE

■ BUSHMASTER .450 RIFLE AND CARBINE

An AR style rifle chambering the .450 Bushmaster. This powerful cartridge, developed in affiliation with Hornady, is tamed by the AR type gas operating system so that recoil is reduced to a heavy thump, and second shot control is retained. The cartridge is adapted from a 6.5mm – .284 case with necking cut off to accommodate the 250-grain Hornady SST Flex Tip .450-caliber bullet. AR type magazine boxes are utilized in the Bushmaster .450, and are fitted with a blue, single stack follower due to the diameter of the cartridge.

With bullet velocity of 2200 fps, accuracy out to 200 yards is exceptional with stopping power ample to take any North American large game. Ballistics approximate the traditional 405-grain .45-70 factory load. The chromoly steel barrels are rifled 1 turn in 24 inches and chrome lined in both bore and chamber for exceptional durability and ease of maintenance. Free Floating Aluminum Forends help deliver optimum accuracy – rifle length is vented for cooling. Forged aluminum receivers; A2 pistol grip and solid A2 buttstock with trapdoor storage compartment are standard features. All operating controls are the same as any AR type rifle, and the Bushmaster .450s are shipped with one 5 round magazine, a black web sling, operators safety manual, and orange safety block in a lockable hard plastic carrying case.

MSRP	EXC.	V.G.	GOOD
1350	1200	1050	900

■ BUSHMASTER GAS PISTON RIFLE

The Bushmaster Gas Piston System Rifles bring new levels of reliability to the "AR" type rifle platform by eliminating carbon build up, gas leaks and heat within the upper receiver. The gas piston system operates by tapping gas pressure off the barrel much like the systems found on AK-47s and FALs. Functions with a wider range of ammunition. Offers improved reliability and control - with cleaner operation and reduced recoil. Keeps carbon build up and powder residue from reaching and fouling the upper receiver and bolt carrier. A detented plug in the gas block allows easy cleaning of the system's hard chrome plated piston. Offered in basic M-4 configuration with a 16 inch barrel.

MSRP	EXC.	V.G.	GOOD
1745	1450	1200	1000

■ BUSHMASTER 6.8 SPC RIFLE

This gas operated semi-automatic packs a bigger punch than the 5.56mm/.223 models – a .270 cal. 6.8mm SPC (Special Purpose Cartridge) specifically developed for the military, but now available commercially. Velocity averages a bit over 2600 FPS (with Hornady 115 Gr.V-Max), and the heavier bullet weights deliver excellent terminal energies. The 6.8 mm SPC was developed from a .30 Remington case, which is shortened slightly to fit the AR15 type magazine. Due to the "fatter" case diameter, magazine capacity in a 30 round AR type shell is reduced to 26 rounds, and 6.8 specific springs and followers are used. The bolt is also different - due again to case diameter. 6.8 mm SPC caliber 16 inch M4 profile barrel with "izzy" brake. Six-position telescoping stocks are fitted to rifles ; other stocks are available as optional installations. 26 round magazine.

MSRP	EXC.	V.G.	GOOD
1295	1100	1000	850

BUSHMASTER 6.8 SPC RIFLE

■ BUSHMASTER M17S

A bullpup style rifle in 5.56mm/.223. It has a 20 inch barrel. The receiver is made from machined aluminum. Uses AR-15 magazines. Discontinued.

EXC.	V.G.	GOOD
750	675	600

BUSHMASTER M17S

■ BUSHMASTER PISTOLS

▶ Carbon 15 Type 21S Pistol

The newest generation of Bushmaster Carbon 15 Pistols - the "S" Series - feature full length picatinny rails with integral iron sights, and cool, comfortable forends for stable firing control. Receivers, forend and other parts are molded of durable, water resistant Carbon 15 composite. Operating controls are similar to any AR15 type firearm, and safety lever markings are color coded for quick, easy identification. The 7-1/4 inch 5.56mm / .223 caliber stainless steel match grade barrel includes an A2 flash suppressor. The total length of the pistol is only 20 inches. The bolt carrier is black oxide finished, and other critical steel parts are manganese phosphate finished for corrosion and rust protection. Upper receiver includes a full length picatinny optics rail with integral dual aperture rear sight (windage adjustable), and an A2 type square post front sight adjustable for elevation. Uses AR-15 magazines.

MSRP	EXC.	V.G.	GOOD
1050	850	750	650

▶ BUSHMASTER Carbon 15 Type 97 Pistol

Features receivers and other parts molded of durable carbon fiber composite, and match grade stainless steel barrels with operating controls similar to any AR-15 type firearm. Receivers and other parts are molded of durable, water resistant Carbon 15 composite. Operating controls are similar to any AR15 type firearm, and safety lever markings are color coded for quick and easy identification. The rear sight is a ghost ring type, and the front sight is a blade machined into the gas block. 7-1/4 inch 5.56mm/.223 caliber stainless steel match grade barrel fluted for lighter weight and improved cooling capability. Includes a quick detach compensator for control of muzzle rise in rapid fire sequences. Fitted with Hogue® overmolded pistol grip for ergonomic hand comfort. Uses AR-15 magazines.

MSRP	EXC.	V.G.	GOOD
990	850	750	650

CARBON 15
TYPE 21S PISTOL

▶ Bushmaster Carbon 15 Type 97S Pistol

The newest generation of Bushmaster Carbon 15 pistols, the "S" Series, feature full length picatinny rails with integral iron sights, and cool, comfortable forends for stable firing control. Receivers, forend and other parts are molded of durable, water resistant Carbon 15 composite. Operating controls are similar to any AR15 type firearm, and safety lever markings are color coded for quick, easy identification. 7-1/4 inch 5.56mm/.223 caliber stainless steel match grade barrel includes an A2 flash suppressor. Upper Receiver includes a full length picatinny optics rail with integral dual aperture rear sight (windage adjustable), and an A2 type square post front sight adjustable for elevation. The forend features an additional picatinny accessory mounting rail for lasers or flashlights, and the pistol grip is a Hogue® overmolded unit for ergonomic comfort. Uses AR-15 magazines.

MSRP	EXC.	V.G.	GOOD
1095	900	800	700

**BUSHMASTER
CARBON 15
TYPE 97 PISTOL**

▶ Bushmaster Carbon 15 9mm Pistol

9x19mm NATO caliber AR type pistol. With a full length picatinny rail including integral iron sights, an M203 type foregrip, and a comfortable neoprene sleeve over the buffer tube, this pistol is ideal for law enforcement, personal protection and unique fun at the range.Receivers, forend and other parts are molded of durable, water resistant carbon fiber composite. Operating controls are similar to any AR-15 type firearm, and safety lever markings are color coded for quick, easy identification. 7-1/4 inch chrome moly steel barrel includes a birdcage flash hider for control of muzzle rise. Bolt carrier, and other critical steel parts are manganese phosphate finished for protection against corrosion or rust. Upper receiver includes a full length picatinny optics rail with integral dual aperture rear sight (windage adjustable). The A2 front post sight is adjustable for elevation. Two quick-detach sling swivel studs are fitted. Carbon 15 pistols are shipped with a 30 round magazine, operating and safety instruction manual.

MSRP	EXC.	V.G.	GOOD
1025	850	750	650

**BUSHMASTER CARBON
15 9MM PISTOL**

CENTURY INTERNATIONAL ARMS
St. Albans, Vermont/ Georgia, Vermont

Century Arms has been known for years as the largest importer of military surplus firearms for the U.S. market. As the overseas supplies of surplus firearms legal for importation has dwindled, Century Arms has expanded their offerings to include a wide variety of semi-automatic versions of classic assault rifles.

■ AKM

Century currently has several variations of the Automat Kalishnikov series available. These are manufactured by Century Arms using U.S. made receivers and barrels and other parts necessary to comply with U.S. code 922(r), along with original AK parts imported from over seas. These are offered with both Draganov style thumbhole stocks as well as standard military pattern stock sets. Some models only accept a 10 round single column magazine and lack the recoil compensator and bayonet mount in order to comply with laws in several states and cities. Others accept the original high capacity magazines but lack the features banned by some laws. The Century catalog numbers are listed to help identify specific models.

Note: AKM Type rifles that accept a 10 round low capacity magazine will not accept standard AK magazines.

▶ **Cut Away GP WASR-10**

CENTURY INTERNATIONAL AKM WITH VERTICAL FOREND (TOP) AND STANDARD CONFIGURATION (BOTTOM)

As above but a cut away rifle for training gunsmiths and others. Allows viewing of internal parts and their functional relationship. Still requires paperwork as any modern firearm. Includes a cut away 10 round magazine. Product ID: RI1071C

NIB	EXC.	V.G.	GOOD
425	350	325	300

▶ WASR-2

Semi-auto rifle low capacity rifle with military style stock, cal. 5.45x39mm. Product ID: RI1172

NIB	EXC	V.G.	GOOD
350	325	300	275

CENTURY INTERNATIONAL WASR-2

▶ WASR-3

Semi-auto rifle, low capacity w/ military style stock, cal. .223. Shipped with two 10 round magazines. Product ID: RI1174

NIB	EXC	V.G.	GOOD
350	325	300	275

▶ WASR-2

Semi-auto rifle, low capacity with Dragunov stock, cal. 5.45x39mm. Shipped with two 10 round magazines. Product ID: RI1158

NIB	EXC	V.G.	GOOD
350	325	300	275

▶ GP WASR-10 LO-CAP

Semi-auto rifle with Dragunov style stock, cal. 7.62x39mm. Shipped with one 5 and one 10 round magazines. Product ID: RI1171D

NIB	EXC	V.G.	GOOD
350	325	300	275

CENTURY INTERNATIONAL GP WASR-10 LO-CAP

▶ WASR 22

Semi-auto rifle with Dragunov style stock, cal. .22LR. Shipped with one 10 round magazine. Product ID: RI1160

NIB	EXC	V.G.	GOOD
350	325	300	275

CENTURY INTERNATIONAL
WASR 22

■ AKM TYPE RIFLES THAT ACCEPT STANDARD CAPACITY MAGAZINES AND DRUM MAGAZINES

▶ GP WASR-10 HI-CAP

Semi-auto rifle with Dragunov style stock, Cal. 7.62x39mm. 16-1/4 inch barrel. Weight is 7-1/2 lbs. Shipped with two 30 round magazines. Product ID: RI1164

NIB	EXC.	V.G.	GOOD
375	325	300	275

▶ WASR-2 HI-CAP

Semi-auto rifle with military stock, Cal. 5.45x39mm. No recoil compensator or bayonet lug. Shipped with two 30 round magazines. Product ID: RI1167

NIB	EXC	V.G.	GOOD
400	375	350	325

▶ WASR-3 HI-CAP

Semi-auto rifle with military style stock, Cal. .223. No recoil compensator or bayonet lug. Shipped with two 30 round magazines. Product ID: RI1168

NIB	EXC	V.G.	GOOD
400	375	350	325

▶ GP WASR-10 HI-CAP SIDE FOLD

Semi-auto rifle with side folding composite stock and original Romanian pattern wood forward pistol grip, Cal. 7.62x39mm. Has recoil compensator and bayonet lug. Shipped with two 30 round magazines and a bayonet. Product ID: RI1203

NIB	EXC	V.G.	GOOD
475	450	525	400

CENTURY INTERNATIONAL GP WASR-10 HI-CAP SIDE FOLD

▶ GP WASR-10 HI-CAP SLIDE STOCK

Semi-auto rifle with CAR-15 style collapsible stock, cal. 7.62x39mm. Wood forearm. Has recoil compensator and bayonet lug. Shipped with two 30 round magazines and a bayonet. Product ID: RI1209

NIB	EXC	V.G.	GOOD
450	425	400	375

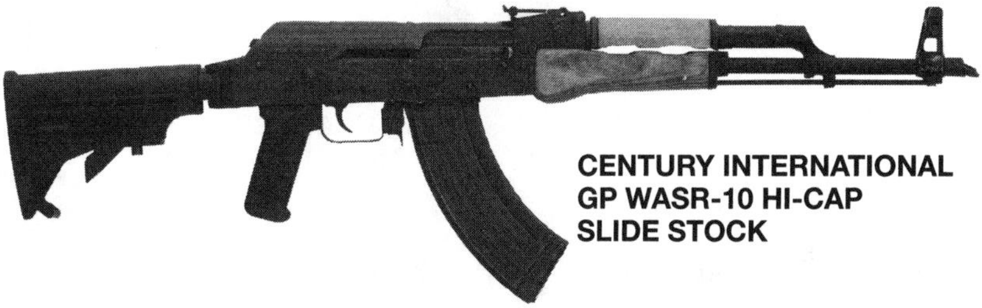

CENTURY INTERNATIONAL GP WASR-10 HI-CAP SLIDE STOCK

■ M70AB2

Sporter with under-folding stock, cal. 7.62x39mm. Based on the Yugoslavian Model 70AB paratrooper rifle with under folding stock. Original parts are refinished to like new condition. Has recoil compensator and bayonet lug. Shipped with two 30 round magazines and a bayonet. Product ID: RI1216

NIB	EXC	V.G.	GOOD
550	500	475	450

CENTURY INTERNATIONAL M70AB2

■ GP WASR-10 HI-CAP

Galil handguard and CAR-15 type collapsible stock, cal 7.62x39mm. Has recoil compensator and bayonet lug. Shipped with two 30 round magazines and a bayonet. Product ID: RI1230

NIB	EXC	V.G.	GOOD
450	425	400	375

■ M72 HEAVY BBL SEMI-AUTO SPORTER

Cal. 7.62x39mm. 21-1/4 inch barrel. Based on the Yugoslavian M72 light machine gun. Folding bi-pod. Has recoil compensator. Shipped with two 40 round magazines. Product ID: RI1233

NIB	EXC	V.G.	GOOD
650	600	575	550

**CENTURY INTERNATIONAL
M72 HEAVY BBL
SEMI-AUTO SPORTER**

■ M70B1 SEMI-AUTO SPORTER

Cal. 7.62x39mm. Same as the Yugoslavian Model 70 rifle. Original wood stock has the issue rubber recoil pad. 16-1/4 inch barrel features a recoil compensator. No bayonet mount. Weight 8-1/2 lbs. Shipped with two 30 round magazines. Product ID: RI1285

NIB	EXC	V.G.	GOOD
525	500	475	450

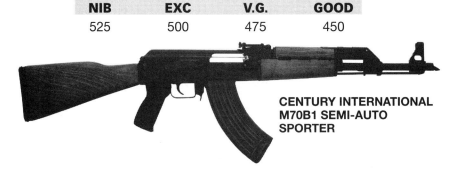

**CENTURY INTERNATIONAL
M70B1 SEMI-AUTO
SPORTER**

■ AMD65

Hungarian AMD65 pattern semi-auto sporter with side folding stock and pistol grip forearm. Cal. 7.62x39mm. Product ID: RI1298

NIB	EXC	V.G.	GOOD
600	550	500	425

CENTURY INTERNATIONAL AMD65

■ CENTURY GP 1975 RIFLE

Cal. 7.62x39mm. It has a T6 adjustable collapsible stock for perfect length adjustment. Top and bottom handguard from Fobus. Accepts 30 round mags. 16-1/4 inch barrel (without compensator). Overall length 34 inches (37.5 inches with fully extended stock). Weight: 6.9 lbs. Product ID: RI1382

NIB	EXC	V.G.	GOOD
575	550	525	500

■ GP WASR-10 ROMANIAN UNDER FOLDER RIFLE

Cal. 7.62x39mm. Has recoil compensator and bayonet lug. Shipped with two 30 round magazines and a bayonet. Product ID: RI1405

NIB	EXC	V.G.	GOOD
475	450	425	400

CENTURY INTERNATIONAL GP WASR-10 ROMANIAN UNDER FOLDER RIFLE OPEN (TOP) AND FOLDED (BOTTOM)

■ AES-10B HI-CAP SEMI-AUTO RIFLE

Cal. 7.62x39mm. Basically an AES-10 with a heavy barrel and bipod to make it look almost exactly like the famous RPK. Comes with two 40 round mags. Barrel: 21-1/4 inches; overall length 40 inches. Weight 10.75 lbs. Product ID: RI1407

NIB	EXC	V.G.	GOOD
500	475	450	425

■ 1975 AK BULLPUP RIFLE

Cal. 7.26x39mm. An AK type rifle reconfigured in bullpup design. Comes with two 30 round magazines. Barrel: 16-1/4 inches, Overall length 27 inches. Weight: 7 lbs. Product ID: RI1420

NIB	EXC	V.G.	GOOD
525	500	475	450

**CENTURY INTERNATIONAL
1975 AK BULLPUP RIFLE**

■ ROMANIAN DRAGUNOV SEMI-AUTO RIFLE

Cal. 7.62x54R. A copy of the classic Russian sniper rifle from the Cold War. 26-1/2 inch barrel. Overall length 45-1/2 inches. Weight 9 lbs. Comes with LPS 4x60 TIP2 scope and mount, compensator and two 10 round magazines. Product ID: RI1342

NIB	EXC	V.G.	GOOD
900	850	800	750

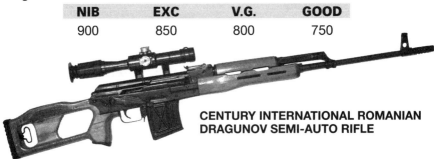

**CENTURY INTERNATIONAL ROMANIAN
DRAGUNOV SEMI-AUTO RIFLE**

■ M-76 SNIPER RIFLE

Cal. 8x57mm. A semi-auto-only version of the famous Yugoslavian M76; has a brand new US-made receiver and barrel. 21-1/2 inch barrel (w/o flash hider), Overall: 44.5 inches. Weight 11.3 lbs. Comes with original scope, mount, and 10 round magazine. Product ID: RI1383

NIB	EXC	V.G.	GOOD
2250	2100	1950	1800

**CENTURY INTERNATIONAL
M-76 SNIPER RIFLE**

NON AK RIFLES

■ CETME

Semi-Auto Sporter, Cal. .308 WIN. Built with original CETME parts kit on a Century Arms receiver. Originally offered with wood stock and forearm. Current model has a synthetic black or camouflage stock and forearm. Product ID: RI1189

Note: *Some owners have reported function issues with early Century Arms CETME sporters. It took them a while to fine tune production and assembly procedures. It is also reported that Century has willingly fixed or replaced affected guns.*

NIB	EXC	V.G.	GOOD
600	550	500	450

**CENTURY INTERNATIONAL
CETME**

■ VZ58 SPORTER SEMI-AUTO RIFLE

Cal. 7.62x39mm. Based on the Czechoslovakian Model Vz-58. The action is not Kalishnikov based. 16 inch barrel. Overall length 35-1/4 inches. Weight 6.9 lbs. 10 round magazines are designed for this model. Standard AKM magazines will not work. Shipped with two 10 round magazines, sling and cleaning kit. Product ID: RI1309

NIB	EXC	V.G.	GOOD
775	725	675	625

CENTURY INTERNATIONAL
VZ58 SPORTER SEMI-AUTO
RIFLE

■ M53 BELT FED SEMI-AUTO RIFLE

Cal. 8mm. Based on the German WWII issue MG-42 machine gun. Comes with 100 round belt and can. Barrel: 21 inches, overall length 48 inches. Weight: 25.5 lbs. Limited production. Product ID: RI1399

NIB	EXC	V.G.	GOOD
2600	2250	2000	1750

CENTURY INTERNATIONAL
M53 BELT FED SEMI-AUTO
RIFLE

■ GOLANI SEMI-AUTO SPORTER RIFLE

Cal. .223. A copy of the Galil rifle. New receiver and barrel with original Galil parts. Comes with a spare 35 round magazine. 21 inch barrel. Overall: 29 inches (folded), Weight: 8.13 lbs.

NIB	EXC	V.G.	GOOD
950	900	850	800

CENTURY INTERNATIONAL GOLANI SEMI-AUTO SPORTER RIFLE OPEN (TOP) AND CLOSED (BOTTOM)

■ L1A1 SPORTER

A semi-automatic version of the FN FAL rifle in 7.62mm/.308. Plastic stock and forearm. Some were made with a thumbhole stock during the 1994 AWB. Discontinued.

EXC.	V.G.	GOOD
600	500	400

■ G-3 RIFLE

A copy of the Heckler and Koch G-3. cal. 7.62mm/.308. Synthetic stock and forearm. Discontinued.

EXC.	V.G.	GOOD
650	550 4	75

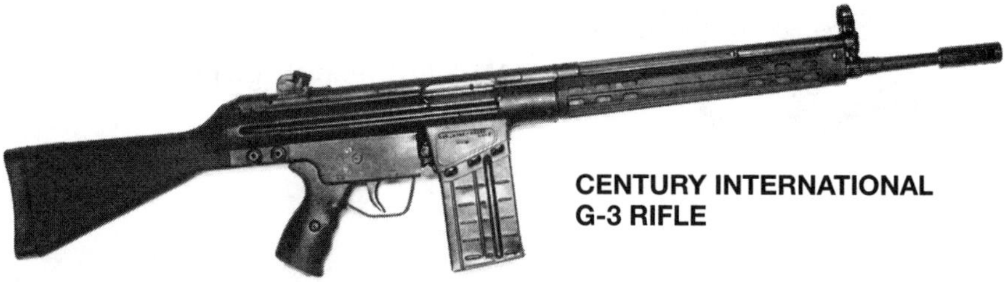

CENTURY INTERNATIONAL G-3 RIFLE

CETME
(Centro de Estudios Técnicos de Materiales Especiales)
Santa Barbara, Spain

Importer: Mars Equipment, Chicago, Illinois

■ CETME

CETME was actually the name of a Spanish government design organization from the 1950s. They designed the CETME rifle using the roller locking system first tried by Germany during WWII in the experimental Mauser StG45. After the war, Mauser engineer Ludwig Vorgrimmler came to Spain and helped design a new rifle. The rifle ended up bearing the name of the design group. Spain adopted the Cetme select fire rifle in 1957. It was chambered in 7.62x51mm. The design was licensed by Heckler and Koch and was adopted by West Germany as the G-3 rifle in 1958. In the early 1960s the semi-automatic CETME Sport rifle was imported to the U.S. by the Mars Equipment Co. of Chicago, Ill. These are the only true Spanish made CETME ever imported. See CETME listings under Century Arms.

EXC.	V.G.	GOOD
3000	2600	2200

MARS EQUIPMENT CETME
RECEIVER MARKINGS

CLARIDGE HI-TEC
North Hollywood, California

■ MODEL S9 PISTOL

A 9mm semi-automatic pistol. It has a 5 inch barrel. 16, 20 and 30 round magazines. Manufactured 1990-93. This design was based on the Goncz pistol and the owner of that design reportedly successfully sued Claridge for patent infringement. The company was forced to cease operations.

EXC.	V.G.	GOOD
450	400	350

**CLARIDGE
MODEL S9**

■ MODEL L9 PISTOL

As above with a 7-1/2 or 9-1/2 inch barrel with a ventilated shroud. Some variations exist. None significantly affects price.

EXC.	V.G.	GOOD
450	400	350

■ C9 RIFLE

A rifle version using the Claridge action. 16-1/8 inch barrel. Wood stock and forearm.

EXC.	V.G.	GOOD
550	500	450

COBRAY INDUSTRIES/ S.W.D. INC.
Atlanta, Ga.

This company was one manufacturer of the MAC-10 pattern semi-auto pistols.

■ M-11 PISTOL

A 9mm semi-automatic pistol. Made from steel stampings. Fires from a closed bolt. Parkerized finish. 12 and 32 round magazines. Guns made until 1994 have a threaded muzzle.

EXC.	V.G.	GOOD
300	250	200

■ M-12 PISTOL

As above but chambered in .380 ACP.

EXC.	V.G.	GOOD
300	250	200

■ TM-11 CARBINE

A 9mm semi-automatic rifle. Constructed from steel stampings. 16-1/4 inch barrel. Back half is covered with a shroud. Metal shoulder stock that can be removed. 12 and 32 round magazines. Factory made steel magazines bring a premium over the more common zytel (plastic) magazines. Based on the M-11 semi-auto pistol. Discontinued.

EXC.	V.G.	GOOD
350	300	250

■ TM-12 CARBINE

As above, but chambered in .380 ACP.

EXC.	V.G.	GOOD
400	350	300

COLT'S PATENT FIRE ARMS MANUFACTURING COMPANY
Hartford, Connecticut

■ AR-15

When Eugene Stoner submitted the early M-16 rifles for government testing in 1958, no one had any idea that it was the beginning of a significant chapter in U.S. gun making history. The first M-16 select fire rifles were made by Armalite on contract for the U.S. Air Force in 1961. When a flood of contracts overwhelmed the Armalite Company the manufacturing rights were transferred to Colt. Colt began filling military orders in 1964. For those interested in learning more about the history and development of this firearm I recommend the book *The Gun Digest Book of The AR-15* by Patrick Sweeney, available from Gun Digest publications.

Colt began offering a semi-automatic version of the new rifle on the civilian market in 1964. This was dubbed an AR-15, which was the name that Armalite had used for the design until the government adopted it as the M-16. It should be noted that while the name "AR-15" has become synonymous with semi-automatic versions of the M-16, Colt holds the trademark on that name.

Pricing for pre ban Colt AR-15 rifles peaked in the 1990s due to demand for rifles with the then-banned features such as the collapsible stock, bayonet lug and flash hider. Since the 2004 expiration of the AWB, the demand for pre-ban rifles has dropped as many buyers can now get new rifles made by several other manufacturers with whatever features they want. Those who insist on owning a Colt made gun are still willing to pay extra for the name.

▶ AR-15 Sporter (Model #6000) Receivers marked SP-1 until 1985

Introduced into the Colt product line in 1964. Similar in appearance and function to the military version, the M-16 but no capability for automatic fire. Chambered for the .223 cartridge. It is fitted with a standard 20 inch barrel with no forward assist, no case deflector, but with a bayonet lug. Weighs about 7.5 lbs. The first production rifles had the three prong flash hider. This was soon changed to the birdcage flash hider. Dropped from production in 1985. Bottom photo shows receiver markings.

EXC.	V.G.	GOOD
1400	1150	900

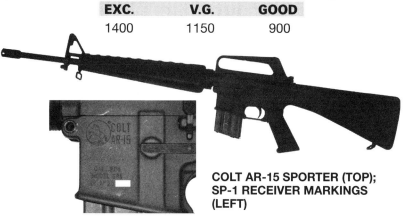

**COLT AR-15 SPORTER (TOP);
SP-1 RECEIVER MARKINGS
(LEFT)**

▶ AR-15 Sporter w/Collapsible Stock (Model #6001)

Same as above but fitted with a 16 inch barrel and sliding stock. Weighs approximately 5.8 lbs. Introduced in 1978 and discontinued in 1985.

EXC.	V.G.	GOOD
1500	1250	1000

▶ AR-15 Carbine (Model #6420)

Introduced in 1985 this model has a 16 inch standard weight barrel. All other features are the same as the previous discontinued AR-15 models. This version was dropped from the Colt product line in 1987.

EXC.	V.G.	GOOD
1250	1100	900

▶ AR-15 9mm Carbine (Model #6450)

Chambered for the 9mm cartridge. Has the collapsible stock. Weighs 6.3 lbs.

EXC.	V.G	GOOD
1500	1250	900

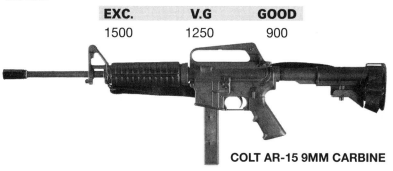

COLT AR-15 9MM CARBINE

▶ AR-15A2 (Model #6500)

Introduced in 1984, this was an updated version with a heavier barrel and forward assist. The AR sight was still utilized. Weighs approximately 7.8 lbs.

NIB	EXC.	V.G.	GOOD
1500	1100	900	800

▶ AR-15A2 Govt. Model Carbine (Model #6520)

Added to the Colt line in 1988, this 16 inch standard barrel carbine featured for the first time a case deflector, forward assist, and the improved A2 rear sight. This model is fitted with a four-position telescoping buttstock. Weighs about 5.8 lbs. Colt restricts this model from civilian sales.

NIB	EXC.	V.G.	GOOD
1600	1250	1000	800

▶ AR-15A2 Gov't. Model (Model #6550)

This model was introduced in 1988; it is the rifle equivalent to the Carbine. It features a 20 inch A2 barrel, forward assist, case deflector, but still retains the bayonet lug. Weighs about 7.5 lbs. Discontinued in 1990.

EXC.	V.G.	GOOD
1250	1000	800

COLT AR-15A2 GOVERNMENT MODEL CARBINE

▶ AR-15A2 H-Bar (Model #6600)

Introduced in 1986, this version features a special 20 inch heavy barrel. All other features are the same as the A2 series of AR15s. Discontinued in 1991. Weighs about 8 lbs.

EXC.	V.G.	GOOD
1250	1000	800

▶ AR-15A2 Delta H-Bar (Model #6600DH)

Same as above but fitted with a 3x9 Tasco scope and detachable

cheekpiece. Dropped from the Colt line in 1990. Weighs about 10 lbs.
Equipped with a metal carrying case.

EXC.	V.G.	GOOD
1800	1500	1250

▶ Sporter Lightweight Rifle

This lightweight model has a 16 inch barrel and is finished in a matte black.
It is available in either a .223 Rem. caliber (Model #6530) that weighs 6.7
lbs., a Model #6430 w/A1 sights, 9mm caliber weighing 7.1 lbs., or a Model #6830 7.65x39mm that weighs 7.3 lbs. The .223 is furnished with two
five round box magazines as is the 9mm and 7.65x39mm. A cleaning kit
and sling are also supplied with each new rifle. The buttstock and pistol
grip are made of durable nylon and the handguard is reinforced fiberglass
and aluminum lined. The rear sight is adjustable for windage and elevation. These newer models are referred to simply as Sporters and are not
fitted with a bayonet lug and the receiver block has different size pins.

EXC.	V.G.	GOOD
850	750	600

▶ Sporter Target Model Rifle (Model #6551)

This 1991 model is a full size version of the Lightweight Rifle. The Target Rifle weighs 7.5 lbs. and has a 20 inch barrel. Offered in .223 Rem.
caliber only with target sights adjustable to 800 meters. New rifles are
furnished with two 5 round box magazines, sling, and cleaning kit.
Same as the Model 6550 except for a rib around the magazine release.
Bottom photo shows receiver markings.

NIB	EXC.	V.G.	GOOD
1350	1200	850	700

COLT SPORTER TARGET
MODEL RIFLE (TOP); RECEIVER
MARKINGS (BOTTOM)

▶ Sporter Match H-Bar (Model #6601)

This 1991 variation of the AR-15 is similar to the Target Model but has a
20 inch heavy barrel chambered for the .223 caliber. This model weighs

8 lbs. and has A2 sights adjustable out to 800 meters. Supplied with two five round box magazines, sling, and cleaning kit.

NIB	EXC.	V.G.	GOOD
1350	1200	850	700

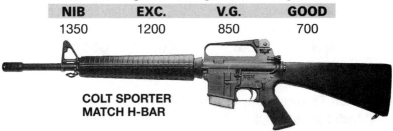

**COLT SPORTER
MATCH H-BAR**

▶ Sporter Match Delta H-Bar (Model #6601 DH)

Same as above but supplied with a 3x9 Tasco scope. Has a black detachable cheekpiece and metal carrying case. Weighs about 10 lbs. Discontinued in 1992. Deduct $150 if there is no scope or hard case.

EXC.	V.G.	GOOD
1350	1200	1000

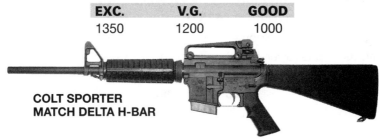

**COLT SPORTER
MATCH DELTA H-BAR**

▶ Match Target H-BAR Compensated (Model MT6601C)

Same as the regular Sporter H-BAR with the addition of a compensator.

NIB	EXC.	V.G.	GOOD
1350	1200	850	700

▶ Sporter Competition H-Bar (Model #6700)

Introduced in 1992, the Competition H-Bar is available in .223 caliber with a 20 inch heavy barrel counterbored for accuracy. The carry handle is detachable with A2 sights. With the carry handle removed the upper receiver is dovetailed and grooved for Weaver-style scope rings. This model weighs approximately 8.5 lbs. New rifles are furnished with two 5 round box magazines, sling, and cleaning kit.

NIB	EXC.	V.G.	GOOD
1200	1100	950	850

▶ Sporter Competition H-Bar Select w/scope (Model #6700CH)

This variation, also new in 1992, is identical to the Sporter Competition with the addition of a factory mounted scope. The rifle has also been selected for accuracy and comes complete with a 3-9X Tasco rubber armored variable scope, scope mount, carry handle with iron sights, and nylon carrying case.

NIB	EXC.	V.G.	GOOD
1350	1200	850	700

▶ Match Target Competition H-BAR Compensated (Model MT6700C)

Same as the Match Target with a compensator.

NIB	EXC	V.G.	GOOD
1350	1200	850	700

▶ AR-15 Carbine Flat-top Heavyweight/Match Target Competition (Model #6731)

This variation in the Sporter series features a heavyweight 16 inch barrel with flat-top receiver chambered for the .223 cartridge. It is equipped with a fixed buttstock. Weight is about 7.1 lbs.

NIB	EXC.	V.G.	GOOD
1350	1200	850	700

▶ AR-15 Tactical Carbine (Model #6721)

This version is similar to the above model with the exception of the buttstock which is telescoping and adjusts to 4 positions. Chambered for the .223 cartridge with a weight of about 7 lbs. A majority of these guns were for law enforcement only.

NIB	EXC.	V.G.	GOOD
1850	1600	1300	1100

▶ Colt Accurized Rifle CAR-A3 (Model CR6724)

This variation was introduced in 1996 and features a free floating 24 inch stainless steel match barrel with an 11-degree target crown and special Teflon coated trigger group. The handguard is all-aluminum with twin swivel studs. Weight is approximately 9.26 lbs.

NIB	EXC.	V.G.	GOOD
1150	1000	900	850

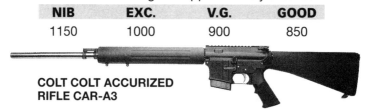

COLT COLT ACCURIZED
RIFLE CAR-A3

COMMANDO ARMS
Knoxville, Tennessee

Formerly known as Volunteer Enterprises. The name was changed in 1978.

■ MARK III CARBINE

A semi-automatic rifle that resembles a Thompson sub-machine gun. 16-1/2 inch barrel with a simulated recoil compensator. .45 ACP caliber. The early versions have an pistol grip/ trigger housing made from metal alloy. Wood stock. Vertical pistol grip in front of magazine. Blued finish. Uses M3 grease gun 30 round stick magazines. Manufactured 1969-78.

EXC.	V.G.	GOOD
550	475	400

■ MARK 45

An improved version of the Mark III. The pistol grip/trigger housing is made from plastic. Wood or synthetic stock. Offered with vertical pistol grip or horizontal forearm. Blued or nickel finish. Uses modified 20 and 30 round Thompson SMG magazines. Will not take a drum magazine. Manufactured from 1978 through the early 1990s.

EXC.	V.G.	GOOD
600	525	450

**COMMANDO ARMS
MARK 45**

■ MARK 9

As above but chambered in 9mm. Uses modified Sten SMG magazines.

EXC.	V.G.	GOOD
550	475	400

CZ USA
Kansas City, Kansas

The U.S. importer for Ceska Zbrojovka products.

■ VZ-58 MILITARY SPORTER

A semi-automatic version of the Czechoslovakian Vz-58 service rifle. Caliber 7.62x39mm. It has a 16-1/8 inch barrel. Total length is 36 inches. Weight is 7-1/2 lbs. 30 round magazine, not interchangeable with AK magazines.

MSRP	EXC	V.G.	GOOD
970	875	800	725

CZ USA VZ-58 MILITARY SPORTER

■ VZ-58 TACTICAL SPORTER

As above but fitted with a synthetic "sporter" stock.

MSRP	EXC.	V.G.	GOOD
990	900	825	750

CZ USA VZ-58 TACTICAL SPORTER

A LITTLE INFORMATION ABOUT THE "NEW" VZ-58 RIFLES:

The Sa vz. 58 was developed by Ing. Jiri Cermak in 1956 and 1957, adopted by the Czechoslovakian army in 1958 and was produced by Ceska Zbrojovka in Uhersky Brod, Czechoslovakia until 1983. Approximately one million Sa vz. 58 rifles were produced during its 20-year production run. As of 2007, it is still the standard issue service rifle in both the Czech Republic and Slovakia.

The new Tactical and Military Sporter models are manufactured by combining original Sa vz. 58 components with a new semi-auto only milled receiver, a new trigger mechanism and new fire control parts. While the appearance of the VZ 58 looks similar to the AK-47, it was inspired by the German StG 44 and initial development was actually based on the 7.92 x 33. Mechanically, the VZ 58 is completely different from the AK-47, and no parts including magazines are interchangeable.

Differences between the VZ 58 Sporter and the AK-47:

- The VZ 58 has a milled receiver, the AK-47 is stamped.
- Even with the milled receiver the VZ 58 is almost one pound lighter than a stamped AK-47.
- The bolt of the VZ 58 stays open after the last round in the magazine has been fired.
- The VZ 58 has a more natural point of aim and is faster handling.
- The safety is more ergonomic making a faster first shot possible with the VZ 58.
- The ejection port is HUGE. There is no chance of an empty case getting stuck in the action of the VZ 58.
- The VZ 58 gas piston can be removed or exchanged without tools.
- The alloy magazine of the VZ 58 is half the weight of the steel AK-47 magazine (.42 lb. vs. .84 lb.).
- VZ 58 is easier to field strip.
- The VZ 58 is striker fired unlike the hammer fired AK-47. This reduces the number of parts and possible points of failure.

DAEWOO
Pusan, Korea

Imported by several companies including Stoeger and Kimber.

■ MAX I AR-100 (K2) 5.56MM RIFLE

The action is a combination of AR-15 type lock up with the gas system of a Kalasnikov. Has an 18 inch barrel. Side folding synthetic stock. Imported 1985-86. Uses AR-15 magazines.

EXC.	V.G.	GOOD
1250	1100	900

■ MAX II (K1A1)

This Daewoo has a different gas system from the MAX I. Made with a retractable wire stock.

EXC.	V.G.	GOOD
1250	1100	900

■ DR200

Introduced in 1996 this is a version of the MAX I with a thumbhole stock. Made to comply with the AWB 1994. Discontinued in 1997.

EXC.	V.G.	GOOD
750	600	500

DOUBLESTAR CORP
Winchester, Kentucky

Current maker of AR-15 type rifles that began business after the expiration of the AWB in 2004.

■ STAR EM-4

Chambered for the .223 cartridge and fitted with a 16 inch barrel. Rifle is supplied with A2 or flat top upper and Colt M4 handguard.

MSRP	EXC.	V.G.	GOOD
915	775	725	650

■ STAR-15

This model has a 20 inch barrel, A2 buttstock, and A2 handguard. Supplied with A2 or flat top upper.

MSRP	EXC.	V.G.	GOOD
775	700	650	600

■ STAR LIGHTWEIGHT TACTICAL RIFLE

Fitted with a 15 inch fluted barrel with permanently attached muzzle–brake. Fitted with a short tactical buttstock. Supplied with an A2 or flat top upper.

MSRP	EXC.	V.G.	GOOD
880	775	725	675

■ STAR CARBINE

This model has a 16 inch match grade barrel. Supplied with either an A2 buttstock or non-collapsing CAR buttstock. Upper receiver is A2 style or flat top.

MSRP	EXC.	V.G.	GOOD
775	700	650	600

■ STAR DS-4 CARBINE

This model features a 16 inch M-4 barrel with six-position buttstock, oval handguard, and A2 flash hider. Weight is about 6.75 lbs. Choice of A2 or flattop upper receiver.

MSRP	EXC.	V.G.	GOOD
875	800	750	675

■ STAR SUPER MATCH RIFLE

Choice of match grade barrel lengths of 16, 20, 22, or 24 inches. Rifle supplied with flat top upper or tactical Hi-Rise upper.

MSRP	EXC.	V.G.	GOOD
875	800	750	675

■ STAR CRITTERSLAYER

This model is fitted with a 24 inch fluted super match barrel with a flat top upper and free floating handguard. Match 2 stage trigger. Fitted with a Harris LMS swivel bipod and Ergo grip with palm swell.

MSRP	EXC.	V.G.	GOOD
1300	1100	1000	900

■ DSC EXPEDITION RIFLE

Offered with a 16 or 20 inch lightweight barrel with integral muzzle-brake. Stock, sights, and receiver are A2 configuration.

MSRP	EXC.	V.G.	GOOD
825	725	675	625

■ DSC STAR-15 CMP SERVICE RIFLE

Fitted with a 20 inch chrome lined heavy match barrel. National Match front and rear sights. CMP free float handguard. National Match trigger. A2 upper receiver.

MSRP	EXC.	V.G.	GOOD
999	900	825	750

■ DSC STAR CMP IMPROVED SERVICE RIFLE

Similar to the above model but with 20 inch Wilson Arms premium grade heavy match barrel. McCormick single- or two-stage Match trigger and Tippie Competition rear sight.

D

MSRP	EXC.	V.G.	GOOD
1299	1100	1000	900

■ DSC STAR 15 LIGHTWEIGHT TACTICAL

This model is fitted with a 16 inch fluted heavy barrel with tactical "shorty" A2 buttstock.

MSRP	EXC.	V.G.	GOOD
880	800	725	650

■ DSC STAR DISSIPATOR

This model features a 16 inch barrel with full length handguard. Available with A2 or flattop upper receiver.

MSRP	EXC.	V.G.	GOOD
875	800	725	675

■ DSC STAR 15 9MM RIFLE

Chambered for the 9mm cartridge and fitted with a 16 inch heavy barrel. A2 or flattop upper receiver. Available with A2 or CAR buttstock.

MSRP	EXC.	V.G.	GOOD
995	900	825	750

DPMS INC.
(DEFENSE PROCUREMENT MANUFACTURING SERVICE)/PANTHER ARMS
Becker, Minnesota

Current manufacturer of AR-15 type rifles that was established in 1996. They offer complete 5.56mm rifles in several configurations. Also available are rifles chambered in .204 Ruger, 6.8 Remington SPC, 7.62x39mm, .243 and .308 Winchester, .260 Remington, .300 Remington SAUM and more. Their current catalog lists over 43 separate variations. DPMS also sells complete kits to build most models as well as stripped lower receivers and upper/lower receiver sets.

■ PANTHER BULL A-15

This AR-15 type rifle is chambered for the .223 cartridge and fitted with a 20 inch stainless steel bull barrel. A2-style buttstock. No sights. Barrel has 1:9 twist. Flat top receiver. Handguard is aluminum free float tube. Upper and lower receivers are hard coated black. Weight is about 9.5 lbs. Each rifle comes standard with two 7 round magazines, sling, and cleaning kit.

MSRP	EXC.	V.G.	GOOD
900	750	700	650

■ PANTHER BULL 24

Similar to the model above but fitted with a 24 inch bull barrel. Flat top receiver. Weight is about 10 lbs.

MSRP	EXC.	V.G.	GOOD
950	800	750	700

■ PANTHER DELUXE BULL 24 SPECIAL

This model is fitted with a 24 inch stainless steel fluted bull barrel. Adjustable A2 style buttstock. Flat top receiver. Adjustable sniper pistol grip. Weight is about 10 lbs.

MSRP	EXC.	V.G.	GOOD
1150	900	850	775

■ PANTHER EXTREME SUPER BULL 24

This model is fitted with a 24 inch stainless steel extra heavy bull barrel (1.150 inch dia.). Skeletonized stock. Flat top receiver. Weight is about 11.75 lbs.

MSRP	EXC.	V.G.	GOOD
1200	925	875	800

■ PANTHER BULLDOG

Fitted with a 20 inch stainless steel fluted bull barrel with black synthetic A2-style buttstock. Flat top receiver. Adjustable trigger. Weight is about 10 lbs.

MSRP	EXC.	V.G.	GOOD
1200	925	875	800

■ PANTHER BULL SWEET 16

This model is fitted with a 16 inch stainless steel bull barrel with flat top receiver. Weight is about 7.75 lbs.

MSRP	EXC.	V.G.	GOOD
875	800	750	700

■ PANTHER BULL SST 16

Similar to the model above but with stainless steel lower receiver. Weight is about 9 lbs.

MSRP	EXC.	V.G.	GOOD
875	800	750	700

■ PANTHER BULL CLASSIC

This model is fitted with a 20 inch 4150 steel bull barrel. Square front post sight, adjustable A2 rear sight. Weight is about 9.75 lbs.

MSRP	EXC.	V.G.	GOOD
900	800	750	700

■ PANTHER ARCTIC

This model is similar to the model above but with 20 inch fluted bull barrel and flat top receiver. Black A2-style buttstock with white coat finish on receiver and handguard. Black Teflon finish on barrel. Weight is about 8.25 lbs.

MSRP	EXC.	V.G.	GOOD
1075	900	825	750

■ PANTHER CLASSIC

Fitted with a 20 inch 4150 steel heavy barrel with square front post sight and A2 rear sight. A2 round handguard. Weight is about 9.5 lbs.

MSRP	EXC.	V.G.	GOOD
775	700	625	575

■ PANTHER DCM

This model is similar to the model above but with 20 inch stainless steel heavy barrel and NM rear sight. DCM free-float handguard. Adjustable trigger. Weight is about 9.5 lbs.

MSRP	EXC.	V.G.	GOOD
1075	800	725	675

■ PANTHER CLASSIC 16 POST BAN

This model is fitted with a 16 inch 4150 steel heavy barrel. A2-style sights. Round handguard. Weight is about 7.25 lbs.

MSRP	EXC.	V.G.	GOOD
775	625	575	525

■ PANTHER FREE FLOAT 16 POST BAN

Similar to the model above with 16 inch barrel but fitted with a vented free-floated barrel and vented free-float tube handguard. Weight is approximately 7.25 lbs.

MSRP	EXC.	V.G.	GOOD
825	675	600	550

■ PANTHER SOUTHPAW POST BAN

This model is fitted with a 20 inch 4150 steel heavy barrel with A2-style sights. Upper receiver has been modified for left-hand ejection. Weight is about 9.5 lbs.

MSRP	EXC.	V.G.	GOOD
875	725	675	600

■ PANTHER RACE GUN

Similar to Panther Bull but with 24 inch fluted bull barrel. Sights: JP Micro adjustable rear, JP front sight adjustable for height. Includes Lyman globe and Shaver inserts.

MSRP	EXC.	V.G.	GOOD
1719	1450	1300	1050

■ PANTHER TUBER

Similar to Panther Bull 24 but with 16 inch barrel with cylindrical aluminum shroud.

MSRP	EXC.	V.G.	GOOD
700	650	600	550

■ SINGLE SHOT RIFLE

AR-15-style single-shot rifle with manually-operated bolt, no magazine.

MSRP	EXC.	V.G .	GOOD
775	675	600	525

■ PANTHER PARDUS

Similar to Panther Post-ban but with 16 inch bull barrel, telescoping butt-stock and tan Teflon finish. Introduced 2006.

MSRP	EXC.	V.G.	GOOD
1200	1000	875	800

■ PANTHER 20TH ANNIVERSARY RIFLE

Similar to Panther Post-ban but with 20 inch bull barrel and engraved, chrome-plated lower receiver. Introduced 2006.

MSRP	EXC.	V.G.	GOOD
2500	2000	1700	1500

■ PANTHER 6.8 RIFLE

Similar to Panther DCM but with 20 inch chrome-moly barrel and chambered for 6.8x43 Remington SPC. Introduced 2006.

MSRP	EXC.	V.G.	GOOD
950	875	800	725

■ PANTHER MARK 12

Similar to Panther but with flash hider and other refinements. Introduced 2007.

MSRP	EXC	V.G.	GOOD
1300	1100	950	875

■ PANTHER SDM-R

Similar to Panther but with stainless steel barrel and Harris bipod. Introduced 2007.

DPMS INC.

MSRP	EXC	V.G.	GOOD
1200	1000	900	825

■ LRT-SASS

Semi-automatic rifle based on AR-15 design. Chambered in .308 Winchester. 18 inch stainless steel barrel with flash hider, collapsible Vitor Clubfoot carbine stock and 19 round detachable magazine. Introduced 2006.

MSRP	EXC.	V.G.	GOOD
1900	1700	1500	1200

■ LR-260

Similar to LRT-SASS but with 24 inch stainless steel barrel and chambered in .260 Remington. Also available with 20 inch chrome-moly barrel as LR-260H. Introduced 2006.

MSRP	EXC.	V.G.	GOOD
1100	975	900	825

■ LR-243

Similar to LR-260 but with 20 inch chrome-moly barrel and chambered in .243 Win. Introduced 2006.

MSRP	EXC.	V.G.	GOOD
1100	975	900	825

■ LR-204

Similar to LRT-260 but chambered in .204 Ruger. Introduced 2006.

MSRP	EXC.	V.G.	GOOD
1100	975	900	825

■ PANTHER A-15 PUMP RIFLE

This model has a 20 inch 4150 steel heavy barrel with A2-style sights. Fitted with an A2 compensator and modified to slide-action. Weight is about 8.5 lbs.

MSRP	EXC.	V.G.	GOOD
1400	1000	900	800

■ PANTHER A-15 PUMP PISTOL

Same as above but fitted with a 10.5 inch barrel. Weight is about 5 lbs.

MSRP	EXC.	V.G.	GOOD
1450	1100	950	825

DSA INC.
Barrington, Illinois

DSA, Inc. began selling its rifles to the public in 1996. Based on actual blueprints of the famous FN/FAL rifle, DSA rifles are made in the US. All SA58 rifles are fitted with fully adjustable gas system, Type I, II, or III forged receiver, hand-lapped barrel, muzzlebrake, elevation adjustable post front sight, windage adjustable rear peep sight with 5 settings from 200 to 600 meters, detachable metric magazine, adjustable sling and hard case.

■ SA58 24 INCH BULL

Fitted with a 24 inch stainless steel barrel with .308 match chamber. Overall length is 44.5 inches. Weight is approximately 11.5 lbs. 20 round magazine. Discontinued.

EXC.	V.G.	GOOD
1500	1250	1000

DSA SA58 21 INCH BULL

■ SA58 FAL BULL BARREL RIFLE

.308 cal. chrome moly, 21 inch premium match grade bull barrel, alloy free float tube with texture finish, standard synthetic or X-series buttstock, standard synthetic pistol grip, type I receiver. 20 round magazine.

MSRP	EXC.	V.G.	GOOD
1745	1500	1250	1000

DSA SA58 24 INCH BULL

■ SA58 FAL MEDIUM CONTOUR RIFLE

.308 cal. 21 inch medium contour barrel with threaded Belgian short flash hider, standard synthetic handguard and pistol grip, standard synthetic or X-series buttstock, type I or type II receiver. 20 round magazine.

MSRP	EXC.	V.G.	GOOD
1595	1250	1000	850

DSA SA58 FAL MEDIUM CONTOUR RIFLE

■ SA58 CARBINE

SA58 FAL carbine rifle, .308 cal. 16.25 inch premium bipod-cut barrel with threaded Belgian short flash hider, standard synthetic handguard and pistol grip, standard synthetic or X-series buttstock, type I or type II receiver. 20 round magazine.

MSRP	EXC.	V.G.	GOOD
1595	1300	1150	1000

DSA SA58 CARBINE

■ SA58 FAL STANDARD RIFLE

.308 cal. 21 inch premium bipod-cut barrel with threaded Belgian short flash hider, standard synthetic handguard and pistol grip, standard synthetic or X-series buttstock, type I or type II receiver. 20 round magazine.

MSRP	EXC.	V.G.	GOOD
1595	1300	1150	1000

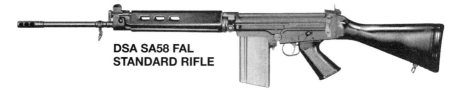

DSA SA58 FAL STANDARD RIFLE

■ SA58 FAL STANDARD PARA RIFLE

.308 cal. 21 inch premium bipod-cut barrel with threaded Belgian short flash hider, standard synthetic handguard and pistol grip, folding para stock, type I or type II receiver. 20 round magazine.

MSRP	EXC.	V.G.	GOOD
1845	1700	1600	1500

DSA SA58 FAL STANDARD
PARA RIFLE

■ SA58 FAL CARBINE PARA RIFLE

.308 cal. 16.25 inch premium bipod-cut barrel with threaded Belgian short flash hider, standard synthetic handguard and pistol grip, folding para stock, type I or type II receiver. 20 round magazine.

MSRP	EXC.	V.G.	GOOD
1845	1700	1600	1500

DSA SA58 FAL CARBINE
PARA RIFLE

■ SA58 FAL TACTICAL CARBINE

.308 cal. 16.25 inch fluted medium contour barrel with threaded A2 flash hider, shortened gas system, short military grade handguard, standard synthetic or X-series buttstock, standard synthetic pistol grip, type I or type II receiver. 20 round magazine.

MSRP	EXC.	V.G.	GOOD
1595	1350	1250	1150

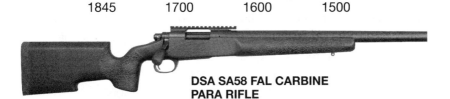

DSA SA58 FAL
TACTICAL CARBINE

■ SA58 FAL PARA TACTICAL CARBINE

.308 cal. 16.25 inch fluted medium contour barrel with threaded A2 flash hider, shortened gas system, short military grade handguard, folding para stock, standard synthetic pistol grip, type I or type II receiver. 20 round magazine.

MSRP	EXC.	V.G.	GOOD
1845	1600	1450	1300

■ SA58 FAL PARA ELITE COMPACT RIFLE

.308 cal. 13 inch barrel with permanently attached long browning flash hider making this a 16 inch barrel semi-auto rifle. Shortened gas system, short military grade handguard, folding para stock, standard synthetic pistol grip, type I or type II receiver. 20 round magazine.

MSRP	EXC.	V.G.	GOOD
1845	1600	1450	1300

■ SA58 SPR (SPECIAL PURPOSE RIFLE)

New for 2008. This model was submitted to the U.S. Army for SASS rifle trials. It features a 19 inch fully fluted premium barrel. Rail interface hand guard. Extended Duty Scope Mount. SPR side folding adjustable stock. Dura coat finish. 20 round magazine.

MSRP	EXC.	V.G.	GOOD
4795	4000	3500	3000

■ SA58 FAL G1 FAL COLLECTORS EDITION

.308/ 7.62mm rifle. 21 inch premium US-made barrel with quick detach long flash hider, bipod cut steel handguard with flush folding g2 bipod, hardwood humpback with proper large sling swivel and steel buttplate, standard synthetic pistol grip, original G1 steel lower receiver. Duracoat black finish on all steel surfaces.

MSRP	EXC.	V.G.	GOOD
1850	1600	1450	1300

**DSA SA58 FAL G1 FAL
COLLECTORS EDITION**

■ SA58 FAL CONGO RIFLE

.308 cal. 18 inch premium bipod-cut barrel with Belgian short flash hider, standard synthetic buttstock and pistol grip, type I or type II receiver with carry handle, Duracoat black finish.

MSRP	EXC.	V.G.	GOOD
1850	1600	1450	1300

DSA SA58 FAL
CONGO RIFLE

■ SA58 FAL PARA CONGO RIFLE

.308 cal. 18 inch premium bipod-cut barrel with Belgian short flash hider, folding para stock, standard synthetic pistol grip, type I or type II receiver with carry handle. Duracoat black finish.

MSRP	EXC.	V.G.	GOOD
2095	1800	1600	1400

■ SA58 FAL T48 COLLECTOR SERIES RIFLE

Based on the T-48 that was tested by the U.S. military in the 1950s. .308 cal. 21 inch premium barrel with long flash hider, European walnut handguard, buttstock and pistol grip, type I receiver with carry handle. Duracoat black finish.

MSRP	EXC.	V.G.	GOOD
1995	1800	1600	1400

DSA SA58 FAL T48
COLLECTOR SERIES RIFLE

■ SA58 FAL PREDATOR RIFLE

Offered in .308, .260 Rem., or .243. 16 inch premium medium carbine or 19 inch medium contour barrel with target crown, standard synthetic or X-series buttstock, standard synthetic pistol grape, OD green handguard, grip and stock. Type I receiver no carry handle cut. Scope mount included.

MSRP	EXC.	V.G.	GOOD
1695	1500	1350	1200

DSA SA58 FAL PREDATOR RIFLE

■ SA58 FAL GRAYWOLF RIFLE

.308 Win cal. 21 inch premium match grade bull barrel with target crown, alloy free float tube with texture finish, standard synthetic or x-series butt-stock, FN saw pistol grip, type I receiver no carry handle cut. Versa-pod model 1 bipod included. Duracoat graywolf and black finish included.

MSRP	EXC.	V.G.	GOOD
2120	1900	1750	1600

DSA SA58 FAL GRAYWOLF RIFLE

■ DS-AR-15 TYPE RIFLES

▶ S1 Rifle

Introduced in 2004 this 5.56 caliber rifle features a 20 inch or 24 inch bull barrel with Picatinny gas black sight base. Flattop receiver. Free floating aluminum handguard. A2 stock. Ten round magazine. Discontinued.

EXC.	V.G.	GOOD
800	725	650

▶ CVI Carbine

Similar to the model above but with a 16 inch barrel with forged front sight base and integral muzzlebrake. D-4 handguard. Fixed CAR buttstock. Ten round magazine. Discontinued.

EXC.	V.G.	GOOD
800	725	650

▶ DS-AR S Series Rifle

Introduced in 2005 this rifle is chambered for the .223 cartridge and fitted with a choice of 16 inch, 20 inch, or 24 inch stainless steel match grade bull barrel. A2 stock with free floating handguard. Flattop receiver, National Match 2 stage trigger. Magazine capacity is 10, 20, or 30 rounds.

MSRP	EXC.	V.G.	GOOD
1154	850	775	700

▶ DS-AR Carbine

Chambered for the .223 cartridge and fitted with a 16 inch D4 barrel with flash hider. Choice of fixed or collapsible stock. Choice of forged flattop or A2 upper receiver. Magazine capacity is 10, 20, or 30 rounds. Introduced in 2005.

MSRP	EXC.	V.G.	GOOD
1054	750	700	650

▶ DS-AR Rifle

As above but with 20 inch heavy barrel with flash hider and fixed stock. Introduced in 2005.

MSRP	EXC.	V.G.	GOOD
1054	750	700	650

▶ DS-AR DCM Rifle

Chambered for the .223 cartridge with Wylde chamber. Fitted with a 20 inch match grade Badger barrel. DCM free float handguard system. National Match two-stage trigger. National Match rear sight. A2 upper receiver. Introduced in 2005.

MSRP	EXC.	V.G.	GOOD
1520	1250	1100	1000

▶ DS-AR CQB MRP

Introduced in 2005 this model features a 16 inch chrome lined barrel with A2 flash hider. Collapsible stock with MRP quad rail. Monolithic rail platform upper. Flattop upper receiver. Supplied with 30 round magazine.

MSRP	EXC.	V.G.	GOOD
2420	1750	1500	1200

▶ DSA Z4 Gas Trap Carbine (GTC)

Introduced in 2005. The AR Gas Trap Carbine features a C.R.O.S., 5.56 NATO, 16 inch M4 profile 1:9 twist chrome lined barrel. A2 flash hider. Flattop upper receiver. Six-position collapsible stock. Z4 mil-.spec forged 7075T6 lower receiver. Mil-spec flattop upper receiver with billet charging handle. Chrome lined picatinny gas block with removable, fixed front sight. Silicone nickle plated gas plug and gas piston. Silicon nickle plated Young bolt carrier. Silicone nickel plated bolt and extractor, cam and firing pin. Flip up rear battle sight. Predator P4X free float tactical rail with sling/bipod mount. Magazine capacity is 10, 20, or 30 rounds.

MSRP	EXC.	V.G.	GOOD
1800	1500	1350	1200

■ TP-9 PISTOL

A 9x19mm semi-automatic pistol based on the Steyr TMP machine pistol. Made in Switzerland by Brugger and Thomet for DSA. 6-1/2 inch barrel. Picatinney rail on top and underneath.

MSRP	EXC.	V.G.	GOOD
1250	1100	950	800

DSA TP-9 PISTOL

EAA
(EUROPEAN AMERICAN ARMORY)
Rockledge, Florida

EAA was formerly an importer of the Izhmash Saiga series of rifles. See: Russian American Armory Co.

■ P.A.P. 7.62 RIFLE

An AK type rifle made by Zastava. 7.62x39mm. 16-3/4 inch barrel. Monte Carlo sporter-type stock. New in 2008. No pricing information available.

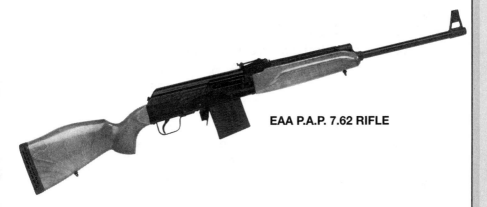

EAA P.A.P. 7.62 RIFLE

EAGLE ARMS
Coal Valley, Illinois

From 1990 to 1995 Eagle Arms manufactured a line of AR type rifles. In 1995 they bought the old Armalite name and continue operations as Armalite. For post 1995 models see the Armalite listing.

■ EA-15 E-1 RIFLE

A-2 type upper receiver with fixed carry handle. Cal. 5.56mm/.223. 20 inch barrel. Manufactured 1990-93.

EXC.	V.G.	GOOD
700	650	600

■ M15 A2 H-BAR RIFLE

As above with a heavier barrel. Manufactured 1990-95.

EXC.	V.G.	GOOD
775	725	675

■ M15 A2 CARBINE

16 inch barrel. Features a CAR type collapsible stock. Changes to fixed stock in 1994. Manufactured 1990-95.

EXC.	V.G.	GOOD
750	700	650

Note: *Deduct $100 for fixed stock version.*

■ M15 A4 EAGLE SPIRIT

Designed for IPSC competition shooting. Flat top receiver. National match 16 inch premium air gauged barrel. Fixed stock. Tubular full length aluminum hand guard. Manufactured 1993-95.

EXC.	V.G.	GOOD
900	800	700

■ M15 A2 GOLDEN EAGLE

Similar to the M15 A2 with an extra heavy stainless 20 inch barrel. National Match sights. Manufactured 1991-95.

EXC.	V.G.	GOOD
900	800	700

■ M15 A4 EAGLE EYE

Designed for silhouette shooting. Flat top receiver. One inch diameter 24 inch free floating barrel. Tubular aluminum hand guards. Weighted buttstock. Manufactured 1993-95.

EXC.	V.G.	GOOD
1000	900	800

■ M15 ACTION MASTER

A match rifle. National match sights and trigger. 20 inch free floating barrel. Solid aluminum hand guard tube. Fixed stock. Manufactured 1992-95.

EXC.	V.G.	GOOD
900	825	750

■ M15 A4 SPECIAL PURPOSE RIFLE

Rifle with flat top receiver with removable carry handle. 20 inch barrel. Manufactured 1994-95.

EXC.	V.G.	GOOD
750	700	650

■ M15 A4 PREDATOR

Flat top receiver with removable carry handle. National match trigger. 18 inch barrel. Fixed stock. Manufactured 1995 only.

EXC.	V.G.	GOOD
900	825	750

ENFIELD AMERICA, INC.
Atlanta, Georgia

■ MP-45

A blowback operated semi-automatic pistol that resembles a submachine gun. Barrels were offered in 4-1/2, 6, 8, 10, or 18 inches. All observed specimens have the shorter barrels. Steel shroud protects the barrel. Parkerized finish. 10, 30, 40 or 50 round magazines. Manufactured 1985 only. Some catalogs also mention a 9mm version. Prices are the same.

EXC.	V.G.	GOOD
450	400	350

**ENFIELD AMERICA
MP-45**

ENTREPRISE ARMS
Irwindale, California

This company currently offers a line of FN/FAL type rifles in 7.62mm/.308. They also sell stripped receivers and parts, so not all Entreprise Arms rifles seen are factory assembled.

■ IMBEL RIFLE

Entreprise Arm Type 03 steel receiver. 21 inch barrel. Zero Climb muzzle brake. Bolt hold open on last shot, adjustable gas system and carry handle. US legal components. Built with Entreprise Arms US made parts and Brazilian Imbel parts. Parkerized finish.

MSRP	EXC.	V.G.	GOOD
899	850	800	750

■ STG58 STANDARD RIFLE

21 inch barrel with muzzle brake. Stamped steel handguards with folding bipod. Black synthetic stock. Carry handle.

MSRP	EXC.	V.G.	GOOD
899	850	800	750

■ STG58C CARBINE

Entreprise Arm Type 01 receiver. Machined aluminum free-floating hand guards. 16 inch barrel with Zero Climb muzzle brake. Bolt hold open on last shot. Adjustable gas system. No carry handle.

MSRP	EXC.	V.G.	GOOD
1399	1200	1100	1000

■ STG58SC SCOUT CARBINE

18 inch barrel with Zero Climb muzzle brake. Stamped steel handguards with folding bi-pod. Black synthetic stock. Bolt hold open. Carry handle.

MSRP	EXC.	V.G.	GOOD
1199	1050	975	900

■ STG58-G2T TARGET RIFLE

Entreprise Arm Type 01 receiver. Machined aluminum free-floating hand guards. 21 inch barrel with Zero Climb muzzle brake, legal configured pistol grip, bolt hold open on last shot, adjustable gas system and no carry handle.

MSRP	EXC.	V.G.	GOOD
1399	1200	1100	1000

■ STG58 C-LW LIGHTWEIGHT CARBINE

Entreprise Arm Type 01 receiver. 16-1/2 inch barrel with Zero Climb muzzle brake. Integral bipod. Bolt hold open on last shot. Adjustable gas system and carry handle.

MSRP	EXC.	V.G.	GOOD
1199	1050	975	900

■ MATCH TARGET STG58C

Entreprise Arm Type 01 receiver. Crosshair front sight. 24 inch barrel. No muzzle break. Bolt hold open on last shot, adjustable gas system. Alumnium free float hand guards. No carry handle.

MSRP	EXC.	V.G.	GOOD
1999	1700	1500	1250

FABRIQUE NATIONAL (FN)
Herstal, Belgium

One of the world's largest manufacturers of firearms. U.S. importers include Browning Arms Co., Steyr, Howco and others

■ FN FAL "G" SERIES (TYPE 1 RECEIVER)

The first FAL to be imported to the U.S. The receivers are capable of accepting select fire parts. These rifles are subject to interpretation by the BATF as to their legal status. A list of BATF legal serial numbers is shown. This information should be utilized prior to a sale in order to avoid the possibility of the sale of an illegal rifle. There was a total of 1,848 legal "G" Series FN FAL rifles imported into this country. All were "grandfathered" and remain legal to possess. "G" series FAL rifles have a wood buttstock and forearm.

▶ Standard

EXC.	V.G.	GOOD
6500	5000	4000

▶ Lightweight

EXC.	V.G.	GOOD
6500	5000	3000

▶ EXEMPTED FAL RIFLES

Following is the final revised listing of FAL rifles, caliber 7.62mm, that are exempt from the provisions of the National Firearms Act.

FN FAL "G" SERIES

G SERIES

Serial Numbers	Units Manufactured
G492 through G494	3
G537 through G540	4
G649 through G657	9
G662 through G673	12
G677 through G693	17
G709 through G748	40
G752 through G816	65
G848 through G1017	170
G1021	1
G1033	1
G1035	1
G1041 through G1042	2
G1174 through G1293	120
G1415 through G1524	110
G1570 through G1784	215
G1800 through G1979	180
G1981 through G1995	15
G3035 through G3134	100
G2247 through G2996	750
Total:	**1,815**

GL SERIES

Serial Numbers	Units Manufactured
GL749	1
GL835	1
GL1095 through GL1098	4
GL1163 through GL1165	3
GL2004 through GL2009	6
GL3135 through GL3140	6
Total:	**21**

STANDARD FAL

Serial Numbers	Units Manufactured
889768	1
889772 through 889777	6
Total Manufactured:	**7**

PARATROOP MODEL

Serial Numbers	Units Manufactured
889800 through 889801	2
889803	1
889805	1
889809	1
Total Manufactured:	**5**
TOTAL EXEMPTED FAL RIFLES:	**1,848**

■ FN-FAL

A gas-operated, semiautomatic version of the famous FN battle rifle. This weapon has been adopted by more free world countries than any other rifle. It is chambered for the 7.62 NATO or .308 and has a 21 inch barrel with an integral flash suppressor. The sights are adjustable with an aperture rear, and the detachable box magazine holds 20 rounds. The stock and forearm are made of wood or a black synthetic. This model has been discontinued by the company and is no longer manufactured.

 The models listed below are for the metric pattern Type 2 and Type 3 receivers, those marked "FN MATCH." The models below are for semi-automatic rifles only. FN-FAL rifles in the " inch pattern" are found in the British Commonwealth countries of Australia, India, Canada, and of course, Great Britain.

FN-FAL HEAVY BARREL

▶ 50.00 21 inch Rifle Model

EXC.	V.G.	GOOD
3000	2500	2000

▶ 50.63 18 inch Paratrooper Model

EXC.	V.G.	GOOD
3500	3000	2750

▶ 50.64 21 inch Paratrooper Model

EXC.	V.G.	GOOD
3500	3000	2750

▶ 50.41 Synthetic Butt with Heavy Barrel

EXC.	V.G.	GOOD
2800	2500	2000

▶ 50.42 Wood Butt with heavy barrel

EXC.	V.G.	GOOD
3500	3000	2750

■ FNC

A lighter-weight rifle chambered for the 5.56mm cartridge. It is a gas-operated semiautomatic with an 18 inch or 21 inch barrel. It has a 30 round box magazine and is black, with either a fixed or folding stock. This model was also discontinued by FN.

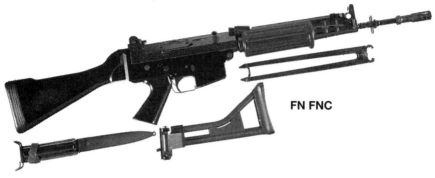

FN FNC

▶ Standard

Fixed stock, 16 inch or 18 inch barrel.

EXC.	V.G.	GOOD
3500	2750	2200

▶ Paratrooper Model

Folding stock, 16 inch or 18 inch barrel.

EXC.	V.G.	GOOD
3700	3000	2500

FAMAS (GIAT)
St. Etienne, France

■ F1

This bull pup design was adopted by France as a battle rifle. Fewer than 100 of a semi-automatic version were imported to the U.S. by Century Arms in the late 1980s. Caliber 5.56mm/.223. 25 round magazine.

EXC.	V.G.	GOOD
8000	7000	6000

FAMAS F1

FEATHER INDUSTRIES, INC.
Trinidad, Colorado

■ AT-22

A blowback operated rifle in .22LR. Removable 17 inch barrel. 20 rd magazine. Collapsible metal stock. Manufactured 1986-95. Rifles made the final year of production had the collapsible stock altered so it could not slide into the retracted position. Late production guns were sold through Mitchell Arms.

EXC.	V.G.	GOOD
375	300	250

■ F-2

Similar to the AT-22 but has a fixed synthetic stock. Made to comply with some state "assault weapon" laws. Manufactured 1992-95.

EXC.	V.G.	GOOD
300	250	200

■ AT-9

A blowback operated 9mm rifle. Has a 16 inch barrel and collapsible metal stock. Magazines offered in 10, 25 and 30 rounds. Manufactured 1988-95.

EXC.	V.G.	GOOD
600	450	350

FEATHER USA
Eaton, Colorado

A new corporation. They bought rights to the old Feather Industries designs. Currently offering a series of firearms based on the AT-22 and AT-9 design available with many optional upgrades and accessories.

■ RAV-22LR

Basically the same rifle as the AT-22 listed above. The wire stock does not slide to a shorter position. It can be removed easily. There are several options in finish, stocks and accessories. Price listed is for the base model.

MSRP	EXC.	V.G.	GOOD
399	350	300	250

■ RAV-22HA

As above but features a tapered bull barrel.

MSRP	EXC.	V.G.	GOOD
549	475	425	375

■ RAV-22HF

A bull barrel model featuring a CAR-15 style sliding buttstock.

MSRP	EXC.	V.G.	GOOD
695	600	550	500

■ RAV-9MM

A new version of the AT-9 listed above. Several options available. Price is for the base model.

MSRP	EXC.	V.G.	GOOD
599	500	450	400

■ RAV-9HA

As above with a tapered bull barrel.

MSRP	EXC.	V.G.	GOOD
759	650	600	550

■ RAV-40S&W

Similar to the base model but in .40 S&W.

MSRP	EXC.	V.G.	GOOD
699	N/A	N/A	N/A

■ RAV-45ACP

Similar to base model but in .45 ACP.

MSRP	EXC.	V.G.	GOOD
759	650	600 5	50

■ RAV-45ACPHA

Similar to above but with tapered bull barrel.

MSRP	EXC.	V.G.	GOOD
899	750	700	650

FEDERAL ENGINEERING
Chicago, Illinois

■ XC-220
A .22LR semi-automatic rifle. Tubular construction. 16-1/2 inch barrel. 28 round magazine. Manufactured 1984-89.

EXC.	V.G.	GOOD
550	450	400

■ XC-450
As above but in .45 caliber. 30 round magazine. Manufactured 1984-89.

EXC.	V.G.	GOOD
750	600	500

■ XC-900
As above but in 9mm. 32 round magazine. Manufactured 1984-89.

EXC.	V.G.	GOOD
700	550	450

FEDERAL ORDNANCE
South El Monte, California

■ M-14
A semi-automatic version of the U.S. service rifle. New manufactured receiver assembled with USGI surplus parts. Wood or fiberglass stock. Chambered in .308/7.62 NATO. Manufactured 1986-91.

EXC.	V.G.	GOOD
800	700	600

FEG
(FEGYVER ES GAZKESZULEKGYAR)
Budapest, Hungary

Imported by Kassnar Imports of Harrisburg, Pennsylvania.

■ SA 85M

This is an AK-47 variation produced in Hungary. Caliber 7.62x39mm. Black laquer finish. Light colored wood stocks. Both fixed and folding stock versions were made. Imported 1987-89.

EXC.	V.G.	GOOD
1500	1250	1000

■ SA-2000-M

Introduced in 1999, this FEG-made AK was imported with a thumbhole stock.

EXC.	V.G.	GOOD
750	625	500

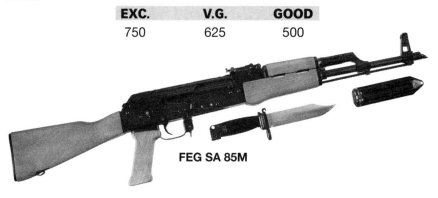

FEG SA 85M

FNH USA Inc.
McClean, Virginia

The U.S. importer for FN Herstal in Belgium. They are the current incarnation of the classic manufacturer Fabrique National.

■ PS-90

A semi-automatic version of the P-90 submachine gun. Chambered for the 5.7x28mm cartridge. 30 and 50 round magazines. Black or green synthetic stock.

MSRP	EXC.	V.G.	GOOD
1300	1200	1100	950

FNH PS-90

■ FS2000

A bullpup style rifle in 5.56mm/.223. 17-3/8 inch barrel. Uses AR-15/M-16 magazines.

MSRP	EXC.	V.G.	GOOD
2100	1850	1700	1600

FNH FS2000, RIGHT AND LEFT VIEWS

FULTON ARMORY
Savage, Maryland

This company manufactures a line of precision M-14 and AR-15 type rifles. They manufacture their own receivers. Most products are custom built to order and pricing changes with each feature. The base model prices are listed here.

■ M-14 SERVICE RIFLE

A new Fulton armory receiver assembled with the customer's choice of a 22 or 18-1/2 inch barrel. Chambered for 7.62mm/.308. The rest of the steel parts are original USGI. Parkerized finish. New military contour walnut stock. Optional feature available for an additional price include: national match trigger, various pattern scope mounts and even a non-functional selector switch for those who want to mirror the full appearance of the military M-14. Uses 10 and 20 round M-14 magazines. Rifle shipped with one 10 round magazine.

MSRP	EXC.	V.G.	GOOD
2500	2200	2000	1800

■ M-14 SUPER SCOUT RIFLE

A new Fulton armory receiver assembled with either a 22 or 18-1/2 inch barrel. Chambered for 7.62mm/.308. The rest of the steel parts are original USGI. Parkerized finish. Includes new Fulton Armory Super Scout Rail Handguard. The new walnut stock is made to original specifications. Uses 10 and 20 round M-14 magazines. Rifle shipped with one 10 round magazine.

MSRP	EXC.	V.G.	GOOD
2800	2500	2250	2000

■ M-14 SOCOM MARK 14 MODEL 0 RIFLE

Tested by the U.S. military. 18- or 22 inch military contour barrel. Chambered for 7.62mm/.308. Includes Sage collapsible stock/accuracy rail system with all Sage stock accessories, tritium front night sight, vortex direct connect flash suppressor, tactical extended bolt release. Uses 10 and 20 round M-14 magazines. Rifle shipped with one 10 round magazine.

MSRP	EXC.	V.G.	GOOD
3500	3250	3000	2750

FULTON M-14 SOCOM MARK 14 MODEL 0 RIFLE

M-14 PEERLESS MATCH/TARGET RIFLE

A new Fulton Armory match grade receiver assembled with a Fulton 22 inch national match stainless steel barrel. Chambered for 7.62mm/.308. Includes National Match trigger modification, national match front and rear sights, and national match operating rod spring guide. The new National Match walnut stock features Includes glass bedding, front end mod, and handguard mod. Uses 10 and 20 round M-14 magazines. Rifle shipped with one 10 round magazine.

MSRP	EXC.	V.G.	GOOD
3300	3100	2800	2500

■ TITAN FAR 308 RIFLE

An AR-10 based system. Dual-finished (hard coat anodized and black Teflon coated) 6066T6 slick-side, no-snag Titan flat top upper receiver. 20 inch or 22 inch stainless steel four groove one-in-ten Heavy barrel, genuine Smith Enterprises USGI Vortex® direct connect flash suppressor. Titan float tube with steel locking ring. The lower assembly begins with a dual-finished (hard coat anodized and black Teflon coated) forged 6061T6 Titan lower receiver. A2 buttstock or an optional Magpul Titan PRS buttstock. Titan SPR hand-filling pistol grip. Fulton Armory-tuned two-stage match trigger. Shipped with a 10 round magazine.

MSRP	EXC.	V.G.	GOOD
1700	1500	1250	1000

FULTON TITAN FAR 308 RIFLE

■ TITAN FAR 308 CARBINE

Dual-finished 6066T6 slick-side no-snag Titan upper receiver. 16 inch or 20 inch stainless steel four groove one-in-ten medium weight barrel. Genuine Smith Enterprises USGI Vortex® direct connect flash suppressor. Titan float tube with steel locking ring. Optional 3 inch to 12 inch rails for all four sides; top rail co-registers with receiver rail. Optional folding/detachable front and rear sights; requires at least one 2 inch top rail. Hard chrome bolt carrier. The lower assemble starts with a Dual-finished (hard coat anodized and black Teflon coated) Forged 6061T6 Titan lower receiver. Command Arms "Fifth Generation" collapsible stock with ambi QD swivel sockets standard. Optional Magpul Titan PRS buttstock. Titan SPR pistol grip. Fulton Armory-tuned two-stage match trigger. Shipped with a 10 round magazine.

MSRP	EXC.	V.G.	GOOD
1700	1500	1250	1000

■ FAR-15 LEGACY

Near-exact replica of the Viet Nam era M16. The Legacy Service Rifle features new, genuine USGI M16A1 chrome lightweight 20 inch barrel in 5.56mm/.223 with 1:12 twist. Original pattern 3-prong M16-type flash suppressor. Military-contractor M16-type "Slick Side" forged upper receiver with no forward assist or case deflector. Forged steel M16 front sight base. M16 front and rear Sights. M16-type triangular handguards. M16-type buttstock with early-type solid buttplate (no door)—CAR stock optional at no extra cost. Chrome plated slick side bolt carrier has no forward assist serrations. Fulton Armory forged lower receiver. Hand-Polished and hand-fitted military trigger. A1 pistol grip.

MSRP	EXC	V.G.	GOOD
900	800	750	700

■ FAR-15 CLASSIC SERVICE CARBINE

Based on the military issue M-4 carbine. Features a choice of flat top or A-2 type upper receiver. Fulton Armory 1:9 heavy contour or M4 contour (chrome lined bore and chamber standard) or 16 inch barrel with Fulton Armory 5.56MM match chamber. (Chrome lined bore and chamber optional) A2 flash suppressor. Forged military numbered flattop or A2 upper receiver. Forged steel front sight base with exclusive windage adjustment. Military-contract forged upper receiver. D-Fender extractor enhancer. Fulton Armory forged lower receiver. Hand-polished and hand-fitted military trigger. A2 pistol grip. Six-position collapsible stock. Choice of Black (standard, or optional Olive Drab (OD) or Tan furniture.

MSRP	EXC.	V.G.	GOOD
800	750	700	650

■ FAR-15 CLASSIC SERVICE RIFLE

Based on the military issue M-16A2, the FAR-15 Classic Service Rifle features a choice of forged flat top or A-2 type upper receiver. Fulton Armory 1:9 heavy contour 20 inch barrel with Fulton Armory 5.56MM match chamber, or Fulton Armory 1:8 heavy contour barrel. A2 flash suppressor. Forged steel front sight base with exclusive windage adjustment. D-Fender extractor enhancer. Fulton Armory forged lower receiver. Hand-polished and hand-fitted military trigger. A2 pistol grip and buttstock. Choice of Black (standard) or optional Olive Drab (OD) or Tan (with A1 buttstock) furniture.

MSRP	EXC.	V.G.	GOOD
800	750	700	650

■ PHANTOM FAR-15 SOCOM EBR (ENHANCED BATTLE RIFLE) CARBINE

AR-type rifle with round and fluted full-float tube; optional 3, 4, 7 or 12 inch Swan/Weaver rails may be mounted on any or all of the four sides. Ambi sling swivel, side or bottom mount. Flip up front sight gas block. Choice of 16 inch Barrels, 1:9 twist heavy or 1:9 twist M-4 contour, all with Fulton Armory 5.56mm match chamber. A2 flash suppressor. D-Fender extractor enhancer. Fulton Armory forged lower receiver. Hand-tuned two-stage Rock River National Match trigger. Ergo tactical grip. Six-position collapsible stock. MagPul fully adjustable buttstock available for an additional $250.

MSRP	EXC.	V.G.	GOOD
1000	950	900	850

■ PHANTOM FAR-15 EBR RIFLE

As above but features a choice of a 20 inch 1:8 or 1:9 twist heavy contour barrel and an A2 buttstock.

MSRP	EXC.	V.G.	GOOD
1050	950	900	850

■ LIBERATOR FAR-15 SOCOM EBR CARBINE

AR-style rifle with Liberator float tube with four full-length Swan/Weaver rails and ambidextrous QD swivel sockets (with one QD swivel). Flip up front sight gas block. Choice of 16 inch barrels: 1:9 twist heavy or 1:9 twist M-4 contour, all with Fulton Armory 5.56mm match chamber. A2 flash suppressor. D-Fender extractor enhancer. Fulton Armory forged lower receiver. Hand-tuned two-stage Rock River NM trigger. Ergo tactical grip. Six-position collapsible stock. MagPul fully adjustable buttstock available for an additional $250.

MSRP	EXC.	V.G.	GOOD
1100	1000	950	900

■ LIBERATOR FAR-15 EBR RIFLE

As above but features a choice of a 20 inch 1:8 or 1:9 twist heavy contour barrel and an A2 buttstock.

MSRP	EXC.	V.G	GOOD
1050	1000	950	900

■ FAR-15 NATIONAL MATCH SERVICE RIFLE

AR-style rifle with Fulton Armory stainless steel 1:8 National Match 20 inch Heavy Match barrel (or add $320 for a Krieger Stainless Steel 1:7.75 NM 20 inch Heavy Match Barrel). National Match A2 flash suppressor with "Safety Locking" set screw. Heavy steel handguard float tube system with full circumferential welds. Northern Competition NM rear sight, 1/4-moa windage and elevation adjustments at no extra cost. Rear sight hooded aperture that will accept lenses. User windage-adjustable PowerWedge front sight base. NM sight with front sight post capture system. Fulton Armory barrel extension/receiver extension fusion. Carpenter steel (not commercial repro) with milled G.I. extractor headspaced bolt carrier group. D-Fender extractor enhancer. Fulton Armory forged lower receiver. Hand-tuned two-stage Rock River NM trigger.

MSRP	EXC	V.G.	GOOD
1200	1100	1025	950

■ ACCUTRON FAR-15 MATCH RIFLE

The Accutron Match Rifle includes Fulton Armory 24 inch stainless steel .812 inch match barrel, 1:8 twist. Accutron reinforced flattop upper receiver. Round float tube handguard with handstop slot. Sculpted gas block. D-Fender extractor enhancer. Hand-tuned two-stage Rock River NM trigger. Accutron SPR match pistol grip. A2 buttstock. Sights and sight bases not Included; sight bases optional, extra.

MSRP	EXC.	V.G.	GOOD
910	850	800	750

■ FAR-15 PREDATOR VARMINT/PRECISION RIFLE

The Predator Varmint Rifle includes Predator reinforced flattop upper receiver. Fulton Armory 1:8, 1:9, or 1:12 20 inch stainless steel or 1:8 NM Heavy Barrel. Optional 24 inch .812 inch stainless steel barrel or Krieger 1:7.75, 1:9, or 1:10 20 inch stainless steel NM heavy barrel or Krieger 1:7.75 24 inch stainless steel .812 inch, or 1:7.75 26 inch .920 inch stainless steel barrel for additional charge. Sculpted gas block. Round and knurled aluminum float tube. D-Fender extractor enhancer. Hand-tuned two-stage Rock River NM trigger. Predator match pistol grip. Lower front sling swivel stud (suitable for bipods).

MSRP	EXC.	V.G.	GOOD
900	850	800	750

GALIL

See IMI.

GALIL

GRENDEL
Rockledge, Florida

■ P-30 PISTOL

A 22 Magnum semi-automatic pistol. Frame constructed mostly of nylon. Matte black finish. It has a 5 inch barrel. 30 round magazine. Manufactured 1990-95.

EXC.	V.G.	GOOD
400	350 3	00

Note: *add $50-80 for each functional 30 round magazine.*

■ R-31 CARBINE

A semi-automatic rifle in .22 Magnum rimfire. It has a 16 inch barrel with muzzle brake, synthetic frame and forearm. Telescoping buttstock. Magazine holds 30 rounds. Discontinued in 1994.

EXC.	V.G.	GOOD
1500	1100	800

GRENDEL P-30 PISTOL

GONCZ ARMAMENT
North Hollywood, California

■ MODEL GA

A 9mm semi-automatic pistol. This was a new design, not based on any other existing firearm. This small manufacturer built these on a prototype and special order basis from 1984-90. There were several minor variations listed in factory listings but it is unclear how many of any type were ever made. The company was taken over by Claridge Hi Tec who went on to produce another model based on this design. The designer Lajos J. Goncz reportedly sued Claridge over patent infringements and forced Claridge to discontinue production.

EXC.	V.G.	GOOD
2500	2000	1500

GONCZ MODEL GA

HECKLER AND KOCH
Oberndorf/Neckar, Germany

■ HK41

The Heckler and Koch model HK41 is a semi-automatic rifle that was first produced in 1966. It is the civilian version of the renowned military and law enforcement G3 automatic rifle that was manufactured by Heckler and Koch, GmbH during the mid to late 1950s, and is the precursor to the HK91 semiautomatic rifle. The HK41 employs the same G3 "roller de-layed blowback system" that is known for its strength, reliability and low recoil. At the time the HK41 was produced, the first digit "4" in Heckler and Koch's model numbering system signified that it is a paramilitary-type semiautomatic rifle, while the second digit "1" identified the type of ammunition the rifle is chambered for as 7.62mm x 51 NATO or .308 cali-ber Winchester. All HK41s were manufactured at the Heckler and Koch, GmbH plant located in Oberndorf am Neckar, Germany. Only a limited number were produced for and imported into the United States. Factory records indicate fewer than 400 model 41s were ever made.

■ HK41 (1966)

Imported in 1966 only by the Sante Fe Division of the Golden State Arms Co in Pasadena, California. These are desirable by collectors as the clos-est copy of a true G-3 and many were converted to full automatic opera-tion before 1986. This has reduced the already limited numbers available on the civilian market.

EXC.	V.G.	GOOD
6000	5000	3800

■ HK41 (1974)

Imported 1974 by SACO (Security Arms Co.) of Arlington, Virginia. The 1974 version of the 1966 HK41 had some internal changes to the receiver and trigger group due to requirements imposed by the BATF, because the 1966 version used some full automatic components.

EXC.	V.G.	GOOD
5000	3750	3000

HECKLER AND KOCH INC.
Arlington, Virginia

Exclusive U.S. importer for H&K products. Formed in 1976.

■ MODEL 91

This rifle is recoil-operated, with a delayed-roller lock bolt. It is chambered for the .308 Winchester/7.62 NATO cartridge and has a 17.7 inch barrel with military-style aperture sights. It is furnished with a 20 round detachable magazine and is finished in matte black with a black plastic stock. This model is a semi-automatic version of the select fire G3 rifle. Some areas of the country have made its ownership illegal. Approximately 48,000 were imported 1975-89.

EXC.	V.G.	GOOD
2500	2200	1850

■ MODEL 91 A3

This model is simply the Model 91 with a retractable metal stock.

EXC.	V.G.	GOOD
2500	2200	1850

■ MODEL 93

This model is similar to the Model 91 except that it is chambered for the .223 cartridge and has a 16.4 inch barrel. The magazine holds 25 rounds, and the specifications are the same as for the Model 91. This is a semi-automatic version of the select fire HK33 rifle. Approximately 18,000 were imported 1975-89.

EXC.	V.G.	GOOD
2700	2500	2100

■ MODEL 93 A3

This is the Model 93 with a retractable metal stock.

EXC.	V.G.	GOOD
2800	2550	2200

■ MODEL 94

This is a carbine version of the Model 93 chambered for the 9mm Parabellum cartridge, with a 16.5 inch barrel. It is a smaller-scaled weapon that has a 15-shot magazine. Many have been converted to full automatic.

EXC.	V.G.	GOOD
3800	3200	2700

■ MODEL 94 A3

This model is a variation of the Model 94 with the addition of a retractable metal stock.

EXC.	V.G.	GOOD
3900	3400	2800

■ SP-89

A large frame semi-automatic pistol in 9mm. Based on the H&K MP-5 submachine gun. 4-1/2 inch barrel. Imported 1991-1994.

EXC.	V.G.	GOOD
3500	3000	2500

■ PSG-1

A precision sniping rifle based on the HK91 with a 25-5/8 inch heavy barrel. Fine tune trigger group. Adjustable buttstock. Sold with a Hensoldt 6x42 scope. Shipped in a fitted case. Discontinued in 1989.

EXC.	V.G.	GOOD
15,000	12,500	9500

■ MODEL SR9

A sporter version of the HK91 made to comply with U.S. law. 19-3/4 inch barrel without flash suppressor. Synthetic stock with thumbhole pistol grip. Imported 1990-94.

EXC.	V.G.	GOOD
1900	1750	1400

■ MODEL SR9 T (TARGET)

SR9 with adjustable MSG90 buttstock, PSG-1 trigger group and hand grip. Imported 1992-94.

EXC.	V.G.	GOOD
3000	2500	2000

■ SR9 TC (TARGET COMPETITION)

SR9 with PSG-1 stock, trigger group and pistol grip. Imported 1993.

EXC.	V.G.	GOOD
7000	5500	4000

■ SL-8-1

A new generation .223/5.56mm rifle based on the Model G36. Gas operated action. Most parts are made from poly carbon fiber. Gray color. Thumbhole stock with cheek rest. 20-3⁄4 inch barrel. 10 round magazine. Introduced in 2000.

MSRP	EXC.	V.G.	GOOD
1600	1400	1250	1000

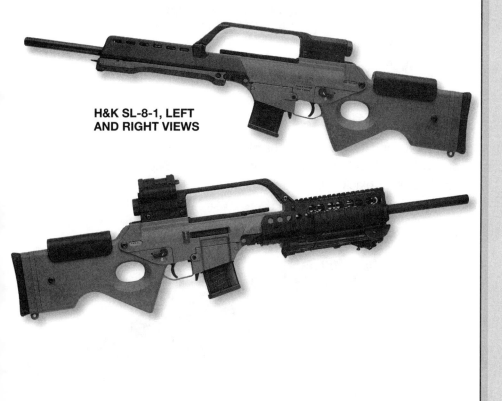

H&K SL-8-1, LEFT AND RIGHT VIEWS

■ SL-8-6

As above with a redesigned stock and sight configuration. Black color.

MSRP	EXC.	V.G.	GOOD
1500	1300	1100	900

**H&K SL-8-6 RIFLE (TOP)
AND RECEIVER MARKINGS
(BOTTOM)**

■ MODEL USC

A semi-automatic blowback operated carbine in .45 ACP. It is based on H&K's UMP submachine gun. 16 inch barrel. Skeletonized synthetic stock. Gray or black color. 10 round magazine. Introduced in 2000.

MSRP	EXC.	V.G.	GOOD
1300	1100	950	800

**H&K MODEL USC RIFLE
AND RECEIVER MARKINGS**

HESSE ARMS
Inver Grove Heights, Minnesota

This company is no longer in business under this name. The resale market in Hesse firearms is extremely soft, so no values are cited here.

■ FAL-H RIFLES

All FAL-H rifles include these features: military spec internal parts, new or as new barrel, military finish, post ban legal muzzlebrake, one magazine, new metric pattern Type 3 receiver, adjustable gas system, refinished or new pistol grip, hard case, carry handle, sling, and manual. All rifles chambered for .308 Winchester cartridge. Additional calibers in .22-250 and .243 are also available. Weights are from 8.5 to 14 lbs. depending on model.

▶ FALO Tactical Rifle

This model features a free floating handguard assembly.

EXC.	V.G.	GOOD
900	800	700

▶ FALO Heavy Barrel

This model features a heavy barrel and is based on the Israeli FALO rifle.

EXC.	V.G.	GOOD
750	650	550

▶ FAL-H High Grade

This model is available in any configuration and features a new walnut stock, pistol grip, and hand guard. Trigger is gold plated.

EXC.	V.G.	GOOD
1050	950	800

This is standard model that is similar in appearance to the original FAL.

EXC.	V.G.	GOOD
750	600	500

▶ FAL-H Congo Rifle

This model features a 16 inch barrel.

EXC.	V.G.	GOOD
800	700	600

▶ FALO Congo Rifle

Similar to the model above but fitted with a 16 inch heavy barrel.

EXC.	V.G.	GOOD
800	700	600

■ HAR-15 RIFLES

All of the HAR-15 rifles have these features: military spec internal parts, heavy match grade barrels, post ban legal muzzle-brake, A2 upper receiver, A2 round handguards with heat shields, A2 stock, A2 lower receiver. Each rifle comes with hard case, manual, and sling. Rifles are chambered for .223 Remington but can be chambered in other calibers as well. These are: .17 Rem. add $145, 9mm NATO add $85, 6mm PPC add $145, 6mmx45 add $95, .300 Fireball add $195; 7.62x39 add $45.

▶ Omega Match

Fitted with a 1 inch diameter stainless steel barrel, adjustable match trigger, E2 stock, flat top receiver, free floating handguard.

EXC.	V.G.	GOOD
800	700	600

▶ HAR-15A2 Standard Rifle

This model has all of the standard features offered for HAR-15 rifles.

EXC.	V.G.	GOOD
575	500	450

▶ HAR-15A2 National Match

This model is fitted with special bolt carrier, adjustable match trigger. Designed as Match grade rifle.

EXC.	V.G.	GOOD
800	700	600

▶ HAR-15A2 Bull Gun

This model is fitted with a 1 inch stainless steel barrel with special front sight base.

EXC.	V.G.	GOOD
650	600	550

▶ HAR-15A2 Dispatcher

Fitted with a 16 inch barrel with full length handguard.

EXC.	V.G.	GOOD
600	550	500

▶ HAR-15A2 Carbine

Fitted with a 16 inch heavy barrel and a non-collapsing stock with short handguard.

EXC.	V.G.	GOOD
500	475	450

▶ M14-H Standard Rifle

This is a semi-automatic version of the M14 rifle chambered for the .308 cartridge. It is fitted with a new receiver, walnut stock or synthetic stock. Each rifle is sold with a sling, annual, and 10 round magazine and an extra original M145 stock.

EXC.	V.G.	GOOD
800	700	600

▶ M14-H Brush Rifle

This model has the same features as the standard rifle but with an 18 inch barrel.

EXC.	V.G.	GOOD
800	700	600

■ MODEL 47 RIFLE

This is a copy of the AK-47 and it is chambered for the 7.63x39 cartridge. It is also available in .223 caliber.

EXC.	V.G.	GOOD
450	400	350

HIGH STANDARD MANUFACTURING CO.
Houston, Texas

This company offers the Mil-Spec series of AR-type rifles.

■ HSA-15 RIFLE A2

Military pattern A2 style. Chambered in 5.56mm/.223. 20 inch barrel. Fixed carry handle. Fixed stock. Has a flash hider and bayonet lug.

MSRP	EXC.	V.G.	GOOD
943	800	700	600

■ HSA-15 CARBINE A2

Ar-type rifle with CAR-15 style handguard. 16 inch barrel. Fixed carry handle. Six-position telescoping buttstock.

MSRP	EXC.	V.G.	GOOD
943	800	700	600

■ HSA-15 FLAT TOP RIFLE A2

Flat top receiver for scope mounting or adjustable sight. Carry handle; standard front sight. 20 inch barrel. Has a flash hider and bayonet lug.

MSRP	EXC.	V.G.	GOOD
920	800	700	600

■ HSA-15 FLAT TOP CARBINE A2

AR-type rifle with A2-style flat top receiver for scope mounting or adjustable sight carry handle. Standard front sight. 16 inch barrel. Has a flash hider and bayonet lug. Six-position telescoping buttstock.

MSRP	EXC.	V.G.	GOOD
920	800	700	600

Hi-Point Firearms
Dayton, Ohio

■ MODEL 995 CARBINE

Introduced in 1996, this economy priced semi-automatic rifle is available in 9mm or .40 S&W. It has a 16-1/2 inch barrel and an overall length of 32-1/2 inches. Weight is 7 lbs. Features include an all-weather black or camo polymer stock. Grip mounted magazine release, quick on/off thumb safety, fully adjustable sights with "Ghost Ring" rear sight and front post. Scope base to allow mounting of a regular rifle scope or red dot scope. 10 round magazines.

NIB	EXC.	V.G.	GOOD
225	200	175 1	50

VARIOUS CONFIGURATIONS OF THE HI POINT MODEL 995 CARBINE

HOLLOWAY ARMS CO.
Ft. Worth, Texas

■ HAC-7

A 7.62mm semi-automatic rifle. An interesting design that has features adopted from the FN FAL, AKM and AR-10. It has a 20 inch barrel. Offered in right or left hand versions. Side folding stock. Uses modified Armalite AR-10 magazines. Approximately 350 were made 1984-85.

EXC.	V.G.	GOOD
3500	3000	2500

HOLLOWAY ARMS HAC-7

IMI
(ISRAEL MILITARY INDUSTRIES)
Israel

The small arms manufacturer for the Israeli military. They have also exported several models to the U.S. IMI products are imported by several companies including Action Arms, Springfield Armory and Magnum Research.

■ UZI CARBINE

A 9mm semi-automatic version of the legendary submachine gun. It has a 16 inch barrel and a collapsible steel stock. Sold with a dummy 10 inch barrel that simulates the appearance of the original SMG.

▶ Model A (Imported 1980-83)

EXC.	V.G.	GOOD
1400	1200	1000

▶ Model B

As above with minor internal changes due to BATF requirements that it not accept the original UZI submachinegun bolt. Also offered in .45 ACP. Imported 1983-89.

EXC.	V.G.	GOOD
1250	1100	950

IMI UZI CARBINE

■ UZI CONVERSION KIT FOR .22LR

With one 12 round magazine. Installs on the B model.

EXC.	V.G.	GOOD
400	325	275

Note: Also see UZI listings under Norinco and Vector Arms.

■ UZI MINI CARBINE

A scaled down version of the Uzi Carbine. 19-3⁄4 inch barrel. Steel stock folds to the side. Imported 1988-89.

EXC.	V.G.	GOOD
2000	1750	1500

■ UZI PISTOL

A 9mm or .45 ACP pistol that resembles the micro UZI submachine gun. 4-1⁄2 inch barrel.

EXC.	V.G.	GOOD
1000	800	650

IMI UZI PISTOL

■ GALIL

An Israeli designed rifle using a refined Kalishnikov (AK-47) action.

▶ Galil Model 386 AR 5.56mm

16-1/8 inch barrel. Side folding stock. 35 round magazine. Importation discontinued in 1989.

EXC.	V.G.	GOOD
2500	2100	1750

IMI GALIL MODEL 386 AR 5.56MM

▶ Galil Model 329 AR 7.62mm

19 inch barrel. Side folding stock. 12- and 25 round magazines. Importation discontinued in 1989.

EXC.	V.G.	GOOD
2600	2200	1850

▶ Galil Model 372 ARM 5.56mm

Heavier version of the AR with a folding bipod.

EXC.	V.G.	GOOD
2750	2500	2200

▶ Galil Model 332 ARM 7.62mm

.308/7.62 NATO version of the AR with a folding bipod.

EXC.	V.G.	GOOD
2700	2550	2300

▶ Hadar II SA 7.62mm

Sporter version of the Galil AR featuring a walnut stock with thumbhole pistol grip. Imported in 1989-90.

EXC.	V.G.	GOOD
1400	1150	850

Note: *Also see Galil entries under Ohio Rapid Fire and Elite Firearms.*

INTERDYNAMICS OF AMERICA
Miami, Florida

■ KG-9

A 9mm semiautomatic handgun with a machine pistol appearance. It has a five inch barrel protected by a perforated steel shroud. The muzzle is threaded. 32 round magazine. Fires from an open bolt. The BATF ruled this model to be illegal to manufacture because it was too easy to modify to full automatic. Manufactured 1981-83.

EXC.	V.G.	GOOD
1000	750	600

■ KG-99

A redesigned version of the KG-9. Striker fired from a closed bolt. Also was available in stainless steel. Manufactured in 1984.

EXC.	V.G.	GOOD
500	425	350

■ KG-9 MINI

As above but has a 3 inch barrel. The muzzle is threaded. Made without the barrel shroud.

EXC.	V.G.	GOOD
500	425	350

INTRATEC
Miami, Florida

This was Interdynamics reorganized under a new name. They were forced out of business in the late 1990s after lawsuits over misuse of their products.

■ TEC-9 OR TEC-DC9

A 9mm semiautomatic hand gun with a machine pistol appearance. It has a five inch barrel protected by a perforated steel shroud. The muzzle is threaded. 32 round magazine. Matte black or stainless steel finish. Manufactured 1985-94.

EXC.	V.G.	GOOD
500	425	350

■ TEC-9 MINI

As above but has a 3 inch barrel. The muzzle is threaded. Made without the barrel shroud.

EXC.	V.G.	GOOD
500	425	350

■ TEC-22 OR SKORPION

A 22LR semi-automatic pistol similar to the Tec-9. 4 inch barrel with threaded muzzle. Does not have the barrel shroud. 30 round magazine. This pistol uses a magazine that is interchangeable with that of the Ruger 10-22 rifle. Manufactured 1988-94

EXC.	V.G.	GOOD
350	300	250

■ AB-10

This is simply a post-ban Tec-9 Mini without the threaded muzzle. Shipped with a 10 round magazine, but also accepts the earlier 32 round version.

EXC.	V.G.	GOOD
300	250	200

■ SPORT-22

Post-ban version of the Tec-22 without the threaded muzzle. Sold with a 10 round rotary magazine but also accepts the earlier high-capacity versions.

EXC.	V.G.	GOOD
275	250	200

J AND R ENGINEERING
South El Monte, California

■ MODEL 68

A 9mm semi-automatic rifle. It has a 16-1/4 inch barrel that ends with a cone shaped flash hider. Wood buttstock and forearm. 31 round magazine. This design first appeared in the 1960s. It was later manufactured by Wilkinson Arms as the Terry carbine.

EXC.	V.G.	GOOD
450	400	350

KEL-TEC CNC INDUSTRIES
Cocoa, Florida

■ SUB-2000 RIFLE

A 9mm or .40 S&W semi-automatic rifle. It has a 16-1/8 inch barrel. The rifle can be folded closed with a length of 16 inches. They offer different grip assemblies that can use different magazines. The standard one takes S&W type magazines. Other grip options include Glock, SIG or Beretta. Introduced 2001.

NIB	EXC.	V.G.	GOOD
406	350	300	275

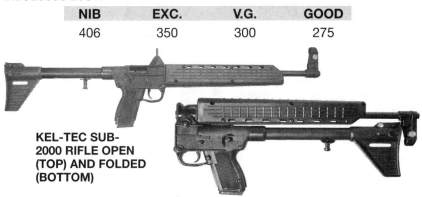

KEL-TEC SUB-2000 RIFLE OPEN (TOP) AND FOLDED (BOTTOM)

■ SU-16A

A semi-automatic rifle in 5.56mm. 18 inch barrel. Picatinny rail for sight mounting. The nylon forearm splits open and folds down to become a bi-pod. The stock can be rotated for storage. Two 10 round or one 30 round magazines can be stored in the buttstock. Accepts AR-15/M-16 series magazines.

NIB	EXC.	V.G.	GOOD
665	550	500	425

KEL-TEC SU-16A OPEN (TOP), FOLDED (MIDDLE) AND WITH BIPOD EXTENDED (BOTTOM)

KEL-TEC SU-16
5.56 mm Rifle

■ SU-16 B

The "B" model retains all the features of the original SU-16, such as integrated bipod, Picatinny rail, and rotating stock with magazine storage. 16 inch barrel. The rear sight is hard coat anodized aluminum and adjustable for windage. The front sight, also aluminum, is removable and accepts standard M-16 posts. Note: The "B" type sights can be purchased as a retrofit for SU-16 owners preferring the M-16 system.

NIB	EXC.	V.G.	GOOD
718	600	500	500

KEL-TEC SU-16 B FOLDED
(TOP) AND OPEN (BOTTOM)

■ SU-16C

Retains most features of the original SU-16, such as integrated bipod, Picatinny rail, and M-16 magazine compatibility. The sights are similar to the "B" inch model, but with the front sight integrated into the gas block. The SU-16C has a true folding stock and can be fired with the stock folded. An reciprocating dust cover and a case deflecting operating handle are also integrated into the rifle. The barrel is 16 inch long and of medium weight. The muzzle is threaded 1/2x28 to accept standard attachments.

NIB	EXC.	V.G.	GOOD
770	650	575	500

KEL-TEC SU-16C OPEN WITH
BIPOD EXTENDED (TOP) AND
FOLDED (BOTTOM)

■ SU-16 CA

The SU-16CA Is a hybrid of the SU-16C and SU-16A rifles. The receiver, 16 inch barrel with 1/2-28 threads, bolt carrier, dust cover, sights, and case deflecting operating handle of the C model are combined with the stock of the A model. The SU-16CA will come with two 10 round magazines that store in the stock just like the A model and has all the same parkerized parts as the C model. Just like the A model the SU-16CA can be folded for storage and it will not fire in the folded position. This allows for it to be purchased in most states that still have an "assault weapons ban."

NIB	EXC.	V.G.	GOOD
770	650	575	500

KEL-TEC SU-16 CA

■ PLR-16

A gas operated, semi-automatic pistol chambered in 5.56 mm NATO caliber. The PLR-16 has a conventional gas piston operation and utilizes the proven M-16 breech locking system. The rear sight is adjustable for windage. The front sight is of M-16 type. An integrated MIL-STD-1913 Picatinny rail will accept a multitude of standard accessories. The muzzle end of the barrel is threaded to accept standard attachments such as a muzzle brake. Except for the barrel, bolt, sights, and mechanism, the PLR-16 pistol is made entirely of high-impact glass fiber reinforced polymer.

NIB	EXC.	V.G.	GOOD
665	575	500	425

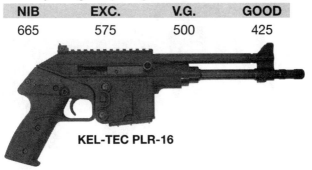

KEL-TEC PLR-16

■ PLR-22

A .22LR blowback operated pistol based on the PLR-16. It has a 10 inch barrel. The total length is 18-1/2 inches. Weight is 2-3/4 lbs. Accepts many

of the accessories for the PLR-16 and SU-16 series. 27 round magazine. Also accepts Atchison M-16 22LR conversion magazines. New for 2008.
Note: *No pricing information available.*

KEL-TEC PLR-22

■ SU-22

Based on the popular SU-16 series. .22LR blowback operated. 16.1 inch barrel with threaded muzzle. Total length is 40 inches. Fixed stock. Weight is 4 lbs. 27 round magazine. Also accepts Atchison M-16 .22LR conversion magazines. New for 2008.
Note: *No pricing information available.*

■ RFB HIGH EFFICIENCY RIFLE

This bullpup design was introduced at the 2007 SHOT show as the SRT-8, (Sniper Rifle Tactical). The name has been changed to RFB (Rifle Forward ejection Bullpup) but as of early 2008 no RFB carbines have been shipped. Factory announcements promise delivery by late 2008. The RFB is chambered in .308. It has a 18 inch barrel. The total length of the RFB is 26 inches. Weight is 8 lbs. No sights. Picatinny rail on top. Uses FAL magazines.
Note: *No pricing information available.*

KEL-TEC RFB HIGH
EFFICIENCY RIFLE

■ RFB TARGET

As above with a 32 inch barrel and a folding bipod. The total length is 40 inches and it weighs 11.3 lbs.
Note: *No pricing information available.*

KIMEL INDUSTRIES
Matthews, North Carolina

■ AP-9 PISTOL

A 9mm semi-automatic pistol with a machine pistol look. Five inch barrel with vented shroud. Magazine inserts in front of trigger guard. Black matte finish. Manufactured 1989-94.

EXC.	V.G.	GOOD
400	350	300

AP-9 PISTOL

■ MINI AP-9

As above except with a three inch barrel without shroud. Made with a matte black or nickel finish.

EXC.	V.G.	GOOD
425	375	325

KNIGHT'S MANUFACTURING CO.
Vero Beach, Florida

This company was established in 1993 by Reed Knight. AR-15 inventor Eugene Stoner was involved in the design of their products. As of early 2008 Knights has suspended most civilian production so they can fill government orders.

■ STONER SR-15 RIFLE

A 5.56mm/.223 flat top rifle with a 20 inch standard weight barrel. Two stage target trigger. Proprietary RAS (rail accessory system) hand guard has accessory rails on four sides. Shipped without fixed sights. A2 type fixed stock. Introduced in 1997.

NIB	EXC.	V.G.	GOOD
1700	1200	1000	800

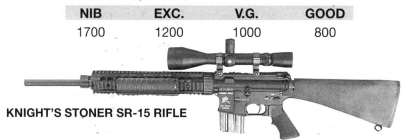

KNIGHT'S STONER SR-15 RIFLE

■ STONER SR-15 M-4 CARBINE

As above with a 16 inch barrel. Flip up rear sight included. RAS hand guard. Choice of fixed or collapsible buttstock.

NIB	EXC.	V.G.	GOOD
1750	1400	1200	1000

■ STONER SR-25 SPORTER

A modernized version of the AR-10 rifle chambered in 7.62mm/.308. It has a flat top receiver with removable carry handle. 20 inch lightweight barrel. Round hand guard. 5, 10, or 20 round magazines. Manufactured 1993-97.

EXC.	V.G.	GOOD
3000	2750	2500

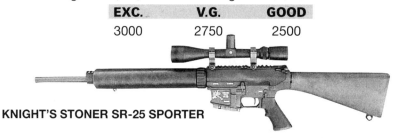

KNIGHT'S STONER SR-25 SPORTER

■ STONER SR-25 CARBINE (OLD VERSION)

As above but with a 16 inch free floating barrel. Flat top receiver with a removable carry handle. Fixed stock. Introduced in 1995.

EXC.	V.G.	GOOD
3000	2750	2500

■ STONER SR-25 CARBINE (CURRENT PRODUCTION)

Features a flat top receiver including flip sight. 16 inch free float barrel and URX hand guard with accessory rails. Two stage match trigger. Fixed or Collapsible buttstock.

NIB	EXC.	V.G.	GOOD
3700	3250	2750	2200

■ STONER SR-25 MATCH RIFLE

Flat top receiver shipped without any sights. Fitted with a 24 inch target contour free floating barrel. Round hand guard with folding bi-pod. Fixed buttstock.

EXC.	V.G.	GOOD
3200	3000	2750

■ STONER SR-25 MK-11 MOD 0

This is a version of the SR-25 that has been adopted as a sniper rifle by the U.S. Marine Corp and the U.S. Army. It features a flat top receiver, 20 inch free float barrel and URX hand guard with accessory rails. Fixed buttstock. Civilian sales have been suspended. Current production goes to fill government orders. No examples found for sale.

KNIGHT'S STONER SR-25 MK-11 MOD 0

LANCASTER ARMS
Goodyear, Arizona

This company produces a series of AK-type rifles and pistols. These are built with a U.S. made receiver and the required number of U.S. made parts combined with original AK parts. The AK series is offered in three receiver thicknesses.

■ AKM-47A

Rifle with a 1mm thick receiver. Cal. 7.62x39mm. Wood stocks. Features Romanian type pistol grip forearm.

NIB	EXC.	V.G.	GOOD
549	500	450	400

■ AKM-47A

Rifle as above with a 1.6mm thick receiver.

NIB	EXC.	V.G.	GOOD
629	575	500	450

■ AKM-47A RIFLE

As above, with milled steel receiver.

NIB	EXC.	V.G.	GOOD
899	825	700	600

■ AKM-47 WITH BULGARIAN STOCK OPTION

Offered with black synthetic, blond wood and red wood furniture. Listing prices for synthetic version. Wood furniture is slightly higher. 1 mm receiver.

NIB	EXC.	V.G.	GOOD
619	550	500	450

■ AKM-47

As above with 1.6mm thick receiver.

NIB	EXC.	V.G.	GOOD
679	600	550	500

■ AKM-47

As above with milled steel receiver.

NIB	EXC.	V.G.	GOOD
899	825	725	625

■ AKM 47T TACTICAL

Has a six-position sliding CAR style stock. Synthetic forearm available in black, green or tan. 1mm thick receiver.

NIB	EXC.	V.G.	GOOD
659	600	550	500

■ AKM 47T

As above with a 1.6mm receiver.

NIB	EXC.	V.G.	GOOD
719	650	600	550

■ AKM 47T

As above with milled steel receiver.

NIB	EXC.	V.G.	GOOD
929	825	750	675

■ CLASSIC POLISH UNDERFOLD

AKM type rifle in 7.62x39mm. Underfolding stock. Wood forearm. 1mm receiver.

NIB	EXC.	V.G.	GOOD
769	700	650	575

■ CLASSIC POLISH UNDERFOLD

As above with 1.6mm receiver.

NIB	EXC.	V.G.	GOOD
819	750	675	600

▶ Classic Polish Underfold

As above with milled steel receiver.

NIB	EXC.	V.G.	GOOD
999	850	775	700

■ POLISH TANTAL

Cal 5.45x39mm. Side folding stock. Synthetic forearm. Wood available at higher cost.

NIB	EXC.	V.G.	GOOD
689	625	550	500

■ POLISH TANTAL

Fixed stock. Choice of blond or red wood.

NIB	EXC.	V.G.	GOOD
769	700	625	550

■ POLISH TANTAL

As above with underfolding stock. Choice of synthetic or wood forearm.

NIB	EXC.	V.G.	GOOD
799	725	650	575

■ AK PISTOL

Cal. 7.62x39mm, 11-1/2 inch barrel. Wood or synthetic pistol grip and forearm. Price listed is for base model.

NIB	EXC.	V.G.	GOOD
619	575	525	475

■ AK PISTOL

7.62x39mm, 9-1/2 inch barrel. Wood or synthetic pistol grip and forearm. Price listed is for base model.

NIB	EXC.	V.G.	GOOD
739	675	625	575

LEADER DYNAMICS
Tasmania, Australia

Imported by World Public Safety of Culver City, California

■ MODEL T2 MK. 5

A 5.56mm/.223 semi-automatic rifle. Many action parts are made from stamped steel. Similar to the Armalite AR-180. 16-1/4 inch barrel. Synthetic stocks. A small quantity was imported 1986-89.

EXC.	V.G.	GOOD
1250	1100	950

**LEADER DYNAMICS
MODEL T2 MK. 5**

■ SAP PISTOL

A handgun using the same action as the Leader rifle. It has a 10-1/2 inch barrel.

EXC.	V.G.	GOOD
1250	1100	950

LEINAD

Another name for the maker of the M-11 semi-automatic pistol series. Pricing on all these is about the same. See: SWD.

LES BAER CUSTOM
Hillsdale, Illinois

This company is a well regarded maker of precision 1911-A1 type pistols as well as their line of AR-15 type rifles.

■ ULTIMATE AR.223 SUPER VARMINT MODEL

AR-type rifle with LBC forged and precision machined upper and lower receivers (available with or without forward assist upper), picatinny style flat top rail, LBC ultimate national match carrier (chromed), LBC ultimate bolt (chromed), LBC ultimate extractor (chromed), Jewell two-stage trigger group, LBC precision machined adjustable free float handguard with locking ring, LBC aluminum gas block with picatinny rail top, LBC bench rest 416 R stainless steel barrel with precision cut rifling (1:9 twist standard, optional twists available including 1:12, 1:8, 1:7) 20 inch length standard (18 inch, 22 inch and 24 inch optional), newly designed LBC custom grip with extra material under the trigger guard corner, Versa Pod, 20 round magazine, LBC ultimate AR .223 rifle soft case, stainless steel barrel, coated on request.

MSRP	EXC.	V.G.	GOOD
1989	1750	1600	1450

■ ULTIMATE AR SUPER VARMINT .204 RUGER

As above but chambered in .204 Ruger.

MSRP	EXC.	V.G.	GOOD
2330	2250	2050	1850

■ ULTIMATE AR.223 SUPER MATCH MODEL

Features include LBC forged and precision machined upper and lower receivers (available with or without forward assist upper), picatinny style flat top rail, LBC ultimate national match carrier (chromed), LBC ultimate bolt (chromed), LBC ultimate extractor (chromed), Jewell two-stage trigger group, four-position free float handguard with integral picatinny rail system, LBC aluminum gas block, LBC bench rest 416 R stainless steel barrel with precision cut rifling (1:9 twist standard, optional twists available including 1:12, 1x8, 1:7) 20 inch length standard (18 inch, 22 inch and 24 inch optional), newly designed LBC custom grip with extra material under the trigger guard corner, Versa Pod Installed, 20 round magazine, LBC ultimate AR .223 rifle soft case, stainless steel barrel, coated on request.

MSRP	EXC.	V.G.	GOOD
2144	1800	1650	1500

LES BAER ULTIMATE AR.223 SUPER MATCH MODEL

■ ULTIMATE AR SUPER MATCH .204 RUGER

As above, but chambered in .204 Ruger.

MSRP	EXC.	V.G.	GOOD
2410	2200	2000	1800

■ ULTIMATE AR.223 M-4 FLAT TOP MODEL

Features include LBC forged and precision machined upper and lower receivers (available with or without forward assist upper), picatinny style flat top rail, LBC ultimate national match carrier (chromed), LBC ultimate bolt (chromed), LBC ultimate extractor (chromed), LBC bench rest 416 R stainless steel barrel with precision cut rifling (1:9 twist standard, optional twists available including 1:12 or 1:8) 16 inch length standard, four-position free float handguard with locking ring and with integral picatinny rail system (12 inch standard) with aluminum gas block covered by rail system, Versa-Pod installed, 20 round magazine, LBC ultimate AR .223 rifle soft case, stainless steel barrel, coated on request.

MSRP	EXC.	V.G.	GOOD
2195	1850	1700	1550

LES BAER ULTIMATE AR.223 M-4 FLAT TOP MODEL

■ ULTIMATE AR.223 IPSC ACTION MODEL

Features include LBC forged and precision machined upper and lower receivers with or without provision for forward assist, picatinny style flat top rail, LBC ultimate national match carrier (chromed), LBC ultimate bolt (chromed), LBC ultimate extractor (chromed), LBC bench rest 416 R stainless steel barrel with precision cut rifling (1:9 twist standard, optional twists available including 1:12, 1:8, 1:7) 20 inch length standard, Jewell two-stage trigger standard (ultra single stage trigger substituted on request), LBC precision machined aluminum free floating handguard with locking ring, LBC aluminum gas block, Versa-Pod installed, 20 round magazine, LBC ultimate ar .223 rifle soft case.

MSRP	EXC.	V.G.	GOOD
2310	2000	1850	1700

LES BAER ULTIMATE AR.223 IPSC ACTION MODEL

■ THUNDER RANCH RIFLE

Features include: LBC forged and precision machined upper and lower receivers, picatinny style flat top rail, LBC ultimate national match carrier (chromed), LBC ultimate bolt (chromed), LBC ultimate extractor, Les Baer custom bench rest 16 inch barrel of 416 R stainless steel with precision cut bench rest rifling and 1:8 twist, barrel is precision fluted in front of gas block for better heat dissipation, Jewell two-stage trigger tuned to 4-1/2 pound pull (total pull weight), special thunder ranch free float handguard with locking ring, sling stud mounted front of free float handguard, nylon weather proof sling and lockable front sling swivel, special detachable carry handle.

MSRP	EXC.	V.G.	GOOD
2499	2200	2000 1	800

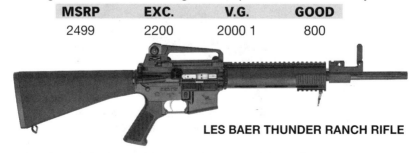

LES BAER THUNDER RANCH RIFLE

■ ULTIMATE CMP COMPETITION RIFLE

CMP legal for service rifle matches. Features LBC forged and precision machined upper and lower receivers, National Match rear sights with hooded aperture, 1/4-minute clicks both windage and elevation, LBC national match carrier (chromed), LBC bolt carrier, LBC extractor, 20 inch LBC precision cut bench rest style 416 R stainless steel barrel, 1:8 twist, Jewell two-stage trigger set at 4-1/2 lbs., special DCM/CMP style free float tube, precision machined front sight housing (drilled and tapped for barrel clamping), lead weight in both stock and forend (total weight is 17 lbs. with lead added), two) 20 round magazines.

MSRP	EXC.	V.G.	GOOD
2840	2600	2400	2200

■ ULTIMATE NRA MATCH RIFLE

Features include LBC forged and precision machined upper and lower (available with or without forward assist upper), picatinny style flat top rail, LBC ultimate national match carrier (chromed), LBC ultimate bolt (chromed), LBC ultimate extractor (chromed), Jewell two-stage trigger group, LBC precision machined adjustable free float handguard with locking ring, hand stop with sling swivel, LBC aluminum gas block, LBC bench rest 416 R stainless steel barrel with precision cut rifling (1:8 twist standard, optional twists available including 1 :7) 30 inch length standard (18 inch, 20 inch, 22 inch and 24 inch optional), newly designed LBC custom grip with extra material under the trigger guard, LBC ultimate AR .223 rifle soft case, one 20 round magazine. Sold without sights.

MSRP	EXC.	V.G.	GOOD
2230	2000	1800	1600

LES BAER ULTIMATE NRA MATCH RIFLE

■ ULTIMATE AR 6.5 GRENDEL M4 STYLE

Except for being chambered in 6.5 Grendel, this model is essentially the same as the .223 caliber, medium weight M4 described above, with the following exceptions:

• It has the same handguard as the Thunder Ranch model;
• Its gas block will include a rail on top to allow mounting add-on sights.

MSRP	EXC.	V.G.	GOOD
2260	2100	1900	1700

■ ULTIMATE AR 6.5 GRENDEL SUPER VARMINT MODEL

Similar to the Ultimate .223 model described above but chambered in 6.5mm Grendel.

MSRP	EXC.	V.G.	GOOD
2135	1950	1750	1550

LES BAER ULTIMATE AR 6.5 GRENDEL SUPER VARMINT MODEL

MARLIN FIREARMS CO.
New Haven, Connecticut

This old-line gun maker has discontinued production of the two models they had that fit in this book. Despite the fact that they were sold with traditional looking wood stocks, the Camp 9 and Camp 45 are included due to the fact that they accept high capacity magazines. Additionally, there are some assault type stocks available from other manufacturers; these have pistol grips and folding stocks.

■ CAMP 9

A semi-automatic rifle in 9mm. Simple blow back operation. 16-1/2 inch barrel. Open sights. Receiver is drilled to allow scope mounting. Marlin made magazines in 4-, 10- and 12 round capacity. The rifle also accepts S&W 59 series magazines.

EXC.	V.G.	GOOD
400	350	300

■ CAMP 45

As above but chambered in .45 ACP. Uses 1911-A1 type magazines.

EXC.	V.G.	GOOD
550	475	400

MICROTECH SMALL ARMS RESEARCH
Bradford, Pennsylvania

■ STG-556

This is basically a copy of the STEYR AUG Rifle chambered in 5.56mm/.223. The STG-556 Sporting Model rifle is a gas-operated semi-automatic bullpup rifle featuring a quick interchangeable barrel available in 14, 16 and 20 inch lengths. The weight is 7-1/2 lbs. The STG-556's innovative design features include a forward assist and last round bolt hold open release. 10, 20, 30 and 42 round magazines.

MSRP	EXC	V.G.	GOOD
2100	1850	1750	1650

MITCHELL ARMS INC.
Santa Ana, California

Note: Mitchell Arms imported a series of .22LR semi-automatic copies of assault rifles. These were made in Italy by Armi Jager or Adler. See Armi Jager. Mitchell Arms also imported some Zastava-made Kalashnikov rifles from Yugoslavia in the late 1989. Importation was banned in 1989.

■ AK-47

Typical pattern. Cal. 7.62x39mm. 16-1/2 inch barrel. Wood stocks. Imported 1989 only. The single shipment of these AK inchs was held in customs for over a year due to the just enacted import ban. BATF required the bayonet lug be removed and the muzzle cap be welded in place before they were released.

EXC.	V.G.	GOOD
1250	1000	900

MITCHELL ARMS
AK-47

■ AK-47 WITH FOLDING STOCK

As with the standard AK-47 above, the folding stock version was also held up by U.S. customs. Mitchell Arms was forced to have a plastic thumbhole stock made for these. The original folding stock was left intact but was welded in the closed position. It was common for these stocks to be restored to functional condition by subsequent owners. Such a restoration would be a violation of 922r regulations unless enough U.S. made parts were added to the rifle.

EXC.	V.G.	GOOD
1350	1150	950

MITCHELL ARMS AK-47
WITH FOLDING STOCK

■ AK-47 IN 7.62X51MM/.308

Similar to above. Fixed stock only. 20 round magazine. Scarce.

EXC.	V.G.	GOOD
1750	1500	1250

Note: *add $200 for each additional 20 round magazine.*

■ M-76 SNIPER RIFLE

A Kalashnikov rifle chambered in 8x57mm Mauser. Side rail scope mount. 10 round magazine.

EXC.	V.G.	GOOD
2000	1750	1500

■ RPK

Patterned after the Soviet RPK light machine gun. Chambered in 7.62x39mm or 7.62x51/.308. Heavy barrel with cooling fins. Folding bi-pod. Scarce.

EXC.	V.G.	GOOD
2500	2000	1750

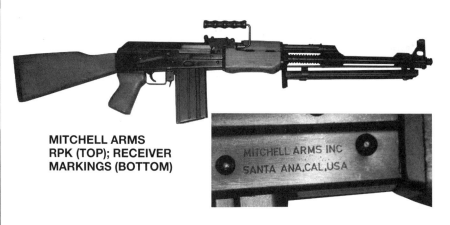

MITCHELL ARMS RPK (TOP); RECEIVER MARKINGS (BOTTOM)

KAHR/AUTO-ORDNANCE MODEL M1SB SHORT-BARRELED SEMI-AUTO RIFLE.

KAHR/AUTO-ORDNANCE MODEL T1-C COMMANDO.

KAHR/AUTO-ORDNANCE MODEL T1 WITH 50-ROUND DRUM.

KAHR/AUTO-ORDNANCE MODEL T1 WITH 30-ROUND STICK MAGAZINE.

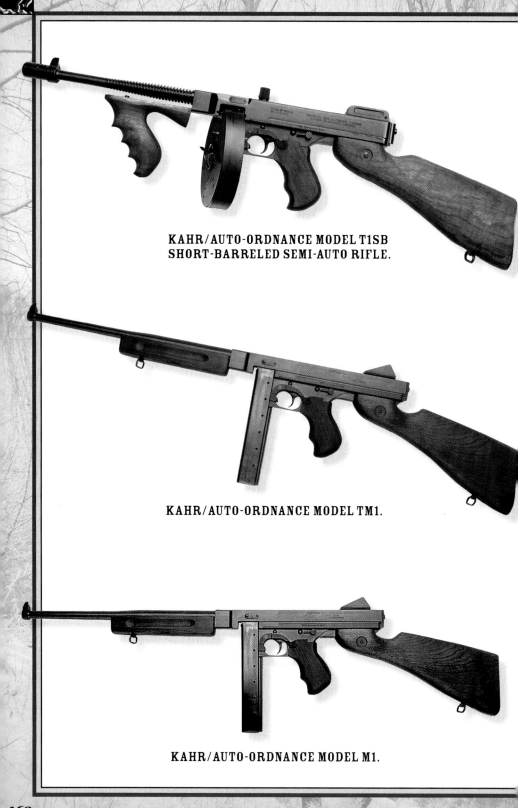

**KAHR/AUTO-ORDNANCE MODEL T1SB
SHORT-BARRELED SEMI-AUTO RIFLE.**

KAHR/AUTO-ORDNANCE MODEL TM1.

KAHR/AUTO-ORDNANCE MODEL M1.

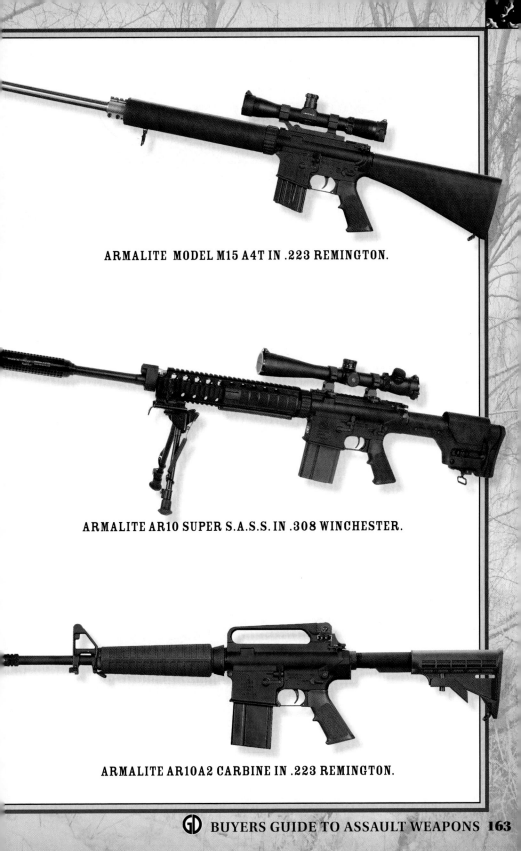

ARMALITE MODEL M15 A4T IN .223 REMINGTON.

ARMALITE AR10 SUPER S.A.S.S. IN .308 WINCHESTER.

ARMALITE AR10A2 CARBINE IN .223 REMINGTON.

ARMALITE AR10 A2 RIFLE IN .223 REMINGTON.

ARMALITE AR10 A4 CARBINE WITH ADJUSTABLE STOCK IN .223 REMINGTON.

ARMALITE AR10 A4 RIFLE IN .223 REMINGTON.

ARMALITE AR10 A4 CARBINE WITH FIXED STOCK IN .223 REMINGTON.

ARMALITE AR10B IN .308 WINCHESTER.

ARMALITE AR10T IN .338 FEDERAL.

BERETTA CX4 CARBINE IN
9MM, .40 S&W, AND .45 ACP.

BUSHMASTER BFI CARBON 15 R21 IN .223.

BUSHMASTER BFI CARBON 15M4 IN .223 REMINGTON.

BUSHMASTER BFI DISSIPATOR
IN .223 REMINGTON.

CENTURY INTERNATIONAL MG53 IN 8MM MAUSER.

CENTURY INTERNATIONAL WASR10 IN 7.62X39.

MARS EQUIPMENT CETME IN .308 WINCHESTER.

CENTURY INTERNATIONAL AK BULL PUP IN 7.62X39.

CENTURY INTERNATIONAL AK SIDE FOLD IN 7.62X39.

CENTURY INTERNATIONAL AMD65 IN 7.62X39.

CENTURY INTERNATIONAL CETME CAMO IN .308 WINCHESTER.

CENTURY INTERNATIONAL GOLANI IN .223 REMINGTON (FOLDED).

CENTURY INTERNATIONAL GOLANI (EXTENDED)

VOLUNTEER ENTERPRISES COMMANDO MK45 IN .45 ACP.

ENFIELD MP45 IN .45 ACP.

FABRIQUE NATIONALE FS2000 IN .223 REMINGTON.

FABRIQUE NATIONALE PS90 IN 5.7X28.

HECKLER & KOCH SL81 IN .223 REMINGTON, LEFT VIEW.

HECKLER & KOCH SL81, RIGHT VIEW.

HI-POINT MODEL 995 CAMO WITH 4X SCOPE, 9MM.

ARMI JAGER MAS 22
IN .22 LONG RIFLE.

CASEY POLACHEK OF MIDWEST GUN AND RANGE IN ELKHART, IN, DISPLAYS
THE MICROTECH STG-556.

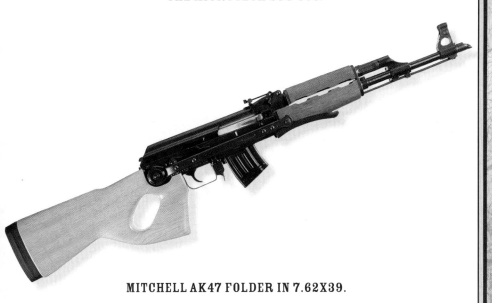

MITCHELL AK47 FOLDER IN 7.62X39.

MITCHELL AK47 FIXED STOCK IN 7.62X39.

NORINCO AK SPORTER IN 7.62X39.

NORINCO TYPE 86 IN 7.62X39.

OHIO ORDNANCE BAR IN 30-06.

POLY TECH LEGEND SPORTER IN 7.62X39.

REMINGTON MODEL 4-15 IN .223 REMINGTON.

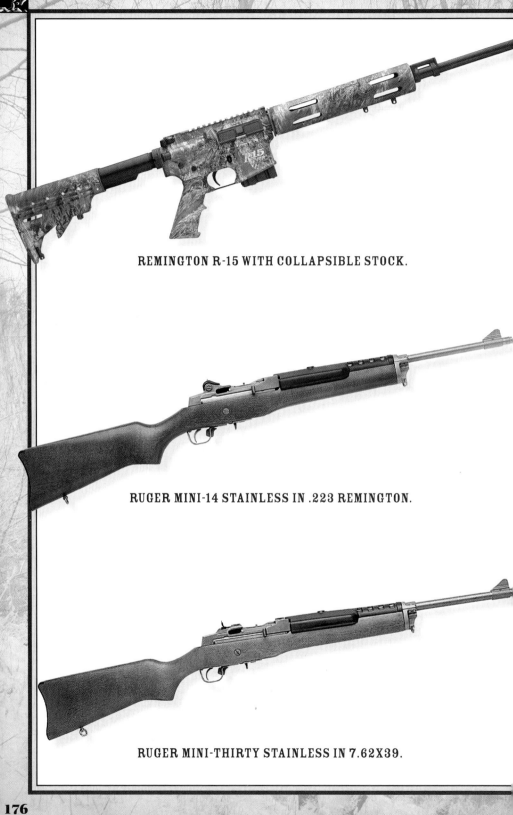

REMINGTON R-15 WITH COLLAPSIBLE STOCK.

RUGER MINI-14 STAINLESS IN .223 REMINGTON.

RUGER MINI-THIRTY STAINLESS IN 7.62X39.

NATIONAL ORDNANCE
El Monte, California

In the 1970s this company manufactured new M-1 carbine receivers and assembled complete rifles with USGI parts.

■ M-1 CARBINE

A basic pattern M-1 carbine. Will be seen with a variety of stock configurations. Caliber .30 M-1.

EXC.	V.G.	GOOD
450	400	350

NORINCO
China

This is a commercial front for the Chinese military arms production factories. The first Norinco products were imported in the mid 1980s. They offered semi-automatic variations of AKM rifles as well as the SKS. These were imported by several companies. Importer names observed include Clayco, CSI, KSI, Labanu, and Sile.

After the 1989 ban on imported "assault weapons" the Norinco product line was altered to comply with "sporting use" criteria in the GCA 1968. This was when the thumbhole stocks appeared on AK type rifles. In 1994, President Clinton banned further import of Norinco produced firearms with rifled barrels. Some sporting shotguns are still imported.

■ NORINCO AKM VARIATIONS

Pre-1989 imports. Rifles with stamped sheet steel receivers were usually made at factory 66. The factory mark is a triangle with 66 in the center. There were a few model markings found on these. The following entries indicate models observed. There were probably more models imported.

▶ AKS

The earliest Norinco AKS were imported by Clayco Sports in 1984. Caliber 7.62x39mm. They have red synthetic stocks. Originally boxed with three 30 round magazines and a bayonet.

EXC.	V.G.	GOOD
1500	1200	1000

▶ AKM/47S, Type 56S

As above. Later import. Light colored wood stocks.

EXC.	V.G.	GOOD
1250	1000	800

● Type 56S-1

As above but with a under folding stock.

EXC.	V.G.	GOOD
1250	1100	900

● Type 84S

An AKS chambered in 5.56mm/.223.

EXC.	V.G.	GOOD
1200	950	850

● Type 84S-1

As above, with an under folding stock.

EXC.	V.G.	GOOD
1250	1100	900

● Type 84S 5

As above with a side folding stock. Black synthetic forearm. Imported in 1989 only.

EXC.	V.G.	GOOD
1500	1200	1000

● Type 86S

A 7.62x39mm AKS in bull pup configuration. Imported in 1989. Only one shipment came in before the ban. Fewer than 2000 imported.

EXC.	V.G.	GOOD
1800	1500	1250

NORINCO TYPE 86S

■ POST 1989 IMPORT BAN AK MODELS

The 1989 ban on imported "assault rifles" caught several importers unprepared. There had been little discussion of such an executive action before it occurred. Some shipments were stuck in customs warehouses while others were on ships that had to be turned back to China. A few importers were allowed to modify rifles already paid for to remove offending characteristics such as the bayonet lug and threaded muzzles. This was when they came up with the thumbhole stocks that eliminate the separate pistol grip. There were even some folding stock versions that had the stock welded in the closed position and a thumb hole stock installed behind it. Others had the folding stock removed, leaving the hole in the receiver where it was.

It did not take long before Norinco began producing rifles that complied with the characteristics imposed by the ban. Model names found on the thumbhole stocked models include MAK-90, NHM-90 or 91. The name "Sporter" will also appear on these.

Warning: *It is common to encounter a post-1989 imported Norinco AK type rifle that has had a standard pistol grip stock set installed. If you are examining a AK type gun that is marked MAK-90, BWK-90, NHM-91, or Sporter be aware that it might be an illegal rifle. According to BATFE regulations, it is not legal to modify an imported rifle to a configuration that cannot be imported, unless enough U.S. made parts are installed. This is a very confusing law.*

▶ MAK-90

Standard AKM type rifle in 7.62x39mm with a thumbhole stock.

EXC.	V.G.	GOOD
500	425	350

NORINCO MAK-90

▶ BWK-90

As above but in 5.56mm with a thumbhole stock.

EXC.	V.G.	GOOD
500	425	350

▶ NHM-90

7.62x39mm with a 16 3/4 inch barrel. Thumbhole stock.

EXC.	V.G.	GOOD
500	425	350

▶ NHM-91

AK type rifle in 7.62x39mm with a 23 1/4 inch barrel and a folding bipod. Thumbhole stock.

EXC.	V.G.	GOOD
550	475	400

▶ AK Hunter

An AKM action with a traditional sporting type stock installed.
7.62x39mm. 19 inch barrel.

EXC.	V.G.	GOOD
400	325	275

▶ NDM86

A copy of the Soviet SVD "Dragonov" sniper rifle. Chambered for
7.62x54Rmm or 7.62x51mm/.308. 24 inch barrel. Skeletonized stock
made from laminated wood. 10 round magazine.

EXC.	V.G.	GOOD
1500	1200	900

■ MODEL 320

A semi-automatic copy of the Israeli UZI submachine gun. Cal 9mm.
16 inch barrel. The only shipment of Model 320s was stopped by the
1989 import ban. The folding metal stocks were replaced with a thumbhole stock and the barrel nut was welded so the barrel could not be
removed.

EXC.	V.G.	GOOD
650	550	450

■ M-14

A copy of the U.S. M-14 service rifle. Chambered for 7.62mm/.308. No
flash hider. Rubber recoil pad.

EXC.	V.G.	GOOD
650	575	500

■ SKS

The standard SKS rifle is chambered in 7.62x39mm and has a fixed 10
round magazine. As such it is not in the purview of this book. However,
since hundreds of thousands were imported in the 1980s and 1990s under the Norinco name they are included here. They do not always have
Norinco stamped on them but that does not affect the price. SKSs were
frequently sold with the folding bayonet attached. After a few years the
BATF ruled that it was not legal to have a bayonet on an SKS unless the
rifle was imported as a Curio and Relic under definitions listed in the GCA
1968. Of course the fact that they had already issued import licenses for
thousands of rifles with the bayonets on them did not seem to matter. The

official view is that a bayonet is not allowed on new rifles imported under the "Sporting Use" criteria.

EXC.	V.G.	GOOD
250	190	150

NORINCO SKS CARBINE

■ SKS CARBINE

This is a SKS that was made with a 16 inch barrel. Some may have been shortened here in the U.S. by the importers. They were sometimes called a "paratrooper" carbine, although there is no indication that any were ever used by any Chinese paratroop forces.

EXC.	V.G.	GOOD
300	250	200

■ NORINCO SKS WITH DETACHABLE MAGAZINE

This version was made to accept AK-47 type detachable magazines. There are three variants. The first was a standard pattern SKS with a 16 inch barrel, with or without the bayonet.

EXC.	V.G.	GOOD
700	600	500

■ NORINCO SKS "SPORTER"

After the ban on importation of "assault rifles," the Norinco SKS was made in a "sporter" configuration. One variation has a Monte Carlo stock; the other has a thumbhole stock. There is no provision for a bayonet.

EXC.	V.G.	GOOD
500	450	400

OHIO ORDNANCE WORKS
Chardon, Ohio

This manufacturer builds semi-automatic versions of famous machine guns.

■ BAR MODEL 1918A3 SELF LOADING RIFLE

A semi-automatic version of the legendary Browning Automatic Rifle. Caliber .30-06. 20 round magazines. Introduced in 1996. Offered with walnut or synthetic stock.

MSRP	EXC.	V.G.	GOOD
3800	3000	2500	2000

OHIO ORDNANCE BAR MODEL 1918A3 SELF LOADING RIFLE

■ COLT BROWNING MODEL 1917 WATER COOLED MACHINE GUN

A semi-automatic version of the famous belt-fed machine gun. Offered in .30-06, 7.65mm or .308. Parkerized finish. Sold with a tri-pod, wooded ammo box, water can and hose and one 250 round cloth belt. Introduced in 2001.

MSRP	EXC.	V.G.	GOOD
5000	4700	4200	3500

Note: *The .308 version is worth approximately $250 more.*

■ M240 SLR

This is a semi-automatic version of the FN MAG M 240 machine gun currently used by the U.S. military. Cal. 7.62mm/.308. Uses disintegrating metal links. Introduced in 2007. Limited production.

MSRP	EXC.	V.G.	GOOD
13,500	12,000	10,000	8500

■ VZ-2000

A semi-automatic version of the Czechoslovakian Vz-58 rifle. Caliber 7.62x39mm. Synthetic stocks. Shipped with four 30 round magazines, bayonet, sling, cleaning kit, manual and extra folding stock.

MSRP	EXC.	V.G.	GOOD
1250	1100	1000	850

OLYMPIC ARMS
Olympia, Washington

This company manufactures several versions of AR-15 type firearms. They are listed here with their Olympic Arms product numbers.

■ 24 AND 20 INCH MODELS

▶ K4B

The same dimensions as the U.S. Military M-16-A2. Semi-automatic. Cal 5.56mm/.223. 20 inch barrel. A2 upper receiver with adjustable sight. Fixed stock.

MSRP	EXC.	V.G.	GOOD
839	750	700	650

▶ K4B-A4

An AR-15 model with a 20 inch barrel, flat top upper receiver, FIRSH quad rail free floating handguard and fixed A2 buttstock.

MSRP	EXC.	V.G.	GOOD
941	850	775	700

▶ K8 Targetmatch

This Targetmatch model features a flat top upper receiver and gas block that have picitinny rails. 20 inch stainless steel bull barrel with satin bead blast finish. Aluminum free floating handguard with knurled surface. Fixed A2 stock.

MSRP	EXC.	V.G.	GOOD
839	750	700	650

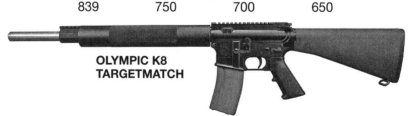

OLYMPIC K8
TARGETMATCH

▶ K8-MAG Targetmatch Magnum

The Targetmatch Magnum is chambered for Winchester Super Short Magnum (WSSM) cartridges. Features a flat top upper receiver and gas block that have picatinny rails. 24 inch bull barrel. Aluminum free floating handguard with knurled surface. Fixed A2 stock.

MSRP	EXC.	V.G.	GOOD
1182	1000	900	800

**OLYMPIC K8-MAG
TARGETMATCH MAGNUM**

▶ Plinker Plus 20

This model is an entry level AR-15 rifle. 20 inch standard weight barrel. All of the same features as Olympic's other AR-15 models but the rear sight is changed to an A1 and no factory installed options are allowed.

MSRP	EXC.	V.G.	GOOD
779	700	650	600

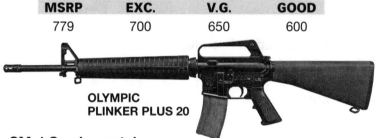

**OLYMPIC
PLINKER PLUS 20**

▶ SM-1 Servicematch

A2 upper and lower receiver are premium quality. 20 inch stainless steel barrel. Free floating hand guard.

MSRP	EXC.	V.G.	GOOD
1099	950	850	750

**OLYMPIC SM-1
SERVICEMATCH**

▶ SM-1P Servicematch Premium

As above but with AC4 pneumatic recoil buffer, Bob Jones inter-changeable sight system. Two-stage match trigger. Front sight post is attached using set screws.

MSRP	EXC.	V.G.	GOOD
1493	1100	1000	900

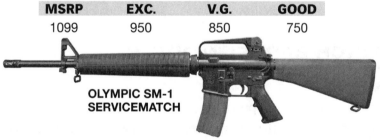

**OLYMPIC SM-1P
SERVICEMATCH PREMIUM**

▶ UM-1 Ultramatch

20 inch Ultramatch broach-cut bull barrel coupled with a free floating handguard and forged receiver for target and competition shooting. Flat top upper receiver and gas block that have picitinny rails. Aluminum free floating hand guard with knurled surface.

MSRP	EXC.	V.G.	GOOD
1150	950	850	750

OLYMPIC UM-1 ULTRAMATCH

▶ UM-1P Ultramatch Premium

HIgh-end target shooting model. 24 inch free floating bull barrel. Pneumatic recoil buffer. Williams set trigger. Harris S series bipod installed.

MSRP	EXC.	V.G	GOOD
1599	1200	1000	850

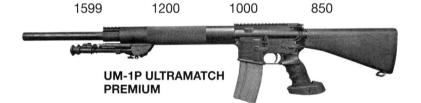

UM-1P ULTRAMATCH PREMIUM

16 INCH BARREL MODELS

▶ GI-16

Identical to our Plinker Plus model. The GI-16 features an A2 forged upper with A1 rear sight, 16 inch button rifled barrel and M4 collapsible stock.

MSRP	EXC.	V.G.	GOOD
743	675	625	575

OLYMPIC GI-16

▶ K10 Pistol Cal. 10mm

10mm in an AR-15 platform with a 16 inch barrel. Uses standard AR-15 lower receivers that accept modified pistol caliber magazines. CAR type collapsible buttstock.

MSRP	EXC.	V.G.	GOOD
869	800	750	700

▶ K16

Features a 16 inch bull barrel, flat top upper, free floating handguard, rail gas block and fixed A2 buttstock.

MSRP	EXC.	V.G.	GOOD
714	675	625	575

▶ K30R 7.62x39mm

New in 2007 is the K30R model featuring 7.62 x 39mm in an AR-15 platform. A2 upper receiver with adjustable sight. 16 inch barrel. Six-position collapsable buttstock.

MSRP	EXC.	V.G.	GOOD
846	800	750	700

▶ K3B

Base model AR-15 carbine. Available in four variants along with a ton of options.

MSRP	EXC.	V.G.	GOOD
815	750	700	650

OLYMPIC K3B

■ K3B-CAR

This K3B variant has an 11.5 inch barrel with a permanently attached 5.5 inch flash suppressor.

MSRP	EXC.	V.G.	GOOD
839	775	750	700

OLYMPIC K3B-CAR

■ K3B-FAR FEATHERWEIGHT CARBINE

As above but with the Featherweight (FAR) barrel which lightens the weight of the carbine significantly without compromising accuracy or quality.

MSRP	EXC.	V.G.	GOOD
880	800	750	700

OLYMPIC K3B-FAR FEATHERWEIGHT CARBINE

■ K3B M-4

Variant of the K3B model and features an M4 contoured barrel and M4 handguards.

MSRP	EXC.	V.G.	GOOD
899	825	775	725

OLYMPIC K3B M-4

■ K3B M-4 A3-TC

Sometimes called the "alphabet gun." The A3-TC variant takes the K3B-M4 and adds a detachable carry handle and FIRSH quad rail free floating handguard.

MSRP	EXC.	V.G.	GOOD
1079	900	850	800

OLYMPIC K3B M-4 A3-TC

■ K40

Pistol caliber .40 S&W in an AR-15 platform with a 16 inch barrel. Olympic Arms pistol caliber models use standard AR-15 lower receivers that accept modified pistol cal magazines. CAR type collapsible buttstock.

MSRP	EXC.	V.G.	GOOD
869	800	750	700

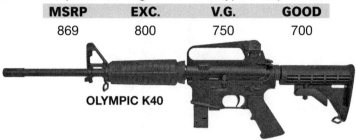

OLYMPIC K40

■ K40GL

Pistol caliber .40 S&W in an AR-15 platform with a purpose-made lower receiver that uses Glock® magazines. CAR type collapsible buttstock.

MSRP	EXC.	V.G.	GOOD
869	800	750	700

■ K45

Pistol caliber 45 ACP in an AR-15 platform with a 16 inch barrel. Olympic Arms pistol cal models use standard AR-15 lower receivers that accept modified pistol cal magazines. CAR type collapsible buttstock.

MSRP	EXC.	V.G.	GOOD
869	800	750	700

■ K68

New model that uses the 6.8 Remington SPC cartridge in an AR-15 platform. Featured with an M4 barrel and collapsible stock.

MSRP	EXC.	V.G.	GOOD
905	825	775	725

■ K7 ELIMINATOR

The K7 eliminates the gap between 16 inch and 20 inch AR-15 models. This model has a 16 inch barrel with the sight radius of a 20 inch model. A gas block is hidden under the handguards to accomodate the 16 inch barrel gas operating system.

MSRP	EXC.	V.G.	GOOD
844	800	750	700

■ K9 GL

Pistol caliber 9mm in an AR-15 platform with a purpose-made lower receiver that uses Glock® magazines. CAR type collapsible buttstock.

MSRP	EXC.	V.G.	GOOD
959	875	825	775

OLYMPIC K9 GL

■ LIGHTWEIGHT TACTICAL FLUTED

The LTF model has fluting along the full length of the barrel increasing heat dissipation. Other options are also included standard: Flat top upper receiver and gas block with picitinny rail. FIRSH quad rail free floating handguard. ACE FX Skeleton stock.

MSRP	EXC.	V.G.	GOOD
1235	1075	950	825

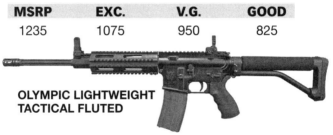

OLYMPIC LIGHTWEIGHT TACTICAL FLUTED

■ LIGHTWEIGHT TACTICAL M4

The LT-M4 model has an M4 barrel. Other options are also included standard: Flat top upper receiver and gas block with picitinny rail. FIRSH quad rail free floating handguard. ACE FX Skeleton stock.

MSRP	EXC.	V.G.	GOOD
1175	1000	900	800

■ MULTIMATCH ML-1

The Multimatch model ML-1 is basically an enhanced standard AR-15 with an Ultramatch barrel, free floating aluminum handguard and M4 collapsible stock.

MSRP	EXC.	V.G.	GOOD
1026	950	900	800

OLYMPIC MULTIMATCH ML-1

■ MULTIMATCH ML-2

The Ultramatch features flat top upper receiver and gas block with picitinny rail. Bull barrel, free floating aluminum handguard and an A2 trapdoor buttstock put the ML-2 model in a class above standard AR-15 carbines.

MSRP	EXC.	V.G.	GOOD
1026	950	900	800

**OLYMPIC
MULTIMATCH ML-2**

■ OA-93-CAR

This AR-15 model features the OA Operations System upper receiver which incorporates a gas piston recoil system into a flat top upper. This allows us to add an aluminum side-folding stock. Discontinued as of September of 2007.

EXC.	V.G.	GOOD
1000	925	850

OLYMPIC OA-93-CAR

■ OA-93-PT

Using the OA Operations System upper receiver incorporates the recoil system into a flat top upper allowing the OA-93-PT model to have a detachable aluminum stock. Discontinued as of September of 2007.

EXC.	V.G.	GOOD
975	900	825

■ PLINKER PLUS

A .22 rimfire version of the AR-15, the Plinker Plus model has all the features of Olympic's current AR-15 models but has an A1 rear sight and does not allow any factory installed options.

MSRP	EXC.	V.G.	GOOD
629	575	525	475

OLYMPIC ARMS

■ AR-15 PISTOLS

▶ K23 P

AR-15 pistol model featuring a 6.5 inch barrel, no buttstock and a padded receiver extension tube.

MSRP	EXC.	V.G.	GOOD
869	800	750	700

OLYMPIC K23 P

▶ K23P-AT-3C Tactical Pistol

AR-15 pistol model featuring a 6.5 inch barrel, no buttstock and a padded receiver extension tube. The A3-TC variant adds a flat top upper with detachable carry handle and FIRSH quad rail free floating handguard.

MSRP	EXC.	V.G.	GOOD
1018	925	850	775

OLYMPIC K23P-AT-3C TACTICAL PISTOL

▶ OA-93

Unique to Olympic Arms, the OA Operations System incorporates the recoil system into a flat top upper receiver eliminating the need for a buttstock. The OA-93 was the first AR-15 pistol on the market.

MSRP	EXC.	V.G.	GOOD
1079	975	900	800

OLYMPIC OA-93

▶ OA-98

A skeletonized, extremely lightweight version of the OA-93. Discontinued as of September of 2007.

EXC.	V.G.	GOOD
950	875	800

P.A.W.S. Inc
Salem, Oregon

This company manufactured some copies of the English Sterling sub-machine gun.

■ ZX6 CARBINE

A semi-automatic carbine chambered for 9mm or .45 ACP. It has a 16 inch barrel. Folding metal stock. Matte black finish. 10 and 32 round magazines. Introduced in 1989.

EXC.	V.G.	GOOD
900	750	600

■ PAWS PISTOL

A short version of the ZX6 without the stock. 4 to 6 inch barrel.

EXC.	V.G.	GOOD
900	750	600

PATRIOT ORDNANCE FACTORY
Phoenix, Arizona

POF manufactures a line of AR-15 type rifles that use a gas piston operating system.

■ P-415 SPECIAL PURPOSE RIFLE

Cal. .223. Features an 18 inch heavy contour barrel, fluted to reduce weight and heat. A3 flattop upper receiver, forged 7075-T6 aircraft aluminum alloy. Gas piston operated, rotating bolt (short stroke system). Reversible piston/gas trap design (adjustable: two modes of fire). C.R.O.S. (corrosion resistant operating system); chrome plated barrel, gas block/tube (billet machined), gas plug (billet machined), gas piston (billet machined), bolt carrier assembly (integral keyed billet machined), silicone nickel plated A3 flattop upper receiver and charging handle.Predator P-12SX tactical rail (slim, extended, full-length rail, w/ urethane spray) or predator P-12X. Timney drop-in 4-lb. single stage trigger group. Ergo pistol grip. Vltor EMOD buttstock. Weight is 8.2 lbs.

MSRP	EXC.	V.G.	GOOD
2095	1850	1700	1550

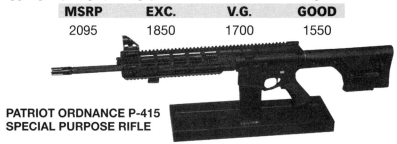

PATRIOT ORDNANCE P-415
SPECIAL PURPOSE RIFLE

■ P-415 RECON CARBINE

Cal. .223. Features a 16 inch heavy contour barrel, fluted to reduce weight and heat. A3 flattop upper receiver, forged 7075-T6 aircraft aluminum alloy. Gas piston operated, rotating bolt (short stroke system). Reversible piston/gas trap design (adjustable: two modes of fire). C.R.O.S. (corrosion resistant operating system) chrome plated: barrel, gas block/tube (billet machined), gas plug (billet machined), gas piston (billet machined), bolt carrier assembly (integral keyed billet machined), silicone nickel plated A3 flattop upper receiver and charging handle. Predator P-12SX tactical rail (slim, extended, full-length rail, with urethane spray) or predator P-12X. Timney drop-in 4-lb. single stage trigger group. Ergo pistol grip. Vltor clubfoot buttstock with mil-spec tube. Weight is 7.8 Lbs.

MSRP	EXC.	V.G.	GOOD
1995	1800	1650	1500

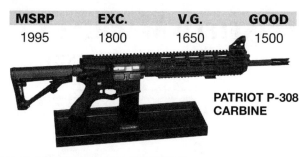

PATRIOT P-308 CARBINE

■ P-415 CARBINE, M-4 TYPE

Cal. .223. Features a 16 inch heavy contour barrel, fluted to reduce weight and heat. A3 flattop upper receiver, forged 7075-t6 aircraft aluminum alloy. Gas piston operated, rotating bolt (short stroke system). Reversible piston/ gas trap design (adjustable: two modes of fire). C.R.O.S. (corrosion resistant operating system) chrome plated: barrel, gas block/tube (billet machined), gas plug (billet machined), gas piston (billet machined), bolt carrier assembly (integral keyed billet machined), silicone nickel plated A3 flattop upper receiver and charging handle. Mil-spec semi-auto trigger. Mil-spec six-position retractable stock. Tango down battle grip. Weight is 6.9 lbs.

MSRP	EXC.	V.G.	GOOD
1595	1450	1300	1150

PATRIOT P-415 RECON CARBINE

■ P-308 CARBINE

Chamber: 7.62X51mm/.308. Features a heavy contour 14.5 inch fluted barrel with permanently attached muzzle device. Gas piston operated, rotating bolt (short stroke system). Reversible piston/gas trap design (two modes of fire). C.R.O.S. (Corrosion resistant operating system) upper is a modular railed receiver. Billet machined 7075-T6 aircraft aluminum alloy. Silicone nickel and black hard coat anodized per mil spec and teflon coated black and charging handle. Timney mfg. Drop-in 4-lb. single stage trigger group. Ergo pistol grip. Vltor, six-position retractable buttstock with mil-spec tube. Ergo ladder rail covers. POF-USA: modular railed receiver, continuous/monolithic top rail, tactical rail system. Uses DPMS, Knight Armament, or original AR-10 "waffle" magazines. Weight is 8.5 Lbs. Also available with a 16-1/2 or a 20 inch barrel.

MSRP	EXC.	V.G.	GOOD
2400	2200	2050	1900

PLAINFIELD MACHINE CO.
Dunnelein, New Jersey

A maker of new production M-1 carbines. No longer in business.

■ SUPER ENFORCER

A handgun based on the M-1 carbine action. 12 inch barrel. Caliber .30M-1. Blued finish with a walnut stock.

EXC.	V.G.	GOOD
550	450	350

■ M-1 CARBINE

EXC.	V.G.	GOOD
475	400	375

■ M-1 PARATROOPER CARBINE

As above with a telescoping wire buttstock

EXC.	V.G.	GOOD
500	450	400

POLY TECHNOLOGIES
Beijing, China

This is another name used by the Chinese arms production network. It might have been a separate branch from Norinco. Poly Tech produced variations of the AK series as well as an M-14 type rifle. Imported by Kengs Firearms Specialists (KFS) of Atlanta, Georgia.

■ AKS

This is a standard AKM rifle chambered in 7.62x39mm and it was made with a stamped receiver. It has a folding bayonet and is the same configuration of the Chinese military issue Type 56.

EXC.	V.G.	GOOD
1250	1100	950

POLY AKS

■ M AKS SIDE FOLDING STOCK

This version takes a standard blade bayonet. Stocks are made from red plastic or light colored wood. It features a side folding stock.

EXC.	V.G.	GOOD
1400	1250	1000

■ LEGEND SERIES MODEL AK-47/S

This is the closest copy of the original AK-47 that was imported. It has a milled steel receiver, instead of the stamped receiver found on the later AKM. Poly Tech made two versions.

▶ Fixed Stock

EXC.	V.G.	GOOD
1400	1175	1050

▶ Under Folding Stock

EXC.	V.G.	GOOD
1500	1250	1100

▶ Post Import Ban Legend

KFS had some rifles caught in customs when the import ban was imposed. These were fitted with a thumbhole stock and the bayonet lug and barrel threads were removed. Later, there were some Poly Tech made milled receiver sporter rifles imported that had the name MAK-90 added to them.

EXC.	V.G.	GOOD
750	625	500

POLY POST IMPORT BAN LEGEND

■ M-14/S

This is a copy of the U.S. M-14 rifle. Chambered in 7.62 NATO/.308. Wood stock. It has a cosmetic flash hider that was made without venting slots. No bayonet mount.

EXC.	V.G.	GOOD
800	700	600

PROFESSIONAL ORDNANCE, INC.
Ontario, California

Note: This company has been purchased by Bushmaster.

■ CARBON-15 PISTOL—TYPE 97

Introduced in 1996 this semi-automatic pistol is built on a carbon fiber upper and lower receiver. Chambered for the 5.56 cartridge it has a 7.25 inch fluted stainless steel barrel. Ghost ring sights are standard. Magazine is AR-15 compatible. Quick detach compensator. Furnished with a 10 round magazine. Weight is approximately 46 oz.

NOTE: This pistol has several options which will affect value.

EXC.	V.G.	GOOD
600	450	325

■ CARBON-15 RIFLE—TYPE 97

Similar to the above model but fitted with a 16 inch barrel, quick detachable buttstock, quick detach compensator, Weaver type mounting base. Overall length is 35 inches. Weight is about 3.9 lbs.

EXC.	V.G.	GOOD
625	500	400

■ CARBON-15 RIFLE—TYPE 97S

Introduced in 2000 this rifle incorporated several new features. Its foregrip is double walled and insulated with a sheet of ultra-lightweight amumina silica ceramic fiber. The recoil buffer has been increased in size by 30 percent for less recoil. A new ambidextrous safety has been added, and a new multi carry silent sling with Hogue grip is standard. Weight is approximately 4.3 lbs.

EXC.	V.G.	GOOD
950	700	550

■ CARBON-15 PISTOL—TYPE 21

Introduced in 1999 this model features a light profile stainless steel 7.25 inch barrel. Ghost ring sights are standard. Optional recoil compensator. A 30 round magazine is standard. Weight is about 40 oz.

EXC.	V.G.	GOOD
600	450	325

■ CARBON-15 RIFLE—TYPE 21

This model is fitted with a 16 inch light profile stainless steel barrel. Quick detachable stock, Weaver mounting base. Introduced in 1999. Weight is approximately 3.9 lbs.

EXC.	V.G.	GOOD
750	600	500

RED ROCK ARMS
(FORMERLY BOBCAT ARMS)
Mesa, Arizona

■ ATR-1

Based on the FN FAL platform. 16-1/4 inch barrel. Caliber 5.56/.223 1-9 twist. Weight is 8 lbs. Aircraft grade, 7075 T6 aluminum receiver is machined from a solid bar to exacting specifications in the U.S. Design specifically to accept AR-15 (M-16) magazines. Last round hold open and paddle magazine release. Original FN FAL gas operated piston breech block unlocking system, proven, reliable field history in Military and Law enforcement applications. Buttstock, forend and grip molded from glass filled nylon for added impact strength and thermal stability. The lower, including the fire control mechanism and all components thereof, are original FN FAL components. Semi-automatic ONLY. The receiver is NOT slotted to accept an auto sear. All primary exterior metal surfaces, except the magazine, are painted with Duracoat brand coatings. Minor parts are finished in black oxide.

MSRP	EXC.	V.G.	GOOD
1400	1250	1175	1100

■ BW5 FSA RIFLE

Based on the H&K MP-5 SMG. Caliber 9mm. Features: High-grade steel receiver is stamped, formed and welded to exacting specifications in the U.S. Paddle magazine release. Delayed blowback operated, roller lock bolt system has a proven, reliable field history in military and law enforcement applications. Button rifled, stainless steel, 9 inch, 3-lug barrel, rifled with 1:10 twist rate and fluted chamber. Billet machined, aluminum, permanently attached, fake suppressor is black anodized and extends the barrel length to 16.5 inches (rifle only). Fixed buttstock and forend molded from glass filled nylon for added impact strength and thermal stability. Pistol polymer buttcap w/ D-ring. The fire control mechanism is housed in a polymer Navy/FBI style lower/grip and has ambidextrous selection for safe and semi-automatic fire. All exterior metal surfaces, except the magazine, are epoxy coated for exceptional durability and finish.

MSRP	EXC.	V.G.	GOOD
1700	1500	1400	1300

■ BW5 FSA PISTOL

Based on the H&K MP-5 SMG. Caliber 9mm. Features include: High-grade steel receiver is stamped, formed and welded to exacting specifications in the U.S. Paddle magazine release. Delayed blowback operated, roller lock bolt system has a proven, reliable field history in Military and Law Enforcement applications. Button rifled, stainless steel, 9 inch, 3-lug barrel, rifled with 1:10 twist rate and fluted chamber. Forend molded from glass filled nylon for added impact strength and thermal stability. Pistol polymer buttcap w/ D-ring. The fire control mechanism is housed in a polymer Navy/FBI style lower/grip and has ambidextrous selection for safe and semi-automatic fire. All exterior metal surfaces, except the magazine, are epoxy coated for exceptional durability and finish.

MSRP	EXC.	V.G.	GOOD
1700	1500	1400	1300

REMINGTON ARMS CO.
Madison, North Carolina

In 2008, this old line manufacturer of sporting arms added a few AR-15 based rifles.

■ R-15 VTR PREDATOR RIFLE CAL. 204 RUGER

A new semi-automatic AR-15-style rifle developed with the predator hunter in mind. It features a 21 inch free-floating button-rifled 0.680 inch muzzle OD ChroMoly barrel with recessed hunting crown for superior accuracy. The fluted barrel design reduces weight and promotes rapid barrel cooling. Clean-breaking single-stage hunting trigger. Receiver-length picatinny rail for adding optics. Ergonomic pistol grip. Fore-end tube drilled and tapped for accessory rails. Full Advantage® MAX-1 HDTM camouflage coverage. Includes a 5 round magazine. Legal for hunting in most states. Compatible with aftermarket AR-15 magazines.

MSRP	EXC.	V.G.	GOOD
999	850	775	700

REMINGTON R-15 VTR
PREDATOR RIFLE CAL. .223

■ R-15 VTR PREDATOR RIFLE CAL. .223

As above but chambered in 5.56mm/.223 Remington.

MSRP	EXC.	V.G.	GOOD
999	850	775	700

■ R-15 VTR PREDATOR CARBINE CAL. .204 RUGER

As above with an 18 inch barrel.

MSRP	EXC.	V.G.	GOOD
999	850	775	700

REMINGTON R-15 VTR PREDATOR
CARBINE CS CAL. .204 RUGER

■ R-15 VTR PREDATOR CARBINE CAL. .223

As above chambered for 5.56mm/.223 Remington.

MSRP	EXC.	V.G.	GOOD
999	850	775	700

■ R-15 VTR PREDATOR CARBINE CS CAL. .204 RUGER

A Predator carbine featuring a CAR style collapsible stock.

MSRP	EXC.	V.G.	GOOD
999	850	775	700

■ R-15 VTR PREDATOR CARBINE CS CALIBER .223

As above but chambered in 5.56mm/.223 Remington

MSRP	EXC.	V.G.	GOOD
999	850	775	700

ROBINSON ARMAMENT
Salt Lake City, Utah

■ XCR SERIES

The XCR was originally designed for military trials in the SOCOM program. Civilian sales began in 2006. The XCR employs a Kalashnikov type gas system. The rifle uses an upper and lower receiver. The upper receiver features picitinny rails on all four sides. The top rail is 17 inches long, providing ample room for any available sighting system. Many features of the XCR can be special ordered. Consult a factory catalog to see the options. The XCR is a multi-caliber weapon system. The base platform is chambered in 5.56 NATO. Other caliber offerings include 6.8SPC, 6.5 Grendel, 7.62x39. The conversions are easily achieved by changing to the appropriately chambered barrel and bolt. Conversions can be done in two-three minutes.

The base model rifle in 5.56mm/.226 has a barrel length of 16 inches. Side folding or fixed stock. The weight is 7-1/2 lbs. The XCR uses M-16 series magazines.

MSRP	EXC.	V.G.	GOOD
1300	1200	1100	1000

Note: *For XCR in calibers other than .223 add 200 to MSRP.*

ROBINSON XCR SERIES

■ M96 EXPEDITIONARY RIFLE

The M96 is based on the Stoner 63 Weapon System designed by Eugene Stoner and used by the U.S Navy Seals in Vietnam. The Stoner 63 inchs receiver, using a variety of modular components, could be configured as a rifle, carbine, a top fed light machine gun, a belt fed squad automatic weapon, or a vehicle mounted weapon. The M96 has been designed with similar modularity in mind but has been simplified for easier maintenance. It is chambered for 5.56mm/.223. The barrel is 20 inches long and included a built-in muzzle brake. The barrel can be quickly changed. Total length is 40 inches. The weight is 8-1/2 lbs. The action is piston driven gas operation. Stainless steel receiver with a matte black finish. Picatinny rails can be added on top of receiver and sides of fore-arm. Front and rear sights are adjustable for windage and elevation. Black, green or tan synthetic stock and forearm. Uses M-16 magazines and drums.

MSRP	EXC.	V.G.	GOOD
1600	1350	1200	1050

**ROBINSON M96
EXPEDITIONARY RIFLE**

■ M96 RECON CARBINE

As above with a 16 inch barrel.

MSRP	EXC.	V.G.	GOOD
1600	1350	1200	1050

■ M96 RECON CARBINE WITH TOP FEED

A M96 carbine that features a Top Feed or "BREN" type magazine system. The top cover features an off set rear sight.

MSRP	EXC.	V.G.	GOOD
1900	1600	1400	1200

■ VEPR SERIES

These Russian made rifles were imported by Robinson Armament. The line has been discontinued. The VEPR Rifles and Carbines are sporting arms based on the famous Soviet designed RPK machine gun. VEPR rifles are manufactured in Russia at the historic Vyatskie Polyany Machine Building Plant (a.k.a. "MOLOT").

■ VEPR II

A 7.63x39mm rifle with a 20-1/2 inch barrel. The total length is 39-3/4 inches. Weight is 9 lbs. Open sights. Russian type scope mount on Left side of receiver. Synthetic stocks. Accepts AK magazines and drums.

EXC.	V.G.	GOOD
1000	850	700

Note: *add $50 for muzzle brake.*

■ VEPR II .223

As above but chambered for 5.56mm/.223.

EXC.	V.G.	GOOD
1000	850	700

**ROBINSON
VEPR II .223**

■ VEPR II .308

A VEPR rifle chambered in 7.62mm/.308. It has a 20-1/2 inch barrel. Available magazines hold 5 or 10 rounds.

EXC.	V.G.	GOOD
1100	975	850

■ VEPR K 7.62X39MM, 223 OR 5.45X39MM

A VEPR II with a 16-1/2 inch barrel. Other features are the same as listed above.

EXC.	V.G.	GOOD
1000	850	700

■ SUPER VEPR .308

A deluxe version of the original VEPR rifle. It has a 21-1/2 inch barrel. Total length is 41 inches. It weighs 8-1/2 lbs. One piece walnut stock with ambidextrous grip and recoil pad. Adjustable sights as well as Weaver Rail. 5 and 10 round magazines.

EXC.	V.G.	GOOD
1250	1100	950

■ VEPR .308 RIFLE

This rifle features a 23-1/4 inch barrel. Total length is 39-3/4 inches. The rifle weighs 8.3 lbs. Checkered walnut stock and forearm. 5 and 10 round magazines.

EXC.	V.G.	GOOD
1100	975	850

■ VEPR .308 CARBINE

This rifle features a 20-1/2 inch barrel. Total length is 39-3/4 inches. The rifle weighs 8.3 lbs. Checkered walnut stock and forearm. 5 and 10 round magazines.

EXC.	V.G.	GOOD
1100	975	850

ROCK RIVER ARMS, INC.
Colona, Illinois

RRA makes a variety of AR-15 type rifles and pistols. The basic models are listed. All can be factory ordered to be assembled with different options. Price will be based on options selected. They also offer lower and upper receiver assemblies.

■ .223/5.56MM RIFLES

▶ CAR A2

This is an AR-15-style rifle chambered for the .223 cartridge. Fitted with a 16 inch barrel with CAR handguards. Two stage trigger. Choice of A2 or non-collapsible buttstock. Choice of black or green furniture. Weight is about 7 lbs.

NIB	EXC.	V.G.	GOOD
925	750	700	650

▶ CAR A2M

Same as above but with mid-length handguard.

NIB	EXC.	V.G.	GOOD
925	750	700	650

▶ CAR A4

Similar to the models above but with flattop receiver and CAR handguard.

NIB	EXC.	V.G.	GOOD
890	725	700	650

ROCK RIVER CAR A4M

▶ **CAR A4M**

Flattop receiver with mid-length handguard.

NIB	EXC.	V.G.	GOOD
890	725	700	650

▶ **Standard A2**

The AR-15-style rifle is fitted with a 20 inch barrel and chambered for the .223 cartridge. Two stage trigger. Fixed stock and full-length hand guard. Weight is about 8.2 lbs.

NIB	EXC.	V.G.	GOOD
945	750	700	650

▶ **Standard A4 Flattop**

Same as Standard A2 but with flattop receiver.

NIB	EXC.	V.G.	GOOD
925	725	700	650

▶ **National Match A2**

This model features a .22 Wylde chamber with a 20 inch Wilson air-gauged match stainless steel barrel. A2 receiver. Two stage trigger. Free float high temperature thermo mold handguard. Match sights. Weight is about 9.7 lbs.

NIB	EXC.	V.G.	GOOD
1165	950	875	800

▶ **National Match A4**

As above but with a flat top receiver and removable carry handle.

NIB	EXC.	V.G.	GOOD
1215	1050	925	850

▶ **Varmint Rifle A4**

This flattop model is fitted with a 16 inch, 18 inch, 20 inch and 24 inch stainless Wilson steel barrel without sights. Fixed stock. Two-stage trigger. Weight is about 9.5 lbs.

NIB	EXC.	V.G.	GOOD
1055	900	825	750

Note: *Add $10 for each barrel length from 16 inch.*

▶ Varmint EOP (Elevated Optical Platform)

Chambered for the .223 with a Wylde chamber and fitted with a Wilson air-gauged bull stainless steel barrel. Choice of 16 inch, 18 inch, 20 inch, and 24 inch barrel lengths. Free float aluminum handguard. National Match two stage trigger. Weight is about 8.2 lbs. with 16 inch barrel and 10 lbs. with 24 inch barrel.

NIB	EXC.	V.G.	GOOD
1080	950	875	800

Note: Add $10 for each barrel length from 16 inches.

▶ Pro Series Government Model

Chambered for the .223 cartridge and fitted with a 16 inch Wilson chrome barrel with A2 flash hider. National Match two stage trigger. A4 upper receiver. Flip-up rear sight. EOTech M951 light system. Surefire M73 Quad Rail handguard, and 6 position tactical CAR stock. Weight is about 8.2 lbs.

NIB	EXC.	V.G.	GOOD
2290	1950	1800	1700

ROCK RIVER PRO SERIES GOVERNMENT MODEL

▶ Tactical CAR A4

This .223 caliber rifle has a 16 inch Wilson chrome barrel with A2 flash hider. A4 upper receiver with detachable carry handle. Two stage National Match trigger. R-4 handguard. Six-position tactical CAR stock. Weight is about 7.5 lbs.

NIB	EXC.	V.G.	GOOD
1015	900	800	700

▶ Elite CAR A4

As above but with mid-length handguard. Weight is about 7.7 lbs.

NIB	EXC.	V.G.	GOOD
1015	900	800	700

▶ Tactical CAR UTE (Universal Tactical Entry) 2

This .223 caliber rifle has a 16 inch Wilson chrome barrel with A2 flash hider. It has a R-2 handguard. The upper receiver is a UTE2 with standard A4 rail height. Two stage trigger and six-position CAR tactical stock. Weight is about 7.5 lbs.

NIB	EXC.	V.G.	GOOD
1000	900	800	700

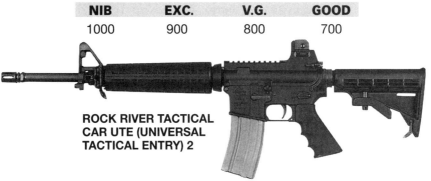

ROCK RIVER TACTICAL
CAR UTE (UNIVERSAL
TACTICAL ENTRY) 2

▶ Elite CAR UTE 2

As above but with mid-length handguard. Weight is about 7.7 lbs.

NIB	EXC.	V.G.	GOOD
1000	900	800	700

▶ Entry Tactical

This .223 model features a 16 inch Wilson chrome barrel with a R-4 profile. A4 upper receiver with detachable carry handle. National Match two stage trigger. Six-position tactical CAR stock. R-4 handguard. Weight is about 7.5 lbs.

NIB	EXC.	V.G.	GOOD
1000	900	800	700

ROCK RIVER
ENTRY TACTICAL

▶ TASC Rifle

This rifle features a 16 inch Wilson chrome barrel with A2 flash hider. A2 upper receiver with windage and elevation rear sight. R-4 handguard. A2 buttstock. Weight is about 7.5 lbs.

NIB	EXC.	V.G.	GOOD
950	850	775	700

The Pro-Series TASC

ROCK RIVER TASC RIFLE

■ 9MM RIFLES

▶ 9mm CAR A2

These are AR-15-style rifles chambered for the 9x19mm cartridge. Fitted with a 16 inch barrel with CAR handguards. Two stage trigger. Choice of A2 or non-collapsible buttstock. Choice of black or green furniture. Weight is about 7 lbs.

NIB	EXC.	V.G.	GOOD
1075	975	900	825

ROCK RIVER 9MM CAR A2

▶ 9mm CAR A4

As above with a flat top receiver.

NIB	EXC.	V.G.	GOOD
1075	975	900	825

ROCK RIVER 9MM CAR A4

■ 6.8MM REMINGTON SPC RIFLES

▶ AR 6.8 SPC CAR A2

Fitted with a 16 inch barrel with CAR handguards. Also available with mid length hand guards. Two stage trigger. Choice of A2 or non-collapsible buttstock. Choice of black or green furniture. Weight is about 7 lbs.

NIB	EXC.	V.G.	GOOD
935	825	775	700

ROCK RIVER LAR
6.8 SPC CAR A4

▶ AR 6.8 SPC CAR A4

As above with a flat top receiver.

NIB	EXC.	V.G.	GOOD
935	825	775	700

■ .458 SOCOM RIFLES

▶ LAR-458 CAR A4

Fitted with a 16 inch barrel with free float aluminum handguards. Two stage trigger. Choice of A2 or non-collapsible buttstock. Choice of black or green furniture. Weight is about 7 lbs.

NIB	EXC.	V.G.	GOOD
1065	975	900	800

ROCK RIVER
LAR-458 CAR A4

■ .308/7.62 NATO RIFLES

▶ LAR-8 A2 Rifle

Fitted with a 16 inch Wilson barrel. Mid length hand guards. A2 type upper receiver. Two stage trigger. Six-position CAR tactical stock. Uses FAL metric or inch magazines.

NIB	EXC.	V.G.	GOOD
1150	1050	975	875

**ROCK RIVER
LAR-8 A2 RIFLE**

▶ LAR-8 A4 Rifle

As above with a flat top receiver.

NIB	EXC.	V.G.	GOOD
1100	1000	925	850

**ROCK RIVER
LAR-8 A4
RIFLE**

▶ LAR-8 Standard Rifle A2

Fitted with a 20 inch Wilson barrel. A2 type buttstock. Uses FAL metric or inch magazines.

NIB	EXC.	V.G.	GOOD
1145	1050	950	850

▶ LAR-8 Standard Rifle A4

As above with a flat top receiver.

NIB	EXC.	V.G.	GOOD
1100	1025	925	850

▶ LAR-8 Varmint A4

Fitted with a 26 inch Wilson stainless steel bull barrel. Free float aluminum handguard. Match trigger. A2 buttstock. Uses FAL metric or inch magazines.

NIB	EXC.	V.G.	GOOD
1350	1200	1075	950

**ROCK RIVER LAR-8
VARMINT A4**

■ LAR PISTOLS

▶ LAR-15 A2 Pistol .223/5.56

Offered with a Wilson 7 or 10-1/2 inch barrel.

NIB	EXC.	V.G.	GOOD
920	850	775	700

**ROCK RIVER LAR-15 A2
AND LAR-15 A4 PISTOLS**

▶ LAR-15 A4 Pistol

As above with a flat top receiver.

NIB	EXC.	V.G.	GOOD
955	850	775	700

▶ LAR-9 A2 Pistol 9mm

Offered with a Wilson 7 or 10-1/2 inch barrel.

NIB	EXC.	V.G.	GOOD
1100	1000	925	850

▶ LAR A4 Pistol 9mm

As above with a flat top receiver.

NIB	EXC.	V.G.	GOOD
1100	1000	925	850

RUSSIAN AMERICAN ARMORY CO.
Scottsburg, Indiana

This company is the current importer for the Saiga series of rifles. These are based on the Kalashnikov design and are the only Russian made AK's currently imported. They are made in Russia by Izhmash. EAA and others have imported these as well. Pricing is the same.

■ SAIGA .308

A semi-automatic rifle based on the Kalishnikov design. Caliber .308. Barrel length is 16-1/4 or 21-3/4 inches. Total length is 37-1/4 or 43-1/4 inches. The weight is 8-1/2 lbs. Wood or synthetic stocks. Magazines hold 8 rounds.

NIB	EXC.	V.G.	GOOD
395	375	325	275

■ SAIGA .308 VER 21

As above fitted with a wooden thumbhole type stock. 21-3/4 inch barrel. New in 2007. No pricing information available.

■ SAIGA RIFLE

Available as a rifle with 20-1/2 inch barrel or a carbine with 16-1/4 inch barrel. Offered in 5.56mm/.223, 5.45x39mm and 7.62x39mm. Black synthetic stocks. Factory magazine capacity is five and ten rounds. Higher capacity magazines are available. The importer has added thumb hole type stocks to the available options for the Saiga. Price for base model rifle in 7.62x39mm.

NIB	EXC.	V.G.	GOOD
325	275	250	200

SABRE DEFENCE INDUSTRIES
Nashville, Tennessee

Sabre manufacturers a line of AR-15 type rifles.

■ A2 NATIONAL MATCH

Sabre A3 upper and matched lower CNC machined from 7075-t6 forgings, cal. 5.56mm/.223. 20 inch barrel. A2 stock, National Match handguards, A2 grip, two-stage match trigger, forged front sights/NM rear sight.

MSRP	EXC.	V.G.	GOOD
1699	1400	1200	1000

**SABRE DEFENSE
A2 NATIONAL MATCH**

■ A4 RIFLE

As above with a flat top upper receiver.

MSRP	EXC.	V.G.	GOOD
1309	1100	950	800

■ COMPETITION DELUXE

Sabre A3 upper and matched lower CNC machined from 7075-t6 forgings, five position stock, tactical handguards, ergo grip, match trigger, flip-up sights, Sabre competition gill-brake. Available with a fluted 16, 18 or 20 inch barrel. Chambered in 5.56 or 6.5 Grendel (add $200).

MSRP	EXC.	V.G.	GOOD
2299	2000	1850	1700

**SABRE DEFENSE
COMPETITION DELUXE**

■ COMPETITION EXTREME

Sabre A3 upper and matched lower CNC machined from 7075-T6 forgings, CTR Stock, tubular free-float handguards, ergo grip, match trigger, 45 degree flip up sights. Cal. 5.56mm. Available with a fluted 16, 18 or 20 inch barrel.

MSRP	EXC.	V.G.	GOOD
1999	1850	1700	1550

■ COMPETITION SPECIAL

Sabre A3 upper and matched lower CNC machined from 7075-t6 forgings, A2 stock, tubular free-float handguards, ergo grip, match trigger, gas block. Available with a fluted 16, 18 or 20 inch barrel. Chambered in 5.56 or 6.5 Grendel (add $200).

MSRP	EXC.	V.G.	GOOD
1799	1650	1500	1350

■ FLAT TOP CARBINE

Sabre A3 upper and matched lower CNC machined from 7075-T6 forgings. 16 inch barrel. CAR round handguards, flip-up sights, ergo grip, single stage mil trigger, six-position collapsible stock.

MSRP	EXC.	V.G.	GOOD
1319	1200	1100	1000

■ HEAVY BENCH TARGET

Sabre A3 upper and matched lower CNC Machined from 7075-T6 forgings, tubular free-float handguards, flip up sights, ergo grip, single stage adjustable trigger, A2 stock, sling swivel stud and bipod. Fitted with a 24 inch 410 stainless steel fluted match-grade heavy barrel, 11-degree target crown. Calibers: 5.56, .204 Ruger or 6.5 Grendel.

MSRP	EXC.	V.G.	GOOD
1829	1700	1550	1400

SABRE DEFENSE HEAVY BENCH TARGET

■ M4 CARBINE

Sabre A3 upper and matched lower CNC machined from 7075-T6 forgings, M4 oval handguards, forged front sights, A2 grip, single stage mil trigger, six-position collapsible stock. 16 inch or 14-1/2 inch barrel with permanent A2 flash hider. Available in 5.56mm, 6.5 Grendel and 7.62x39mm.

Price for base model 5.56mm.

MSRP	EXC.	V.G.	GOOD
1149	1000	850	700

■ M4 FLAT TOP

As above, fitted with flip up sights.

MSRP	EXC.	V.G.	GOOD
1349	1175	1000	825

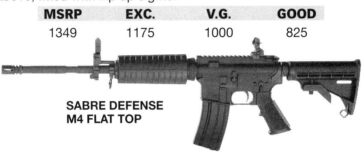

**SABRE DEFENSE
M4 FLAT TOP**

■ M4 TACTICAL

Sabre A3 upper and matched lower CNC machined from 7075-T6 forgings, multi-rail handguards, CTR mil-spec tube, flip-up sights, ergo grip, single stage mil trigger. 16 inch or 14-1/2 inch barrel with permanent A2 flash hider. Available in 5.56mm, 6.5 Grendel and 7.62x39mm. Price for base model 5.56mm.

MSRP	EXC.	V.G.	GOOD
1969	1750	1600	1450

■ M5 CARBINE

Sabre A3 upper and matched lower CNC machined from 7075-T6 Forgings, six-position collapsible stock, mid-length hand guards, ergo grip, single stage mil trigger, forged front sights. 16 inch or 14-1/2 inch barrel with permanent A2 flash hider. Available in 5.56mm, 6.5 Grendel and 7.62x39mm. Price for base model 5.56mm.

MSRP	EXC.	V.G.	GOOD
1299	1175	1000	825

■ M5 FLAT TOP

As above, fitted with flip up sights.

MSRP	EXC.	V.G.	GOOD
1259	1150	1000	850

■ M5 TACTICAL

Sabre A3 upper and matched lower CNC machined from 7075-T6 forgings, CTR mil-spec tube, multi-rail handguards, flip-up sights, EOTech 552, ergo grip, single stage mil trigger. 14-1/2 inch barrel with permanent A2 flash hider. Available in 5.56mm, 6.5 Grendel and 7.62x39mm. Price for base model 5.56mm.

MSRP	EXC.	V.G.	GOOD
2999	2750	2500	2250

■ PRECISION MARKSMAN RIFLE

Sabre A3 upper and matched lower CNC machined from 7075-T6 forgings. Fluted 20 inch barrel. Cal. 5.56mm. Mid-length gas system, rail handguards, ergo tactical deluxe grip with palm rest, match trigger, Leupold 6.5 - 20x50 Mark 4 LR/T M1 Illuminated tactical scope, Magpul PRS stock. Add $200 for 6.5 Grendel.

MSRP	EXC.	V.G.	GOOD
3599	3250	3000	2750

SABRE DEFENSE PRECISION MARKSMAN RIFLE

■ SPR

Sabre A3 upper and matched lower CNC machined from 7075-T6 forgings, 16, 18 or 20 inch fluted barrel. Five-position stock, tactical handguards, ergo grip, match trigger, flip up sights, bipods. Add $200 for 6.5 Grendel.

MSRP	EXC.	V.G.	GOOD
2499	2250	2000	1750

■ VARMINT

Sabre A3 upper and matched lower CNC machined from 7075-T6 forgings, 20 inch fluted barrel, tubular free float handguards, ergo grip, match trigger, A2 stock, sling swivel stud.

MSRP	EXC.	V.G.	GOOD
1709	1550	1400	1250

SAIGA
Izhmash, Russia

See Russian American Armory

SIG ARMS AG
Neuhausen, Switzerland

■ PE-57

A semi-automatic version of the Stgw57 Swiss service rifle. Chambered in 7.5x55mm. 18-3/4 inch barrel. Folding bipod. Wood stock. Approximately 4000 were produced. Discontinued in 1988.

EXC.	V.G.	GOOD
5000	4500	4000

■ SIG AMT

A version of the PE-57 but chambered in 7.62mm/.308. Fewer than 3000 were produced. Discontinued in 1988.

EXC.	V.G.	GOOD
6000	5250	4500

SIG AMT

■ SIG 550

A semi-automatic version of the current Swiss service rifle. The 550 has an 18 inch barrel. Synthetic side folding stock and forearm. One small lot was imported in 1988, just before the import ban.

EXC.	V.G.	GOOD
8500	7500	6500

■ SIG 551

A semi-automatic version of current Swiss service rifle. The 551 has an 16 inch barrel. Synthetic side folding stock and forearm. One small lot was imported in 1988, just before the import ban.

EXC.	V.G.	GOOD
10,000	8500	7500

SIG SAUER
Exeter, N.H.

■ SIG556

A U.S. produced version of the SIG 550, chambered for 5.56mm/.223. It has a 16 inch barrel. Gas piston operation. Flat top receiver with picatinney rail and flip up sights. CAR-15 type sliding buttstock. Uses AR-15/M-16 series magazines.

NIB	EXC.	V.G.	GOOD
1565	1250	1100	975

■ SIG 556 SWAT

As above with a Magpull CTR adjustable buttstock and a quadrail forearm.

NIB	EXC.	V.G.	GOOD
1800	1400	1200	1050

SMITH & WESSON
Springfield, Massachusetts

In 2006 S&W entered the par military rifle market with the release of the Military and Police (M&P) line. These are based on the AR-15 pattern.

■ M&P 15 RIFLE

Cal. 5.56mm/.223. 16 inch barrel. A2 upper receiver. Six-position telescoping buttstock.

NIB	EXC.	V.G.	GOOD
1304	1000	925	850

S&W M&P 15 RIFLE

■ M&P 15A RIFLE

As above with a flat top receiver. Rear folding sight.

NIB	EXC.	V.G.	GOOD
1320	1000	925	850

■ M&P 15T TACTICAL RIFLE/M&P M15FT WITH FIXED STOCK

Flat top receiver. Folding rear sight. Free float handguard has picatinny rails on four sides. Six-position collapsible stock. M15FT version has the stock fixed in the extended position, to comply with some state laws.

NIB	EXC.	V.G.	GOOD
1754	1250	1100	950

S&W M&P 15T TACTICAL RIFLE/ M&P M15FT WITH FIXED STOCK

■ M&P 15PC RIFLE

Cal. 5.56/.223. 20 inch heavy barrel. Free float round hand guard. Flat top receiver. Fixed stock.

NIB	EXC.	V.G.	GOOD
2173	1900	1750	1500

S&W M&P 15PC RIFLE

■ M&P 15X

The M&P15X is designed with a new four-rail drop-in tactical hand guard for easy accessory insertion and removal. The black anodized rifle measures 35 inches in length when fully extended and measures a compact 32 inches with the stock collapsed. The rifle is standard with an A2 post front sight, a rear Troy folding battle sight, and a 30 round detachable magazine.
Note: *Pricing not yet available.*

■ M&P 15 OR

The M&P15OR (Optics Ready) rifle features a gas block with integral Picatinny-style rail for additional sight mounting. The rifle is without standard sights, providing users with a broad platform for additional optics, lights or other aiming devices. The black anodized rifle measures 35 inches in length when fully extended and measures a compact 32 inches with the stock collapsed. The M&P15OR is standard with a 30 round detachable magazine.
Note: Pricing not yet available.

■ M&P 15 FT

The M&P15FT (Fixed Tactical) features a fixed-position stock and a 10 round detachable magazine making it compliant for sale in Connecticut, Massachusetts, Maryland, New Jersey and New York. The rifle is standard with a front and rear Troy folding battle sight.
Note: *Pricing not yet available.*

SPITFIRE MFG CO
Phoenix, Arizona

■ SPITFIRE CARBINE

This was probably the first .45-caliber semi-automatic rifle made to look like a submachine gun. It resembles the Model 1928 Thompson. It fires from an open bolt, just like real SMGs. In fact, it was so easy to convert these to full-automatic that in 1968 the BATF ruled that they were machine guns. This means that they had to be registered just like a machine gun. If a Spitfire was not registered by the close of the 1968 amnesty it is considered "contraband" today. Values below are for registered examples.

NIB	EXC.	V.G.	GOOD
1600	1200	925	850

SPRINGFIELD ARMORY USA
Geneseo, Illinois

Note: *In January of 1993, Springfield Inc. purchased the inventory, name, patents, trademarks, and logo of the Springfield Armory Inc. and intends to carry on the tradition of quality products and service in the future. Products, services, and distribution patterns remain unchanged. They are currently using the name Springfield Armory U.S.A.*

■ RIFLES

▶ M1A Basic Rifle

Chambered for .308 Win. and fitted with a painted black fiberglass stock. Barrel length is 22 inches without flash suppressor. Front sights are military square post and rear military aperture (battle sights). Magazine is a 5, 10, or 20 round box. Rifle weighs 9 lbs.

NIB	EXC.	V.G.	GOOD
1250	1050	900	800

SPRINGFIELD ARMORY M1A
BASIC RIFLE

▶ M1A Standard Rifle

This model is chambered for the .308 Win. or .243 cartridge. Also fitted with a 22 inch barrel but with adjustable rear sight. Fitted with a walnut stock with fiberglass hand guard, it comes equipped with a 20 round box magazine. Weighs 9 lbs.

NIB	EXC.	V.G.	GOOD
1500	1250	1050	900

SPRINGFIELD ARMORY
M1A STANDARD RIFLE

▶ M1A-A1 Bush Rifle

Chambered for .308 or .243 cartridge with choice of walnut stock, black fiberglass, or folding stock (no longer produced). Fitted with 18.25 inch barrel. Rifle weighs 8.75 lbs.

NIB	EXC.	V.G.	GOOD
1400	1200	1000	900

Note: *Add $250 for folding stock.*

▶ M1A Scout Squad Rifle

This .308 model is fitted with an 18 inch barrel and a choice of fiberglass or walnut stock. Military sights. Supplied with 10 round magazine. Weight with fiberglass stock is about 9 lbs., with walnut stock about 9.3 pounds. Camo finish

NIB	EXC.	V.G.	GOOD
1600	1350	1200	1000

SPRINGFIELD ARMORY M1A SCOUT SQUAD RIFLES

▶ M1A National Match

Chambered for .308 as standard or choice of .243 cartridge. Fitted with a medium weight National Match 22 inch glass bedded barrel and walnut stock. Special rear sight adjustable to half minute of angle clicks. Weighs 10.06 lbs.

NIB	EXC.	V.G.	GOOD
2050	1750	1400	1250

SPRINGFIELD ARMORY M1A NATIONAL MATCH

▶ M1A Super Match

This is Springfield's best match grade rifle. Chambered for .308 as standard and also .243 cartridge. Fitted with special oversize heavy walnut stock, heavy Douglas match glass bedded barrel, and special rear lugged receiver. Special rear adjustable sight. Weighs 10.125 lbs.

NIB	EXC.	V.G.	GOOD
2500	2000	1750	1500

Note: *For walnut stock and Douglas barrel add $165. For black McMillan stock and Douglas stainless steel barrel add $600. For Marine Corp. camo stock and Douglas stainless steel barrel add $600. For adjustable walnut stock and Douglas barrel add $535. For adjustable walnut stock and Krieger barrel add $900.*

SPRINGFIELD M1A SUPER MATCH

▶ M1A Model 25 Carlos Hathcock

Introduced in 2001 this model features a match trigger, stainless steel heavy match barrel, McMillan synthetic stock with adjustable cheek pad, Harris bipod, and other special features. Chambered for the .308 cartridge. Weight is about 12.75 lbs. A special logo bears his signature.

NIB	EXC.	V.G.	GOOD
4650	3500	2800	2200

▶ M21 Law Enforcement/Tactical Rifle

Similar to the Super Match with the addition of a special stock with rubber recoil pad and height adjustable cheekpiece. Available as a special order only. Weighs 11.875 lbs.

NIB	EXC.	V.G.	GOOD
2400	1750	1350	900

▶ M1A SOCOM 16

This M1A1 rifle features a 16.25 inch barrel with muzzlebrake. Black fiberglass stock with steel buttplate. Forward scout-style scope mount. Front sight post has tritium insert. Weight is about 9 lbs. Introduced in 2004.

NIB	EXC.	V.G.	GOOD
1525	1250	1100	1000

SPRINGFIELD ARMORY M1A SOCOM 16

▶ M1A SOCOM II

Introduced in 2005 this model features a full length top rail and short bottom rail for accessories. Weight is about 11 lbs.

NIB	EXC.	V.G.	GOOD
1700	1450	1250	1100

▶ M1A SOCOM Urban Rifle

Similar to the SOCOM but with black and white camo stock. Introduced in 2005.

NIB	EXC.	V.G.	GOOD
1725	1475	1250	1100

▶ SAR-48

This is a semi-automatic copy of the FN-FAL rifle. Chambered for the .308 Win. cartridge. It is fitted with a 21 inch barrel and has a fully adjustable rear sight. Weight is approximately 9.5 lbs. Made in Brazil by Imbel. Import stopped by the 1989 ban.

EXC.	V.G.	GOOD
1400	1250	1000

▶ SAR-48 Heavy Barrel

As above with a heavier barrel and folding bipod. Based on an Israeli pattern FAL light machine gun.

EXC.	V.G.	GOOD
1750	1400	1150

▶ SAR-4800 Sporter

This is a post ban version of the SAR-48 with a thumbhole stock. Made in Brazil by Imbel. Imported by Springfield Armory.

EXC.	V.G.	GOOD
1100	900	750

▶ SAR-4800 Match 5.56 Sporter

A version of the FAL chambered in 5.56mm/.223. Made in Brazil, by Imbel. Imported briefly in the 1990s.

EXC.	V.G.	GOOD
1400	1200	1000

▶ SAR-8

This semi-automatic rifle is similar in appearance to the HK-91. It is chambered for the .308 Winchester and is of the recoil operated delayed roller-lock design. It was assembled by Springfield Armory using a cast aluminum receiver made by DC Industries in Bloomington, Minnesota. Barrel length is 18 inches and the rear sight is fully adjustable. Weight is about 8.7 lbs.

EXC.	V.G.	GOOD
900	750	600

▶ SAR-8 Sporter

This is a copy of the HK G-3 that uses a stamped steel receiver, as found on the original HK made guns. Manufactured in Greece by EBO and imported by Springfield Armory. Synthetic thumbhole stock.

EXC.	V.G.	GOOD
1200	1000	800

▶ SAR-8 Tactical

Similar to the above model but fitted with a heavy barrel. Synthetic Draganov type stock with adjustable cheek rest. Round handguard with folding bipod. Fewer than 100 imported into US.

EXC.	V.G.	GOOD
1350	1100	900

■ M-60 SA 1 SEMI AUTOMATIC

A semiautomatic version of the M-60 machine gun. Cal 7.62 NATO. Belt fed. Limited production in the late 1980s.

EXC.	V.G.	GOOD
7500	6000	4500

STAG ARMS
New Britain, Connecticut

Note: All Stag rifles are available in left hand configuration. The prices are approximately $25-$40 higher than the right handed models listed here.

■ STAG-15 MODEL 1 PRE-BAN

Basic M-4 Carbine pattern. Cal. 5.56mm/.223. 16 inch M-4 barrel with flash hider and bayonet lug. A2 upper receiver with adjustable rear sight. Six-position collapsible buttstock.

MSRP	EXC.	V.G.	GOOD
949	875	825	750

STAG-15 MODEL 1
PR- BAN

■ STAG-15 MODEL 2 PRE-BAN

As above but with a flat top upper receiver. Includes MI ERS flip type rear sight assembly.

MSRP	EXC.	V.G.	GOOD
925	850	800	750

STAG-15 MODEL 2
PRE-BAN

STAG-15 MODEL 2 T

As above but with a A.R.M.S. sight system and Samson MRFS-C four sided hand guard.

MSRP	EXC.	V.G.	GOOD
1125	950	875	800

STAG-15 MODEL 3 PRE-BAN

M-4 type carbine featuring a flat top receiver and gas block with picatinny rails. Six position collapsible buttstock.

MSRP	EXC.	V.G.	GOOD
895	825	775	725

STAG-15 MODEL 3
PRE-BAN

STAG-15 MODEL 4 PRE-BAN

An A-2 type rifle featuring a 20 inch barrel. Flash hider and bayonet lug.

MSRP	EXC	V.G.	GOOD
1015	875	800	725

STAG-15 MODEL 4 PRE-
BAN

STAG 6.8 MODEL 5 PRE-BAN

Cal. 6.8 SPC. 16 inch barrel. Flat top receiver with picitinny rail. Six position collapsible buttstock. 25 round magazine.

MSRP	EXC.	V.G.	GOOD
1045	900	825	750

STAG-15 MODEL 6 PRE-BAN SUPER VARMITER

24 inch heavy barrel. No flash hider. Flat top receiver with picatinny rail. Two stage trigger. Free float round hand guard. A2 type fixed stock.

MSRP	EXC.	V.G.	GOOD
1055	950	875	800

STERLING ARMAMENT LTD.
Dagenham, England

■ MARK VI CARBINE

A 9mm semi-automatic carbine based on the Sterling sub machine gun. 16 inch barrel. Folding stock. 10 and 32 round magazines. Limited importation until 1989, when it ceased altogether.

EXC.	V.G.	GOOD
2500	2200	1700

■ PARAPISTOL MK7

A pistol version of the Sterling SMG. It was made with a 4 inch or 9 inch barrel. No stock. 10 and 32 round magazines. Limited importation until 1989.

EXC.	V.G.	GOOD
1500	1200	900

STEYR
Austria

■ AUG

A 5.56mm semi-automatic rifle. Bullpup configuration, with magazine located in front of hand grip. 20 inch barrel. Integral Swarovski 1.5x scope. Green composite stock. Import discontinued in 1989.

EXC.	V.G.	GOOD
3500	3000	2500

■ AUG POLICE MODEL

A shipment of AUGs with a 16 inch barrel and black stock was stopped by the 1989 import ban. The importer, Sports South, was eventually allowed to sell them to law enforcement officers only. Many have found their way into civilian hands.

EXC.	V.G.	GOOD
4000	3500	3000

■ AUG USR

A post-1989 import ban version of the AUG. The only difference from the original AUG is a stock piece behind the pistol grip as well as in front, and the 20 inch barrel has no flash suppressor. About 3000 were imported in the early 1990s.

EXC.	V.G.	GOOD
2750	2250	1800

STEYR AUG

STURM, RUGER AND CO.
Southport, Connecticut

■ MINI-14

A 5.56mm/.223 semi-automatic carbine. Basically a scaled-down M-14 rifle. 18-1/2 inch barrel. Blued or Stainless steel. Introduced in 1975. Now discontinued. Originally sold with a birch stock and handguard. Handguard was later changed to a synthetic material with steel liner. 5, 10, 20 or 30 round magazine.

Note: *Ruger has a long standing corporate policy not to sell high capacity magazines for the Mini-14 series to the public. Ruger factory 20 and 30 round magazines are restricted to law enforcement sales only. Many end up on the civilian market anyway. Add $30-$60 for each high capacity magazine with Ruger trademark on the base.*

▶ Blued

EXC.	V.G.	GOOD
500	400 3	00

▶ Stainless Steel

EXC.	V.G.	GOOD
575	475	400

RUGER MINI-14 STAINLESS

■ MINI-14 GB MODEL

This is a Mini-14 shipped from the factory with a folding stock with pistol grip, flash hider and bayonet mount. There are also restricted, by Ruger, to law enforcement sales only. Many have filtered onto the civilian market.

EXC.	V.G.	GOOD
1100	950	800

■ GB MODEL 5829

This is a recent addition to Ruger's restricted line. It has a CAR-15 sliding stock and the forearm has integral picatinny rails. Receiver is marked "Restricted Law Enforcement Govt Use Only."

NIB	EXC.	V.G.	GOOD
1250	950	850	750

■ MINI-14 RANCH RIFLE

A Mini-14 with scope mounting bases machined into the receiver. Birch stock. Ruger 1 inch rings are included.

▶ Blued

NIB	EXC.	V.G.	GOOD
830	600	500	400

▶ Stainless

As above, but also offered as the All Weather model with a black synthetic stock.

NIB	EXC.	V.G.	GOOD
894	650	575	500

■ MINI-14 TARGET RIFLE

Introduced in 2008 this Mini 14 has a 22 inch barrel. Offered with a Hogue black synthetic stock or a laminated thumbhole stock. Comes with Ruger rings.

NIB	EXC.	V.G.	GOOD
1035	875	750	600

■ MINI-30

A Mini-14 Ranch rifle chambered in 7.62x39mm. 18-1/2 inch barrel. Sold with Ruger rings. Introduced in 1987.

▶ Blue

NIB	EXC.	V.G.	GOOD
730	500	450	325

Stainless, with black synthetic All Weather stock

NIB	EXC.	V.G.	GOOD
894	650	575	500

■ MINI 6.8

A Mini-14 Ranch rifle chambered in 6.8mm Remington SPC. Black All Weather stock.

NIB	EXC.	V.G.	GOOD
894	775	650	575

■ POLICE CARBINE

A 9mm or .40S&W semi-automatic rifle. 16-1/4 inch barrel. Synthetic black stock. 10 and 15 round magazines. Introduced 1998. Discontinued.

EXC.	V.G.	GOOD
550	475	400

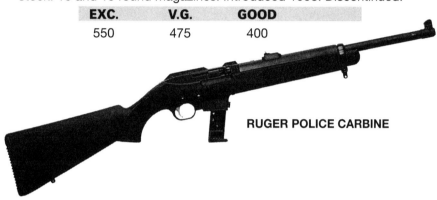

RUGER POLICE CARBINE

S.W.D. INC.
Atlanta, Georgia

■ COBRAY M/11

A 9mm pistol based on the MAC-10 SMG pattern. Sheet metal construction. Parkerized finish. Pistols made before 1994 have a threaded muzzle. three round synthetic magazine.

NIB	EXC.	V.G.	GOOD
375	300	250	200

■ M/11 CARBINE

As above with a 16-1/4 inch barrel. Removable steel stock. Discontinued in 1995.

EXC.	V.G.	GOOD
450	375	300

■ COBRAY M/12

A .380 version of the M/11.

EXC.	V.G.	GOOD
350	300	250

TENNESSEE GUNS
Louisville, Tennessee

■ SKORPION VZ-61

A semi-automatic copy of the Czechoslovakian Vz-61 machine pistol. Caliber 7.65mm/.32 automatic. It has a 4-1/2 inch barrel, with a total length of 10-1/2 inches. Unloaded weight is under 2-1/2 pounds. 10- and 20 round magazines. Made in the Czech Republic. Imported by TN Guns.

NIB	EXC.	V.G.	GOOD
850	800	725	650

**TENNESSEE GUNS
SKORPION VZ-61**

TNW FIREARMS
Vernonia, Oregon

This company manufactures semi-automatic versions of famous machine guns.

■ SEMI-AUTO M2HB

Based on the legendary Browning M-2 machinegun in .50 caliber. The modified original Browning M2 heavy-barrel has been remanufactured using genuine G.I. parts. Specs and design of this remanufactured weapon are very close to the original. Intended for sharpshooters, re-enactors or military vehicle enthusiasts. Fires commercial ammunition or blanks. All components internal and external are finished with a gray military type parkerization process. The M3 tripod is finished in current mil spec coating. Each M2HB includes an original IM2 training manual, headspacing gauge, 200 .50-caliber links, left and right hand feed mechanism and ATF approval letter. Several mounting and barrel configurations are available. Introduced in 1997.

NIB	EXC.	V.G.	GOOD
7000	6500	6000	5500

TNW SEMI-AUTO M2HB

■ SEMI-AUTO MG-34

This modified original German MG34 has been remanufactured using genuine parts to shoot semi-auto only and cannot be converted to full auto. It shoots closed bolt. Fires commercial 8mm ammunition. Includes belts and BATF approval letter. This firearm will shoot semi-auto only and cannot be converted to full-auto. This firearm is BATF approved and may be legally owned in all states except California.

NIB	EXC	V.G.	GOOD
3800	3600	3400	3200

TNW SEMI-AUTO MG-34

■ BROWNING 1919 SEMI-AUTO

The Browning Model 1919 was the workhorse of the U.S. and allied armies. They were used in aircraft, tanks and front line infantry and saw action from WWII through Vietnam. This modified original Browning 1919-A4 has been remanufactured using genuine G.I. parts to shoot semi-auto only and cannot be converted to full-auto. This firearm is BATF approved and may be legally owned like any other rifle and in all fifty states. Fires commercial ammunition or blanks. All components internal and external are finished with a gray military type parkerization process. The tripod is finished in current milspec coating. Each 1919 comes with 250 links, a training manual and BATF approval letter. 30-06 or .308 caliber. Also offered in 1919A6 configuration with shoulder stock and bipod.

NIB	EXC.	V.G.	GOOD
1900	1750	1600	1450

TNW BROWNING 1919 SEMI-AUTO

TRANSFORMATIONAL DEFENCE INDUSTRIES INC. (T.D.I.)
Virginia Beach, Virginia

■ KRISS VECTOR CRB/SO

This revolutionary design is based on a .45 caliber submachine gun offered by the same company. Here is some text from the product announcement:

"The KRISS Vector CRB/SO is an ATF-approved, 38-State legal (folding stock), 16 inch barrel semi-auto version of the KRISS Vector SMG. The KRISS Vector CRB/SO shares the same milspec frame, Super V operating system, materials and rugged housing as the KRISS Vector SMG. Same light weight. Same maneuverability. Same simple and easy to maintain Super V mechanism that reduces felt recoil by more than 60% and reduces barrel elevation by more than 95%. Non-folding stock and California versions will follow in mid-2008. Offering the same acclaimed shootability of its fully-automatic SMG (sub-machine gun) sibling, the new KRISS Vector CRB/SO (Special Ops) is the only semi-automatic firearm that actually helps the operator dramatically improve accuracy in the field or on the range. By re-vectoring the forces of recoil and significantly reducing muzzle climb, the innovative KRISS Super V technology provides a more compact and lighter-weight operating system creating a firearm that can be handled more effectively, more accurately and for longer periods of time, allowing the operator to put more rounds on target more often."

.45 ACP caliber. 16 inch barrel. Total length is 34-3/4 inches with the stock in open position. Weight is 5.0 pounds. Picatinny accessory rail on top. Uses Glock 21 magazines with capacity of 10, 13 and 30 rounds."

Note: *Pricing not yet available.*

TDI KRISS VECTOR CRB/SO, VARIOUS CONFIGURATIONS

U.S. ORDNANCE
Reno, Nevada

This company is the licensed U.S. manufacturer of M-60 series of machine guns for military and law enforcement sales. They also offer a line of semi-automatic versions of famous belt-fed machine guns.

■ M-60 STANDARD SEMI-AUTO

The M60 is a gas operated, disintegrating link, belt fed, air-cooled machine gun in semi-auto configuration. Chambered for 7.62mm Nato/ .308 Winchester. It fires from an closed bolt and features a 22 inch quick-change barrel. The barrel is Stellite-lined and chrome plated for long service. Each gun comes with 200 links, manual, cleaning kit, sling, and a one-year warranty.

NIB	EXC	V.G.	GOOD
13000	12000	11000	10000

■ M-60 E4 MODEL 1 SEMI-AUTO

The M60E4/Mk43 Mod1 features a redesigned machined aluminum top cover with an integrated picatinny rail and an aluminum rail interface system handguard provides for mounting optics, infrared laser systems and other sensors giving the weapon 24 hour capability. Fail-safe reversible piston, positive-lock gas cylinder extension. Barrel changing handle eliminates need for heat mittens. Lightweight, one-hand operated receiver mounted bipod eliminates the weight of a bipod on the spare barrel. Lightweight forearm/pistol grip for improved control and protection during firing. Feed cover eliminates charging jams and improves operator safety. Lightweight trigger assembly with ambidextrous safety switch and winter trigger guard allows gun to be fired with winter gloves. New flat spring on trigger assembly prevents accidental detachment of the assembly. Lightweight buttstock with hinged shoulder rest and improved buffer attachment mechanism provides for fail-safe attachment of the buttstock to the receiver. Each gun comes in a custom Storm i3300 case with 200 links, manual, cleaning kit, sling, and a one-year warranty.

NIB	EXC.	V.G.	GOOD
13500	12000	10500	9000

■ M-60D ENHANCED SEMI-AUTO

The M60D is a gas operated, disintegrating link, belt fed, air-cooled machine gun. It fires from an closed bolt and features a quick-change barrel. The barrel is Stellite-lined and chrome plated for long service. Unlike the earlier version, the M60D Enhanced does not require a mitten to change barrels. The carrying handle is located on the barrel similar to the M60E3 and M60E4 versions to ease quick barrel changes. The M60D model differs from the standard M60 in that the buttstock and trigger grip assemblies are replaced with spade grips and a spade trigger assembly. The rear sight is replaced with a ring sight to assist in acquiring and tracking targets. This permits aimed fire from a pedestal or other similar mount. Other parts are required to adapt the gun to the ammunition feed system. The M60D Enhanced incorporates a bipod mounted on the front of the receiver instead of mounted on the barrel. The bipod is the same one used on the M60E4 therefore increasing interchangeability. The new bipod is lighter but just as strong as the original and reduces the weight and bulk of the spare barrels. The M60D Enhanced also incorporates some of trie features found on the M60E4 feedcover, which permits the user to load the weapon with the bolt in the closed position. Each gun comes with 200 links, manual, cleaning kit, sling, and a one-year warranty.

NIB	EXC.	V.G.	GOOD
14000	12500	11000	9500

■ MODEL 1919

A semi-automatic version of the Browning Model 1919 machinegun. Manufactured in A4 or A6 configuration. Recoil operated, semi-auto. Gray parkerized finish. Caliber: 7.62x51mm NATO/.308 Winchester. Weight: A4 approximately 31 lbs., A6 approximately 32.5 lbs., Length: A4 approximately 41 inches, A6 approximately 53 inches. Barrel Length approximately 24 inches. Sights: front flip-up blade, rear leaf adjustable. Stock: A6 Israeli marked metal detachable.; Handgrip: A6 Israeli marked, wood and metal detachable. Feed Device: Cloth or metal linked belts.

NIB	EXC.	V.G.	GOOD
1900	1750	1600	1450

UNIVERSAL FIREARMS
Hialeah, Florida/
Jacksonville, Arkansas

This company has manufactured a version of the U.S. Carbine Cal. .30 M-1 since the 1960s. The early guns consisted of a new receiver with USGI surplus parts. As the sources for original parts dried up they began manufacturing their own parts. At some point they re-engineered the receiver, trigger housing, and slide. The newer guns only have partial parts interchangeability with the G.I. M-1 Carbines. The factory model numbers are listed; however, these numbers do not always appear on the firearms. All can use U.S.G.I. M-1 carbine magazines.

■ EARLY M-1 CARBINE
Assembled with a Universal receiver and all U.S.G.I. carbine parts.

EXC.	V.G.	GOOD
500	425	350

■ MODEL 1000
The base model G.I. carbine copy. 18 inch barrel. Blue finish. Birch stock. Usually found with a steel handguard.

EXC.	V.G.	GOOD
400	350	300

■ MODEL 1010
As above, but nickel plated.

EXC.	V.G.	GOOD
450	400	350

■ MODEL 1015
As above, but gold plated.

EXC.	V.G.	GOOD
500	425	350

■ MODEL 1005 DELUXE
M-1 carbine with a polished blue finish and Monte Carlo style stock.

EXC.	V.G.	GOOD
425	375	325

■ MODEL 1006 STAINLESS STEEL

M-1 carbine made from stainless steel.

EXC.	V.G.	GOOD
500	450	400

■ MODEL 1256 FERRET

M-1 carbine chambered for 256 Winchester Magnum.

EXC.	V.G.	GOOD
400	350	300

■ MODEL 5000 PARATROOPER

M-1 carbine with a folding or collapsible stock.

EXC.	V.G.	GOOD
475	425	375

■ MODEL 5006 PARATROOPER STAINLESS

As above, made from stainless steel.

EXC.	V.G.	GOOD
525	475	400

■ 1981 COMMEMORATIVE CARBINE

Commemorates the 40th anniversary of WWII, 1941-81. A limited production carbine, sold in a case with accessories.

NIB	EXC.	V.G.	GOOD
600	400	350	300

■ MODEL 3000 ENFORCER PISTOL

A pistol version of the M-1 Carbine with an 11-1/4 inch barrel. Discontinued in 1983.

▶ Blued finish

EXC.	V.G.	GOOD
550	475	400

▶ **Nickel finish**

EXC.	V.G.	GOOD
600	550	500

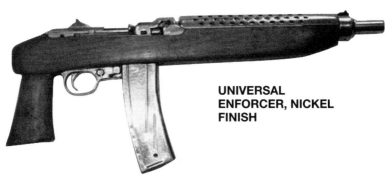

UNIVERSAL
ENFORCER, NICKEL
FINISH

▶ **Gold finish**

EXC.	V.G.	GOOD
700	600	500

▶ **Stainless Steel**

EXC.	V.G.	GOOD
650	550	450

VALKYRIE ARMS, LTD.
Olympia, Washington

■ U.S. M-3A1 GREASE GUN, PISTOL VERSION

.45 ACP semi-automatic. A faithful replica of this well-known U.S. subma-chine gun. 8 inch barrel. Uses original M-3 magazines.

MSRP	EXC.	V.G.	GOOD
950	800	700	600

VALKYRIE U.S. M-3A1 GREASE GUN, PISTOL VERSION

■ M-3 A1 CARBINE VERSION

As above but has a 16-1/2 inch barrel and a collapsible wire stock. Dis-continued.

EXC.	V.G.	GOOD
850	750	650

VALKYRIE M-3 A1 CARBINE VERSION

■ M-3 A1 CARBINE OSS VERSION

As above but with simulated suppressor over the barrel. Discontinued

EXC.	V.G.	GOOD
900	800	700

Note: *Valkyrie Arms discontinued its semi-automatic Browning M1919 belt fed replicas in January of 2008. No examples could be found to es-tablish a price range.*

VALMET, INC.
Jyvaskyla, Finland

Valmet semi-automatic rifles were imported from 1968 until 1989. Importers include Stoeger, Interarms, and Odin International. Valmet rifles are all variations of the AKM, but their quality is considered to be superior to many other makers.

■ M-62S

A copy of the Finnish M-62 service rifle in 7.62x39mm. Milled receiver. 16 5/8 inch barrel with flash hider and bayonet mount. Manufactured with a walnut or tubular steel stock. 15 or 30 round magazines.

EXC.	V.G.	GOOD
2500	2200	1900

■ MODEL 71S

As above but chambered in 5.56mm/.223. 16-1/4 inch barrel with flash hider and bayonet mount. Walnut or synthetic stock. Synthetic forearm. 15-, 30- or 40 round magazines.

EXC.	V.G.	GOOD
1500	1350	1200

VALMET MODEL 71S

■ MODEL 76S 5.56

A 5.56mm/.223 AKM type rifle. 16-1/4 inch barrel with flash hider and bayonet mount. Synthetic stock and forearm.

EXC.	V.G.	GOOD
1500	1350	1200

■ MODEL 76 FS

As above, with a side folding stock.

EXC.	V.G.	GOOD
1700	1500	1300

■ MODEL 76S 7.62

A 7.62mm/.308 AKM type rifle. Has a 20-1/2 inch barrel with flash hider and bayonet mount. Synthetic stock and forearm.

EXC.	V.G.	GOOD
1750	1500	1250

■ MODEL 78

Caliber 7.62 Nato/.308. 24-1/2 inch heavy barrel with folding bi-pod. Wood or synthetic stock and forearm. 20 round magazines.

EXC.	V.G.	GOOD
2000	1750	1500

Note: *Add $100-200 for each original 20 round magazine.*

■ MODEL 78 5.56MM

As above but chambered in 5.56mm/.223.

EXC.	V.G.	GOOD
2000	1750	1500

■ MODEL 82

A bullpup style semi-automatic rifle in 5.56mm/.223.

EXC.	V.G.	GOOD
1700	1450	1200

VECTOR ARMS
North Salt Lake, Utah

■ UZI BASED FIREARMS

▶ UZGI Carbine
This is a semi-auto 9mm version of the famous UZI rifle produced by IMI, using a U.S. made Group Industries receiver. Comes with an 16 inch barrel (an 18 inch barrel is available for Michigan residents). Comes with a folding stock and black furniture. Takes the standard UZI mags. Receiver is heat treated for durability. Parkerized finish. Comes with one 25 round mag.

NIB	EXC.	V.G.	GOOD
700	650	600	550

▶ UZ FSP Full Size Pistol
This is a 9mm, semi-auto pistol version of the full size rifle. It has a 10 inch barrel and a sling loop on the butt instead of a stock. Parkerized finish. Comes with one 25 round mag.

NIB	EXC.	V.G.	GOOD
675	625	575	525

▶ UZ GI GG Grease Gun Rifle
This is the .45 ACP version of the 9mm rifle above. Due to .45 UZI mags not being available any more, this model has a converted lower that allows this rifle to accept 30 round Grease Gun mags instead. This is a plus since the .45 UZI mags only held 16 rounds maximum and these hold 30 rounds.
Note: This lower is designed for most grease gun mags although some mags might require "tweaking" to work in this gun.

NIB	EXC.	V.G.	GOOD
725	675	625	600

▶ UZGIFXW Carbine with Fixed Stock
For a more traditional look, this 9mm rifle, with a fixed wood stock is great. It provides more stability and more comfort for your cheek. It

has an 16 inch barrel with black grips and a parkerized finish. Choices of wood are walnut, gray laminate, and brown-stained poplar. These stocks can be removed with a screwdriver and a folding stock installed if wanted. Comes with one 25 round mag. Also available in .45 ACP for an $85 upcharge. Comes with one 30 round grease gun mag.

NIB	EXC.	V.G.	GOOD
700	650	600	550

▶ UZMR Mini Rifle

This custom order, 9mm mini carbine rifle is made from a U.S. made Group Industries receiver, shortened to make it mini length. It is then heat treated for more strength. It comes with a side folding stock and a 16 inch barrel, black furniture and parkerized finish. It takes the standard UZI mags. Comes with one 25 round mag.

NIB	EXC.	V.G	GOOD
1100	1000	850	700

▶ UZMP Mini Pistol

This custom order, 9mm mini is the pistol version of the mini carbine rifle. IMI did not make a mini pistol. The receiver is a U.S.-made, Group Industries receiver, shortened to mini length and then heat treated for durability. It comes with the full-auto length ported barrel (7.75 inch), and has a sling loop on the butt end. Comes with black furniture and a parkerized finish. It takes the standard UZI mags. One 25 round mag is included.
Note: A stock cannot be legally added to this weapon without extending the barrel to 16 inch and welding a stock bracket on the back of the gun.

NIB	EXC.	V.G.	GOOD
950	850	775	700

■ FIREARMS BASED ON HECKLER AND KOCH DESIGNS

▶ V51 R Rifle

Based on the H&K Model 51. Caliber .308. Barrel extension added to comply with 16 inch barrel laws. Comes with standard barrel thread, M15x1.0, MP5 replica hand guard, SEF lower and full auto bolt carrier. One 20 round mag included.

NIB	EXC.	V.G.	GOOD
1100	1000	925	850

▶ V51LS

V51 Rifle with 16 inch barrel and fake suppressor. Comes with standard barrel thread, M15x1.0, MP5 replica handguard, SEF lower and full auto bolt carrier. One 20 round mag included.

NIB	EXC.	V.G.	GOOD
1200	1050	975	900

VECTOR V51LS

■ V51L

V51 Rifle w/16 inch barrel and flash hider. Comes with standard barrel thread, M15x1.0, MP5 replica handguard, SEF lower and full auto bolt carrier. One 20 round mag included.

NIB	EXC.	V.G.	GOOD
1200	1050	975	900

■ V51P V-51 PISTOL

Cal. 308 V51. Same specs as the V51 with no stock attachment provision. 8 1/2 inch barrel. Comes with standard barrel thread, M15x1.0, MP5 replica handguard. SEF lower and full auto bolt carrier.

NIB	EXC.	V.G.	GOOD
1200	1050	975	900

■ V53L

Based on the H&K 53. cal. .223. V-53. With a 16 inch barrel with standard flash hider. Comes with standard barrel thread, M15x1.0 and MP5 replica handguard. One 40 round magazine included.

NIB	EXC.	V.G.	GOOD
1475	1300	1200	1100

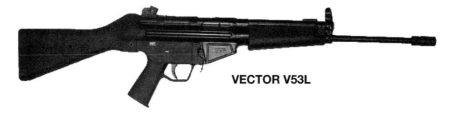

VECTOR V53L

■ V53LS

The V-53LS is a V-53 with a 16 inch barrel and slip-on fake suppressor. The fake suppressor is a copy of the SOCOM suppressor made for the military. It screws on over the long barrel and has three set screws. Comes with standard barrel thread, M15x1.0, MP5 replica handguard. One 40 round magazine included.

NIB	EXC.	V.G.	GOOD
1550	1400	1300	1200

■ V53NS

This version features a plastic "Navy lower" trigger housing, original paddle mag release and barrel extension to comply with the 16 inch barrel rule. Comes with standard barrel thread, M15x1.0, and MP5 replica handguard. Comes with a 40 round aluminum mag.

NIB	EXC.	V.G.	GOOD
1400	1300	1200	1100

■ V53 PISTOL

Cal. .223. Same specs as the V53 but no stock attachment provision. 8-1/2 inch barrel. Comes with one 40 round aluminum magazine.

NIB	EXC.	V.G.	GOOD
1425	1300	1200	1100

VECTOR V53 PISTOL

■ AK-47 TYPE FIREARMS

▶ AK 103

U.S. made on a DC Industies 7.62x39 receiver using the 103 style side-folding black polymer stock and Bulgarian parts kit. Blued finish. Comes with one 30 round mag.

NIB	EXC.	V.G.	GOOD
850	750	650	550

▶ Yugo Krinkov pistol

This pistol is made on a DC Industries or Global receiver using a Yugo 7.62x39 Krink parts kit. Finish is black Guncote paint. Beautiful Blonde wood furniture.

NIB	EXC	V.G	GOOD
900	800	700	600

▶ RPK-74

Vector 5.45x39 semi-auto RPK made with Bulgarian Parts kits and a 1.6mm NODAK Spud precision receiver. Black paint finish. Comes with bipod and flash hider on standard Ak threads.(M14x1.0 left-hand) Has laminated wood furniture and a 40 round magazine. This rifle does not accept bayonets. Also available with poly furniture which is in good, not excellent condition.

NIB	EXC.	V.G.	GOOD
1000	900	800	700

VECTOR RPK-74

▶ AKUP

This Vector AK47, in caliber 7.62x39, has an under-folder stock and comes with black poly furniture. Standard threads on barrel (M14x1.0 left-hand) and a slant break. Parkerized finish. Accepts the older milled style bayonets, not the newer AKM style. Built from Polish, Hungarian, or Bulgarian parts kits. Comes with one 30 round magazine.

NIB	EXC.	V.G.	GOOD
750	700	650	600

▶ AKUW

This Vector AK47, 7.62x39, has an under-folder stock and comes with medium blonde wood furniture. Standard threads on barrel (M14x1.0 left-hand) and a slant break. Parkerized finish. Accepts the older milled style bayonets, not the newer AKM style. Built from Polish, Hungarian, or Bulgarian parts kits. Comes with one 30 round magazine.

NIB	EXC.	V.G.	GOOD
750	700	650	600

VECTOR AKUW

▶ AKSW

This Vector AK47, 7.62x39, has a side-folding stock. Comes with black poly handguards or medium blonde wood handguards. Standard threads on barrel and a slant break. Parkerized finish. Accepts the older milled style bayonets, not the newer AKM style. Built from Polish, Hungarian, or Bulgarian parts kits. The side-folder stock can interchange with a fixed stock if desired. Comes with one 30 round magazine.

NIB	EXC.	V.G.	GOOD
600	550	500	450

▶ AKFP

This Vector AK47, 7.62x39, has a fixed black poly stock and black poly furniture. Standard threads on barrel and a slant break. Parkerized finish. Accepts the older milled style bayonets, not the newer AKM style. Built from Polish, Hungarian, or Bulgarian parts kits. The stock can interchange with a side-folding stock if desired. Comes with one 30 round magazine.

NIB	EXC.	V.G.	GOOD
600	550	500	450

▶ AKFW

As above but with a blonde wood stock and hand guard.

NIB	EXC.	V.G.	GOOD
600	550	500	450

▶ AMD

The AMD, 7.62x39mm rifle. Made with the required U.S. parts including the extended flash hider that is welded on to achieve the 16 inch barrel length. Black poly furniture and parkerized finish. One 30rd mag included.

NIB	EXC.	V.G.	GOOD
700	650	600	500

▶ RPD Semi-auto

Now available from Vector, a drum/belt fed semi-auto RPD. Comes with a 100 round drum mag (with belts) and bipod. Made from Bulgarian parts kits on an American receiver. Fires 7.62x39 ammunition. ATF approved.

NIB	EXC	V.G.	GOOD
2100	1950	1800	1650

VECTOR RPD SEMI-AUTO

VEPR

See: Robinson Armament.

VOLUNTEER ENTERPRISES
Knoxville, Tennessee

See: Commando Arms.

WALTHER
Ulm, Germany

Currently imported by Smith and Wesson.

■ MODEL G22

A 22LR semi-automatic rifle. Bullpup design has the action located in the buttstock. Adjustable sights and scope mount rails. 20 inch barrel. 10 round magazines.

NIB	EXC.	V.G.	GOOD
400	350	300	250

WEAVER ARMS CORP.
Escondido, California

■ NIGHTHAWK CARBINE

A 9mm semi-automatic rifle that fires from a closed bolt. It has a 16 inch barrel. Collapsible shoulder stock. Magazines holding 25, 32, 40 or 50 rounds were available. Approximately 1500 were produced 1987-90.

EXC.	V.G.	GOOD
1000	850	700

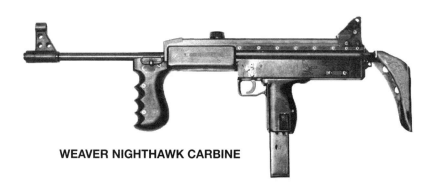

WEAVER NIGHTHAWK CARBINE

WILKINSON ARMS CO.
Covina, California/Parma, Idaho

Entrepreneur Ray Wilkinson manufactured a series of high capacity para-military designs. He started in Covina, Ca. and later mover to Parma, Idaho. His products were named after his daughters: Terry, Linda and Sherry. (The Sherry is a Baby Browning-sized .22 LR pistol.)

■ TERRY CARBINE

9mm semi-automatic rifle. It has a 16-1/4 inch barrel that ends with a cone shaped flash hider. Wood forearm. Synthetic or wood buttstock. 31 round magazine. This design first appeared in the 1960s and was manufactured by J&R Engineering of S. El. Monte, California, as the Model 68. Ray Wilkinson bought rights to the design and made some improvements.

EXC.	V.G.	GOOD
500	425	350

WILKINSON TERRY CARBINE

■ LINDA PISTOL

A 9mm semi-automatic pistol. A streamlined version of the Terry carbine action. 8-3/8 inch barrel. Wood forearm.

EXC.	V.G.	GOOD
550	475	400

**WILKINSON
LINDA PISTOL**

■ LINDA CARBINE

A 9mm semi-automatic rifle. It has a 16-3/16 inch barrel with perforated alloy shroud. Detachable tubular buttstock.

EXC.	V.G.	GOOD
550	475	400

WILKINSON LINDA CARBINE

WILSON COMBAT
Berryville, Arkansas

This manufacturer of precision 1911-A1 pistols also offers a line of AR-15 type rifles.

■ UT-15 TACTICAL CARBINE

Features include: forged upper (flat top) and lower receivers. Premium Wilson combat match-grade fluted barrel, 16-1/4 inch OAL with Wilson tactical muzzle brake. Free-float ventilated quad rail aluminum handguard. Ergo ergonomically correct pistol grip. Crisp 3-3.5-lb. trigger pull with JP trigger/hammer group. Premium mil-spec bolt and bolt carrier, NP-3 coated. Hard anodized finish on receivers and mil-spec black manganese phosphate (parkerized) on barrel and steel components. Six position mil-spec collapsible stock. Accepts all M-16/AR-15 style magazines. Includes one 20 round magazine.

MSRP	EXC.	V.G.	GOOD
1785	1500	1250	1000

WILSON COMBAT UT-15 TACTICAL CARBINE

■ M-4 T TACTICAL CARBINE

Features include forged upper (flat top) and lower receivers. 16-1/4 Inch premium Wilson Combat match grade M-4 style barrel. Wilson tactical muzzle brake. Ergo ergonomically correct pistol grip. Crisp 3-3.5-lb. trigger pull with JP trigger group. Premium mil-spec bolt and bolt carrier. Hard anodize finish on receivers. Mil-spec black manganese phosphate (parkerized) on barrel and steel components or Armor-Tuff® finish. Six position mil-spec collapsible stock. Accepts all M-16/AR-15 style magazines. Includes one 20 round magazine.

MSRP	EXC.	V.G.	GOOD
1785	1500	1250	1000

■ SS-15 SUPER SNIPER TACTICAL RIFLE

Features include forged upper (flat top) and lower receivers. Premium Wilson Combat match grade 20 inch super sniper barrel. Free floated aluminum handguard. Ergo ergonomically correct pistol grip. Crisp 3-3.5-lb. trigger-pull with JP trigger/hammer group, premium mil-spec bolt and bolt carrier. Hard anodized finish on receivers. Mil-spec black manganese phosphate (parkerized) or Armor-Tuff finish on steel components. Accepts all M-16/AR-15 style magazines; includes one 20 round magazine.

MSRP	EXC.	V.G.	GOOD
1799	1500	1250	1000

WISE LITE ARMS
Ft. Worth, Texas

This company builds a series of semi-automatic only versions of famous machineguns and submachine guns. All designs are BATFE approved. Their models feature a newly made receiver as well as original parts that have been re-built to function as a semi-automatic only. Most models are built in limited quantities due to shortages of imported parts. Other models can be custom built if the customer supplies a parts kit. Contact the manufacturer for a list of additional models.

■ BROWNING MODEL 1919 .30-06

A semi-automatic version of the famous WWII era belt fed machine gun. Sideplates are riveted, as on the original guns. Matte blue or parkerized finish. Weight 35 lbs.

NIB	EXC.	V.G.	GOOD
1600	1400	1200	1000

■ RUSSIAN DEGTYAREV DP28 LIGHT MACHINE GUN

These rifles look and feel just the like the original but will function only in a semi-automatic operation. The parts are of Polish origin. Each gun is fit with a patented semi-auto receiver and built to exacting standards with over 50 hours of hand fitting required for each gun. Each rifle comes fully assembled with four 47 round pan magazines, cover, sling, and wooden shipping crate. These guns are now shipping but in very low quantity. Only a limited number of rifles will be built.

NIB	EXC.	V.G.	GOOD
2800	2600	2300	2000

WISE LITE RUSSIAN DEGTYAREV DP28 LIGHT MACHINE GUN

■ RUSSIAN PPSH-41 SEMI-AUTOMATIC RIFLE

Semiautomatic version of one of the most recognizable guns of WWII. The "papa-shaw" or burp gun was one of the best submachine guns ever produced, and saw extensive action from Stalingrad to the Chosin Reservoir. This rugged gun is chambered in 7.62x25mm and accepts 36 round stick or 50 round drum magazines. The barrel/shroud has been extended to 16 inch length to comply with ATF regulations. Includes one 36 round round stick mag. Re-enactor's version also available with removable blank firing adapter. Weight is 12 pounds.

NIB	EXC.	V.G.	GOOD
899	800	700	600

WISE LITE RUSSIAN PPSH-41 SEMI-AUTOMATIC RIFLE

■ RUSSIAN PPS-43 SEMI-AUTOMATIC PISTOL

The WWII replacement to the PPSH-41, the model PPS-43 is made from stamped steel. Caliber is 7.62x25mm. In order to maintain the original appearance of this model, the over top folding stock is welded in the closed position. Accepts the 36 round stick magazines. Does not use the drum magazines. Re-enactors version also available with removable blank firing adapter.

NIB	EXC.	V.G.	GOOD
775	700	600	500

WISE LITE RUSSIAN PPSH-41 SEMI-AUTOMATIC RIFLE

■ FINNISH KP-44 SEMI-AUTOMATIC PISTOL

The Finnish KP-44 is chambered in 9mm Luger. It was copied from the Russian PPS-43. Stamped steel construction. In order to maintain the original appearance of this model, the over top folding stock is welded in the closed position. The barrel is 10 inches long, with an overall length of 24 inches. Accepts 36 round stick or 50 round drum magazines.

NIB	EXC.	V.G.	GOOD
775	700	600	500

Assault Weapon Cartridges

Assault weapons are chambered in a variety of cartridges, ranging from the humble .22 rimfire to the mighty .50 Browning Machine Gun (BMG). The following section of this book is intended to acquaint the reader with the most frequently-encountered cartridges that are chambered in today's assault weapons. The list is necessarily incomplete because every week, new assault weapons are introduced that are chambered for "boutique" or proprietary cartridges that have not yet achieved wide distribution. The cartridges discussed below are arranged according to caliber, from the smallest to the largest. Where calibers are identical, cartridges are listed in order from least to most powerful.

The following data is from *Cartridges of the World*, 11th Edition, originally written by Frank C. Barnes and edited by Stan Skinner (Krause Publications, 2006) and is used with permission of the publisher.

204 Ruger

Introduced in 2004 as a joint Hornady-Ruger project for varmint and target shoot-  ing, the 204 Ruger became the first 20-caliber cartridge to be produced on a large commercial scale. The 204 Ruger is the fastest production cartridge ever offered. Remarkably, it also offers excellent barrel life. After shooting approximately 500 prairie dogs with the Ruger and Dakota rifles chambered for the 204 Ruger, the field research editor found it to be an accurate, low-recoil round, superbly suited for long-range varminting. The 204 Ruger received the Academy of Excellence 2004 Cartridge of the Year Award.

22 Long Rifle

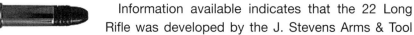 Information available indicates that the 22 Long Rifle was developed by the J. Stevens Arms & Tool Co. in 1887. It is the 22 Long case with a 5.0-grain blackpowder charge (likely with a granulation similar to what we would now call FFFFg) and a 40-grain bullet instead of the original 29-grain. The Peters Cartridge Co. is supposed to have first manufactured it, especially for Stevens. If this is true, then why does the 1888 Stevens catalog refer to a UMC 22 caliber Long rimfire rifle cartridge? This would be a gross ingratitude at best. This 1888 catalog lists the No. 1, 2, 9 and 10 model break-open rifles as available in the new chambering with increased rifling twist. The New Model Pocket or Bicycle rifle also chambered it. The 1888 Marlin-Ballard catalog

recommends the new 22 Long "Rifle" cartridge for its No. 3 Gallery rifle as being more accurate than the common 22 Long or Extra Long.

At one time, the 22 Long Rifle was available in black, semi-smokeless and smokeless-powder loads. Remington introduced the first high-velocity type in 1930. Both the 40-grain solid and a 35/38-grain hollowpoint bullet have been available for many years. The original case was not crimped, a feature that did not appear until 1900. Space does not permit a discussion of the different loads and types of 22 Long Rifle cartridges or the rifles and handguns that chamber it. Suffice to say, it is the most accurate and highly developed of any rimfire cartridge ever.

The 22 Long Rifle is the most popular match cartridge in existence, and also the most widely used small game and varmint cartridge. The high-velocity hollowpoint is the best field load and will do a good job on rabbit-sized animals out to 75 yards. Beyond that, it is unreliable. The Long Rifle is a great favorite of poachers for killing game out of season with close-up head shots. The modest report does not alarm or alert passersby or officials. At close range, the high-velocity load with the solid-lead bullet will penetrate 6 inches of soft pine and has a maximum range of nearly two miles. Maximum range is achieved at the relatively low angle of between 25-30 degrees, so one must be very careful. Humans shot with the 22 Long Rifle often show little immediate distress, survive without complications for several days, then die very suddenly. This is mentioned because many individuals regard 22 rimfires as playthings, not powerful enough to be dangerous. Careless shooting with the 22 rimfire has probably led to the closure of more areas to hunting and caused more trouble than any other cartridge. Use your head and be careful! There is also a 22 Long Rifle shot cartridge, loaded by most companies and useful mostly for rat and other pest control.

22 Magnum/22 Winchester Magnum Rimfire/22 WMR

The 22 Magnum Rimfire was introduced in 1959 by Winchester, but they didn't market a gun to shoot it until well into the following year. However, Ruger and Smith & Wesson advertised revolv-
ers for the new round before the end of 1959 and Savage chambered their Model 24, a 22-410 over/under combination gun, for the Magnum Rimfire shortly thereafter. The discontinued slide-action Winchester Model 61 was the first rifle of their manufacture available for the new round. At present there is a wide variety of single shot and repeating rifles, pistols and

revolvers of American and European manufacture available in 22 Magnum Rimfire caliber. Standard bullet is a jacketed 40 grain type although Federal introduced a 50 grain bullet in 1988 and CCI has recently introduced a hyper-velocity loading with a 30-grain bullet and Federal soon joined the "hyper-velocity" fray with their similar loading.

The 22 Winchester Magnum Rimfire is an elongated and more powerful version of the older 22 WRF. Case dimensions are the same except for length, and the WRF can be fired in any gun chambered for the Magnum Rimfire. It is not a safe practice to rechamber older guns for the new round. The 22 WRF is loaded with outside lubricated lead bullets while the 22 WMR is loaded with jacketed bullets. With a 40-grain thin-jacketed bullet at about 1900 fps, this is the most potent rimfire cartridge currently available. It is more powerful than the 22 Winchester Centerfire, forerunner of the 22 Hornet. Claimed ballistics in a 6 inch pistol barrel exceed any other rimfire fired from a rifle. Thus it is a very effective 125-yard varmint or small game cartridge, although overly destructive of animals intended for the pot unless solid bullets are used. CCI also loads a shot version.

5.45 Soviet

This is a Russian cartridge introduced about 1974 for use in the new AK-74 assault rifle. There are both fixed-stock and folding-stock

versions and the 5.45mm rifle has a redesigned flash reducer/muzzle brake that distinguishes it from the earlier AK-47. The cartridge has a more slender case and a thicker rim than the 7.62x39mm (M43) cartridge. The bullet is 0.221- to 0.222 inch in diameter and weighs from 53 to 54 grains. This bullet is almost 1 inch long and has a very sharp spitzer point, a boattail base, a mild steel core and a short lead filler on top and an air space in the nose. The bullet is designed to be unstable in tissue, producing a more severe wound. The British used somewhat the same idea in the design of their MKVII 303 bullet used in World War II. Casualty reports from Afghanistan, where the new 5.45mm cartridge and rifle first appeared, tend to confirm the lethality of the bullet. Muzzle velocity is approximately 2950 fps.

The first 5.45mm Soviet cartridges publicly available to western military intelligence were brought out of Afghanistan by Galen Geer while on assignment for *Soldier of Fortune* magazine in 1980, and the first information made public was in the October 1980 issue of *Soldier of*

Fortune. Until that time, the existence of a new Russian military cartridge was mostly rumor. Later, the round was withdrawn from service in Afghanistan. Cases are lacquered steel with Berdan primers.

The Russians apparently designed this cartridge as the result of experience on the receiving end of the U.S. M-16 rifle and 5.56mm round in Vietnam. The 5.45mm Russian is a well-designed cartridge for its intended purpose. The long, thin boattail bullet reduces aerodynamic drag to the minimum and results in higher-retained velocity at long range. The bullet is designed to be stable in flight and provide good accuracy at all ranges out to maximum, but unstable on contact so as to tumble easily, which enhances lethality. It is a better-designed military bullet than the original bullet used in the United States. M193 5.56mm cartridge. However, the new 5.56mm SS109 (M855) NATO standard round with its heavier bullet and improved shape probably has an edge over the Soviet bullet.

.223 Remington/5.56 NATO

The 223 Remington first appeared in 1957 as an experimental military cartridge for the Armalite AR-15 assault rifle. In 1964, it was

officially adopted by the U.S. Army as the 5.56mm Ball cartridge M193. It is used in the selective-fire M16 rifle which is based on the original AR-15 design. The cartridge was the work of Robert Hutton, who was technical editor of *Guns & Ammo* magazine and had a rifle range in Topanga Canyon, California. One of the requirements for the cartridge was that the projectile have a retained velocity in excess of the speed of sound (about 1,080 fps at sea level) at 500 yards, something you could not achieve with the [earlier] 222 Remington. Working with Gene Stoner of Armalite, Bob Hutton designed a case slightly longer than the 222 and had Sierra make a 55-grain boattail bullet. This combination met the design requirements. All this was documented in the 1971 issue of the *Guns & Ammo Annual*.

Originally an alternative military cartridge, the 223 (5.56x45mm) is now the official U.S. and NATO military round. We should note here that NATO forces, including the United States, have standardized a new 5.56x45mm round with a heavy bullet and the M193 is no longer standard.

Shortly after the military adopted this cartridge, Remington brought out the sporting version, which has largely replaced both the 222 Remington and Remington Magnum in popularity. Practically every manufacturer of bolt-action rifles has at least one model chambered for the 223. In addition, there are a large number of military-type semi-auto rifles available in this caliber. At one time, the Remington Model 760 pump-action was available in 223.

5.7x28

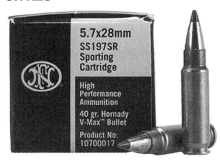

Developed in the late 1980s by FN for its new P90 personal defense gun, this cartridge is intended to replace the 9x19mm Parabellum pistol cartridge. Claimed ballistic performance is much superior to the 9mm cartridge. As yet, no major country has adopted this new chambering.

The 5.7x28mm cartridge is somewhat similar in shape to the commercial 221 Fireball cartridge. However, the two are not interchangeable. A sharply pointed Ball bullet weighing only 23 grains is used, as intended range is limited. Despite this, this bullet has been designed to penetrate helmets and body armor at 50 meters without breaking up.

243 Winchester

The 243 Winchester was introduced by Winchester in 1955 for their Model 70 bolt-action and Model 88 lever-action rifles. The 243 was quickly adopted by Savage for their Model 99 lever- and Model 110 bolt-action rifles. All of the British and European manufacturers began chambering bolt-action rifles for this round. In fact, even Remington, who developed their own 6mm, had to recognize the popularity of the 243 and start chambering their rifles for it. The 243 (6mm) Winchester is nothing more than the 308 Winchester case necked-down. Original development and publicity was due largely to the efforts of gun writer, the late Warren Page, who along with other wildcatters worked out a similar version before Winchester. The 243 is probably chambered in more different rifles than any other cartridge, except possibly the 30-06 Springfield. All other manufacturers of rifles offer this caliber.

260 Remington

Inclusion of this cartridge presents us with a bit of a problem. Along about 1996, A-Square—a bona fide member of SAAMI—submitted drawings, chambering specifications, chambering reamers, sample cartridges and all other necessary materials and data describing a new factory chambering to be adopted into the SAAMI fold. A-Square requested that the chambering be named "6.5-08 A-Square," as specified on the sample cartridge headstamp. Many months later, Remington submitted a memo to SAAMI wherein it mentioned that it intended to eventually standardize a 6.5mm version of the 308 Winchester as the 260 Remington. Since SAAMI subsequently chose to christen this chambering as "260 Remington," a disinterested observer would have to conclude that something was a bit rank, somewhere. *[Editor's note: Ballistics for this cartridge, which eventually became standardized as the 260 Remington, approximate those of low-end 6.5x55 Swedish loads but in a medium-length case, as opposed to the much longer case of the Swedish. Bullets for the 260 Remington, however, are generally much shorter than thiose for the 6.5x55 Swedish because of the former's shorter case.]*

6.8 Remington SPC

The 6.8 mm Remington SPC (or 6.8x43mm) is a new rifle cartridge that was developed with collaboration from individual members of US SOCOM (United States Special Operations Command).

Based on the .30 Remington cartridge, it is midway between the 5.56x45mm NATO and 7.62x39mm in bore diameter and velocity with more energy than both. It is particularly adaptable to current 5.56 mm NATO firearms the cartridge overall length being the same.

Though ballistics similar to the 1950's era .280 British, improved powders allow the 6.8 mm to have a smaller case. The 6.8 mm SPC (Special Purpose Cartridge) has a muzzle velocity in the 2,400 feet per second (730 m/s) range from a 16 inch (406 mm) barrel using a 115-grain bullet. The 6.8 mm Remington SPC is designed to deliver 44% greater energy than the 5.56 mm NATO at 100-200 meters.

30 Mauser/7.63 Mauser

The 30 Mauser cartridge was developed by American gun designer Hugo Borchardt for the first successful commercial, automatic pistol of the same name. The Borchardt pistol was made by Ludwig Loewe & Co.

(later DWM) of Berlin, Germany. Both pistol and cartridge were introduced in 1893. The Borchardt automatic pistol was later redesigned and emerged as the well-known Luger pistol. This cartridge was adopted by Paul Mauser for his famous Model 1896 pistol with increased power for his more rugged design. It has been used mainly in the Mauser M1896 military automatic pistol and various imitations or copies manufactured in Spain and China.

Until the 357 Magnum cartridge came along, the 30 Mauser was the high-velocity champion of the pistol world. It has a flat trajectory that makes long-range hits possible, but lacks stopping power because of the light, full-jacketed bullet. However, it has been used successfully for hunting small game and varmints at moderate ranges. Handloading with softpoint or hollowpoint hunting bullets improves performance considerably. At one time, both Remington and Winchester loaded this cartridge, but it has been dropped. Fresh supplies of this cartridge were recently imported from Portugal by Century International Arms.

7.62x25 Tokarev

The 7.62x25mm Tokarev was the official Soviet pistol cartridge adopted in 1930 for the Tokarev Model TT-30 and modified Model TT-33 automatic pistols. The pistols are a basic Browning-type design similar to the Colt 45 Auto pistol. However, these incorporate many original features, to simplify manufacturing processes, and must be considered an advance over Browning's original patented design. These pistols often have a crude finish, but are well made and of excellent design. These have a 4 1/2 inch barrel and a magazine capacity of eight rounds. Large quantities have been sold as military surplus. Some were made in Communist China and Hungary, as well as in Russia. The Hungarian-made Tokarev, in a modified form called the Tokagypt, is chambered for the 9mm Parabellum cartridge. The Chinese began exporting both pistols and ammunition to the United States in 1987 at very

reasonable prices.

The cartridge is very similar in dimension to the 7.63mm (30) Mauser and most brands of Mauser ammunition can be fired in the Tokarev pistol. The 7.62mm Tokarev is a fair field cartridge for small game with good velocity and flat trajectory, but needs softpoint bullets for maximum effectiveness. The handloader can use loading data for the 7.63 Mauser. The Speer 30-caliber Plinker bullet of 100 grains makes a good hunting bullet, but because it is slightly heavier than the standard weight, it must be loaded to lower velocity.

Chinese and Russian ammunition are steel-cased and Berdan-primed with corrosive primers. Such ammunition is not reloadable. Recently, Hansen Cartridge has imported quantities of 7.62x25mm ammunition with reloadable cases and non-corrosive Boxer primers.

30 Carbine

In 1940, the U.S. Ordnance Department concluded that a light carbine would have advantages over the 45-caliber pistol in many combat situations. Various designs were submitted by a number of private manufacturers and, in the end, Winchester's offering was selected. The semi-auto 30 M1 Carbine was officially adopted in 1941. The cartridge, a modification of the 32 Winchester Self-Loading round of 1906, was hardly a revolutionary new design, but it served the purpose. At about the same time, the Germans developed their StG 44 assault rifle and the 7.92mm Kurz cartridge. The M1 Carbine is not an assault rifle. The military insists it was designed to fulfill a different purpose.

For a few years, starting in 1966, the Marlin Model 62 Levermatic was available in 30 Carbine caliber. Iver Johnson, Plainfield and others manufactured several versions of the M1 carbine for the sporting trade. Federal, Remington and Winchester load softpoint sporting ammunition. One version of the Ruger Blackhawk single-action revolver is available in 30 Carbine.

7.5 Swiss

The first Swiss 7.5mm cartridge was adopted in 1889 for the Schmidt-Rubin straight-pull rifle of the same year. The original loading used a 0.299 inch diameter, 213-grain paper-patched lead bullet and a charge of 29 grains of semi-smokeless powder. Muzzle velocity was 1970 fps. Later, a steel-capped, hollow-base lead bullet was used, followed by a 190-grain copper or iron-jacketed, round-nose bullet with a smokeless powder loading (Model 90/03). In 1911, the 174-grain spitzer boattail bullet was adopted and the diameter increased to 0.308 inch. Golden State Arms Corp. once imported Japanese-made cases with Boxer primer pockets for loading sporting ammunition. Both unprimed cases and loaded rounds are available from Norma.

The 7.5mm Swiss military cartridge is another of the surplus items that has become well known to American shooters only since the end of the war. The Swiss army made a number of improvements in the straight-pull, Schmidt-Rubin rifle and the older, less desirable, models were sold off as obsolete surplus. The original Model 89 with rear-locking lugs, a very long receiver and a protruding box magazine was one of those. The improved Model 1911 with shorter receiver, forward-located locking lugs and a less conspicuous magazine is another. The 190-grain load develops about 37,000 psi breech pressure and the 174-grain load about 45,500 psi, and uses a slightly larger-diameter bullet. The 1911 cartridge, considerably more powerful than the older loading, should not be used in the Model 89 rifle. In a suitable action, the 7.5mm Swiss cartridge can be loaded to deliver performance equal to the 308 Winchester and is suitable for the same range of applications. Reloadable cases can be readily made by necking-up 284 Winchester brass. The 284's rebated rim works just fine in the Schmidt-Rubin rifle.

7.62x39

Anecdotal reports from U.S. forces involved in combat in Iraq and Afghanistan in recent years indicate the six-decade old 7.62x39 cartridge and AK47 rifle may be more effective in combat than the U.S. M4 carbines firing the 5.56x45 cartridge. In 2003, Steve Holland and Cris Murray, individuals associated with special forces and marksmanship units, developed

a special purpose cartridge to improve combat effectiveness in short-barreled (16.5 inch) M4 carbines used for special operations. The resulting 6.8 SPC (Special Purpose Cartridge) achieved favorable results in actual usage, but has not been officially adopted by the U.S. Army as of 2005. The cartridge is under review by the U.S. Marine Corps and FBI.

This cartridge is the standard military chambering for the Russian armed forces. It has become a modern favorite of U.S. sportsmen by virtue of the thousands of new and used SKS and AK 47-type carbines being imported and sold at very low prices. Ruger, Sako, and others are now making sporting rifles in this chambering. For example, the Ruger Mini Thirty semi-auto carbine and bolt-action M77 rifle are both offered in 7.62x39mm.

All major American ammunition manufacturers now offer this cartridge with a softpoint bullet, brass case, and non-corrosive Boxer primer. Imported, low-cost, surplus military ammunition from present and former Communist countries is usually steel cases with corrosive Berdan primers.

While previous military cartridges generally made suitable hunting rounds with proper bullets, many writers condemn the 7.62x39 out of hand as being unsuited for hunting anything beyond small game. In short, they claim it is very much like the M1 Carbine cartridge — fine for military use, but useless for hunting. However, best 125- and 150-grain spitzer loads in this cartridge typically match best 30-30 FP or RN load energy at 100 yards, and at 200 yards, there is no comparison — this little round bests the 30-30 by 20 percent.

Still, the 7.62x39 is definitely a close-range number suitable for deer, javelina and the like. With the best handloads and the proper bullet, it can do even better. It can be loaded to good advantage with 150-grain bullets and then becomes a very good 30-30 class deer rifle. Youthful shooters and women will appreciate its low recoil and mild report. Aftermarket bullet manufacturers now offer suitable bullets. Bore diameter is nominally .311 inch but .308 inch diameter bullets can be used with good results and most reloading dies will accommodate this by including expander balls for both bullet sizes.

308 Winchester/7.62 NATO

Introduced by Winchester as a new sporting cartridge in 1952, the 308 is nothing more than the NATO 7.62x51mm military round. This was a very smart move, to tack the Winchester name on what was sure to become a popular sporting number. Practically every manufacturer of high-powered sporting rifles chambers the 308, since it will work through medium- or standard-length actions. The Model 70 bolt-action and 88 lever-action Winchester were the first American sporting rifles so chambered. It was adopted as the official U.S. military rifle cartridge in 1954, although guns for it were not ready until 1957.

In power, the 308 Winchester is superior to the 300 Savage and almost equal to the 30-06. It delivers about 100 fps less muzzle velocity than the larger 30-06 with any given bullet weight. Most authorities consider the 308 suitable for most North American big game, although it's on the light side for moose or brown bear. This chambering is a favorite of target shooters and has a reputation for excellent accuracy. It is the basis for a number of wildcat cartridges that have been adopted as factory chamberings: 243 Winchester, 6.5-08, 7mm-08 Remington, 358 Winchester and the rimmed versions 307 Winchester and 356 Winchester. All major domestic and foreign ammunition companies offer this cartridge.

7.62x54Rmm Russian

This cartridge was adopted in 1891 with the Model 1891 Mosin-Nagant bolt-action rifle. Its 150-grain spitzer bullet was adopted in 1909. This cartridge was standard issue in the Russian army during World War II. It is still standard issue for medium machineguns

and the SVD sniper rifle. It was also adopted by Finland, China and most ex-satellite nations. It remains one of the few rimmed military cartridges still in standard issue.Early in World War I, Winchester made M95 lefer-action muskets and Remington made rolling block rifles for imperial Russia. Later, Russian Nagant rifles were manufactured in the United States by New England Westinghouse Co. and also by Remington and Winchester. After the war, a large number of surplus rifles were sold commercially and Remington loaded a 150-grain bronze-point hunting round. Additional Russian Nagant rifles and carbines have been sold in surplus stores since the end of World War II. Many of these rifles were captured during the Korean conflict. Surplus Moisin rifles are being imported from China, Finland, Hungary, Poland, Romania and Russia.

The 7.62x54Rmm Russian cartridge has been kicked around since about 1919 and is fairly well known to American shooters. Remington discontinued loading this round about 1950. It was recently offered by Norma and Lapua. Various surplus military ammunition (corrosive Berdan primed, steel-cased) has recently been imported into the United States. Russian military cartridges use Berdan primers, usually of 6.45 mm (0.254 inch) diameter.

With the 150-grain bullet, the 7.62mm Russian is in the same class as the 30-06. However, since the rifle has a shorter magazine, it will not do as well as the 30-06 when loaded with heavier bullets. Although military bullets measure 0.309- to 0.311 inch in diameter, rifles with tighter bores will shoot 0.308 inch bullets just fine. However, many rifles have grossly oversized bores (the editor owns a pair with 0.316 inch groove diameter). In such rifles, 0.308 inch jacketed bullets are hopelessly inaccurate; 0.311 inch bullets will shoot with a modicum of accuracy. Properly sized cast bullets will shoot with impressive accuracy (minute-of-angle groups are no problem). Unfortunately, there is no ready source of appropriate commercial jacketed or cast bullets sized large enough for these specimens and others with bores running larger than about 0.313 inch. Standard working pressure is about 45,000 psi.

32 ACP/7.65 Browning/32 Automatic

 Designed by John Browning for his first successful automatic pistol, this cartridge was first manufactured by FN in Belgium, and introduced in 1899. It was marketed in the United States when Colt turned out a pocket automatic on another Browning patent in 1903. The 32 Automatic is one of

the more popular pistol cartridges ever developed. In the United States, Colt, Remington, Harrington & Richardson, Smith & Wesson and Savage chambered pistols for this cartridge. In Europe, every company that made automatic pistols chambered the 32 ACP (Automatic Colt Pistol). It was also used in the German Pickert revolver. In Europe, it is known as the 7.65mm Browning, while in the United States it is designated 32 Automatic or 32 ACP.

This cartridge uses a semi-rimmed cartridge case and a 0.308 inch diameter bullet. The 32 Automatic is the minimum cartridge that can be seriously considered for self-defense. In the United States, it is used exclusively for small pocket-type guns and is not considered adequate for police or military use. However, in Europe it is often used in police pistols and as an alternative but unofficial chambering for military sidearms. As a hunting cartridge, it is not powerful enough for anything larger than small game.

Loading tables generally give bullet diameter of the 32 Automatic as 0.312 inch or 0.314 inch. It is actually closer to 0.308 inch, and this is important if you handload. Effective small game loads can be made by using 100-grain 30-caliber rifle bullets intended for light loads and plinking, such as the Speer 30-caliber Plinker. All major ammunition makers offer this cartridge. Winchester recently introduced a load with a jacketed hollowpoint bullet. Other makers have followed suit.

338 Federal

In collaboration with Sako Rifles, Federal Cartridge's engineers and ballisticians have developed the 338 Federal, which necks up the proven 308 Winchester case to accept a .338 caliber bullet. This design, which is the first to bear the name "Federal" on the headstamp, is intended to provide big-bore wallop with moderate recoil for today's light weight, short bolt-action rifles. The 338 Federal was made available in 2006 in Federal's Premium line of ammunition.

380 ACP/380 Auto/9mm Kurz

This cartridge was designed by John Browning and introduced in Europe by FN of Belgium in 1912 as the 9mm Browning Short, and was added to the Colt Pocket Automatic line in 1908. Several governments have adopted it as the official military pistol cartridge. These include Czechoslovakia, Italy and Sweden. It is also much used by European police. Colt, High

Standard, Remington and Savage have made pistols in this chambering in the United States. In Europe, Browning, Beretta, Bayard, CZ, Frommer, Astra, Star, Llama, Walther and others made or make 380 Automatic-chambered pistols. This cartridge is also called 9x17mm.

This is another cartridge that has been very popular because of the light, handy pistols that are chambered for it. The 380 Auto has more stopping power and is a far better cartridge for almost any purpose than the 32 Auto. It is about the minimum pistol cartridge considered adequate for police or military use. For self-defense it is not as powerful as the 9mm Luger, 38 Auto and a few others, but this is offset to a certain extent by the reduced size and weight of the arms it is used in. For hunting or field use, it will do a good job on rabbits, birds or other small game. It offers high velocity, as compared to most light handguns, which is an advantage for field use. With cast or swaged half-jacketed bullets of hunting type, it will do a good job on small game, but not many shooters want to bother handloading it.

9mm Luger/9mm Parabellum/9x21

The 9mm Luger, or 9mm Parabellum, was introduced in 1902 with the Luger automatic pistol. It was adopted first by the German Navy in 1904 and then by the German Army in 1908. Since that time, it has been adopted by the military of practically every non-Communist power. It has become the world's most popular and widely used military handgun and submachinegun cartridge. In the United States, Colt, Smith & Wesson, Ruger and many others chamber the 9mm, as do many foreign-made pistols. In 1985, the 9mm Luger was adopted as the official military cartridge by U.S. Armed Forces, along with the Beretta Model 92-F (M-9) 15-shot semi-auto pistol.

Although the 9mm Luger delivers good performance for police, military or sporting use, it was not popular in the United States until fairly recently. The principal reason was that no American-made arms were chambered for it initially. In 1954, Smith & Wesson brought out its Model 39 semi-automatic in this chambering and Colt chambered its lightweight Commander for the 9mm Luger in 1951. This, plus the influx of military pistols chambered for the 9mm greatly increased both popularity and acceptance in this country. Currently the 9mm Luger is the most widely used cartridge in the United States. A principal complaint has always been that the 9mm Luger lacks stopping power as a defensive cartridge. However, the only automatic pistol cartridge with proven stopping power is the 45 Automatic. For hunting use, the 9mm Luger is adequate for most small game if hollowpoint bullets are used. Modern premium type JHP loads can dramatically improve performance. A variety of 9mm loadings are offered by every major U.S. ammunition maker.

40 Smith & Wesson/40 S&W

This cartridge was developed as an in-house joint venture between Winchester and Smith & Wesson within six months from the time it was first discussed in June 1989. Mr. Bersett at Winchester and Mr. Melvin at S&W were primarily responsible for this cartridge's development and standardization. At that time, the FBI had been working with the 10mm Automatic, developing a load that met its criteria for bullet diameter, weight and velocity. The folks at Winchester and Smith & Wesson realized that the power level the FBI had settled on could easily be achieved using a much shorter cartridge. This would facilitate accuracy and allow use of a smaller, more comfortable grip frame.

Until quite recently, none of the factory loads available actually took full advantage of this cartridge's potential. Several now offered actually generate about 500 fpe in typical guns. This is serious power for such a small package and rivals the best the 45 Automatic can offer. However, such a powerful and compact package requires comparatively high pressures. High peak pressure and a short barrel equate to high noise and muzzle blast. Nevertheless, for its purpose, this has to be considered a superior cartridge design. It has already completely eclipsed the similar 41 Action Express.

45 ACP/45 Automatic

 This cartridge was developed by John Browning in 1905 and adopted by the United States Ordnance Dept., with the Colt-Browning automatic pistol, in 1911. It has also been made the official military handgun chambering by several other governments, notably Argentina, Mexico and Norway. The 45 Automatic is the most powerful military handgun cartridge in use today. It is also one of the most difficult to master. The Colt Government Model auto-pistol and its copies, as well as the Colt and Smith & Wesson Army Model 1917 revolvers are the principal arms chambered for the 45 Automatic in the United States. Ruger, S&W, Springfield Armory, Glock, Numrich and many other companies now also offer guns in this chambering. Several submachineguns have

used it. About 1943, a number of Reising semi-automatic rifles were marketed in this chambering. Imitations of the Colt auto pistol have been made in Argentina, China, Korea, Norway, Spain and the United States. It was replaced as of 1985 as the official U.S. military handgun cartridge by the 9mm Parabellum. However, it remains in U.S. Marine Corps service and has proven increasingly popular with police agencies in the United States.

The 45 Automatic has been proven in combat all over the world as having excellent stopping power. It has also developed into a first-class match cartridge with accuracy equal to the best. It requires practice for the average person to develop skill with this cartridge, particularly when fired in some untuned semi-automatics. It is used far more for target shooting than hunting, its curved trajectory limiting its effective range. Despite this, it is quite adequate for any small or medium game. Like all the other semi-auto pistol cartridges, it is a better hunting round with softpoint and hollowpoint bullets. A number of police departments have switched from the 38 Special to the 45 Automatic in the last few years. All major and minor commercial ammunition manufacturers offer this cartridge. After several years of declining sales, it is enjoying a resurgence of popularity.

450 Bushmaster

Note: *The following description is taken from the Hornady website (www. hornady.com).*

"Nicknamed "The Thumper," the new 450 Bushmaster is the most radical cartridge ever chambered in production AR-15 type firearms. Hornady has brought big bore performance to the most popular semi-automatic rifle in America — and this innovation will open a whole new world of hunting to the battleproven platform. Hornady engineers, working closely with the design team from Bushmaster, built the cartridge to wring every last ounce of performance from the AR-15 platform without sacrificing strength or reliability. The NEW 450 Bushmaster is well suited to hunting any game in North America and it bear country. By simply switching uppers, the shooter can go from the prairie dog towns of South Dakota to Kodiak country in Alaska! The 450 Bushmaster fires Hornady's 0.452" 250 gr. SST (now featuring our Flex Tip™ technology). The overall cartridge matches the 223 Remington at 2.250". Its sleek profile makes for surprisingly fl at trajectories and tremendous downrange energy. The new, soft polymer tipped SST™ bullet eliminates tip deformation and also initiates expansion over a wide range of impact velocities. Put it all together, and you have a cartridge that will give your AR series rifle a serious attitude adjustment!"

458 SOCOM

After a bloody 1993 battle in Mogadishu, Somalia, several individuals addressed the opportunity to increase single-hit stopping power from U.S. military's M-16 and M-4 family of rifles and carbines. Maarten ter Weeme (Teppo Jutsu LLC) developed the 458 SOCOM cartridge to provide the equivalent of 45-70 firepower from M-16 rifles. The 458 SOCOM hurls big chunks of metal at substantial velocity from unaltered lower receivers and magazines—in full auto, and suppressed if desired. During testing, the cartridge defeated Level IIIa protective vests.

The 458 SOCOM uses the 50 AE as the parent case, lengthened to 1.575 inches (40mm), necked to accept .458 inch bullets, and featuring a rebated .473 inch rim. It accepts readily available 458-caliber bullets ranging from 250 grains to 600 grains, and in a wide variety of bullet styles and construction. Using standard M-16 lower receivers and unmodified magazines, ten 458 SOCOM rounds will fit into a military 30 round M-16 magazine; the 20 round magazine will hold seven rounds. In 16 inch barreled rifles, the 600-grain subsonic load works well with a 1:14 rifling twist. The 300-grain bullets do better with a 1:18 twist. Cor-Bon supplies loaded 458 SOCOM ammunition; Starline offers new brass cases, CH Tool and Die list reloading dies and Teppo Jutsu LLC provides reloading data.

50 Beowulf

In 1999, Bill Alexander (Alexander Arms) designed the 50 Beowulf to be the biggest possible cartridge that could be chambered in the AR-15 family of rifles and carbines. No contemporary cartridges existed when Bill reworked the 50 AE parent cartridge case, extended it slightly

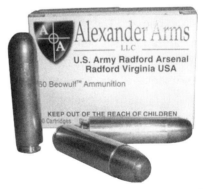

and rebating the rim to fit an AR-15 bolt face. For close range and brush hunting, the 50 Beowulf is superbly suited for wild hogs and even larger game. Over 5000 rifles have been chambered for the 50 Beowulf.

The 50 Beowulf delivers exceptional stopping power at short-to-medium ranges using 1/2 inch diameter bullets, ranging in weight from 325 grains to 400 grains at velocities from 1900 to 2050 feet per second. The 50 Beowulf shares the .445 inch case rim dimension with the military 7.63x39 cartridge case. Seven cartridges will fit into an Alexander

Arms-supplied magazine dimensioned to fit into the magazine well in the AR15's lower receiver. The cartridge performs well in a 16 inch barrel using a 1:19 twist. Factory loads do not exceed 33,000 psi. Alexander Arms supplies rifles, magazines, ammunition, reloading dies and brass.

50 Browning Machine Gun/50 BMG

The 50 BMG was invented by its namesake and adopted into United States military service in 1918 for John M. Browning's famous heavy machinegun. Browning's attentions in this area were prompted by a battlefield need recognized during World War I. There have been other developments and at least once the Pentagon was considering dropping the 50 BMG in favor of more modern and generally bigger chamberings. However, the 50 BMG has remained. The advent of saboted loads, generating 4,500 fps muzzle velocities with devastating armor-penetration capabilities, and its performance in the Gulf War has seemed to cement its continued existence as a stable part of NATO's arsenal.

Battlefield use is against light-armored vehicles to ranges of a mile or more, and used against the unprotected, it is effective to several times that range.

There has long been interest in the 50 BMG as a quasi-sporting round. Today, the most significant sporting use for this chambering is long-range accuracy shooting with some competitions exceeding one mile. The 1000-yard 50-caliber record, as of this writing, is a five-shot group of just under 3 inches on centers. Several bolt-action rifles are currently available for the big fifty. The 50 BMG easily launches the 750-grain bullets available for it at 2,700 fps. The lighter 647-grain bullets available can be launched at 3000 fps. For obvious reasons, sporting rifles chambered for the big fifty uniformly feature muzzlebrakes and weigh 20 pounds or more. Recoil is a bit harsh until the rifle's weight approaches 30 pounds.

The only commercial ammunition that has ever been available for the 50 BMG is from PMC. Components and specialized tools and equipment to handload this cartridge are available to the advanced reloader.

APPENDIX I
Federal Firearms Regulations That Address Assault Weapons

Below is the text of major laws that affect this type of firearm. The first, the infamous Assault Weapon Ban of 1994, is no longer in effect. However, several states and cities have bans in effect that mirror these definitions.

Note also that the law addressed the assembly of assault-style firearms from aftermarket components. These restrictions are still in effect. This is an area of considerable importance given the great number of aftermarket suppliers.

■ FEDERAL ASSAULT WEAPON BAN OF 1994 H.R.3355 VIOLENT CRIME CONTROL AND LAW ENFORCEMENT ACT OF 1994 (ENROLLED AS AGREED TO OR PASSED BY BOTH HOUSE AND SENATE)

SEC. 110102. RESTRICTION ON MANUFACTURE, TRANSFER, AND POSSESSION OF CERTAIN SEMIAUTOMATIC ASSAULT WEAPONS.

(a) RESTRICTION- Section 922 of title 18, United States Code, is amended by adding at the end the following new subsection: `

(v)(1) It shall be unlawful for a person to manufacture, transfer, or possess a semiautomatic assault weapon. `

(2) Paragraph (1) shall not apply to the possession or transfer of any semiautomatic assault weapon otherwise lawfully possessed under Federal law on the date of the enactment of this subsection. `

(3) Paragraph (1) shall not apply to-- `(A) any of the firearms, or replicas or duplicates of the firearms, specified in Appendix A to this section, as such firearms were manufactured on October 1, 1993; `(B) any firearm that-- `(i) is manually operated by bolt, pump, lever, or slide action; `(ii) has been rendered permanently inoperable; or `(iii) is an antique firearm; `(C) any semiautomatic rifle that cannot accept a detachable magazine that holds more than 5 rounds of ammunition; or `(D) any semiautomatic shotgun that cannot hold more than 5 rounds of ammunition in a fixed or detachable magazine. The fact that a firearm is not listed in Appendix A shall not be construed to mean that paragraph (1) applies to such firearm. No firearm exempted by this subsection may be deleted from Appendix A so long as this subsection is in effect.

(4) Paragraph (1) shall not apply to-- `(A) the manufacture for, transfer to, or possession by the United States or a department or agency of the United States or a State or a department, agency, or political subdivision of a State, or a transfer to or possession by a law enforcement officer employed by such an entity for purposes of law enforcement (whether on or off duty); `(B) the transfer to a licensee under title I of the Atomic Energy Act of 1954 for purposes of establishing and maintaining an on-site physical protection system and security organization required by Federal law, or possession by an employee or contractor of such licensee on-site for such purposes or off-site for purposes of licensee-authorized training or transportation of nuclear materials; `(C) the possession, by an individual who is retired from service with a law enforcement agency and is not otherwise prohibited from receiving a firearm, of a semiautomatic assault weapon transferred to the individual by the agency upon such retirement; or `(D) the manufacture, transfer, or possession of a semiautomatic assault weapon by a licensed manufacturer or licensed importer for the purposes of testing or experimentation authorized by the Secretary.'.

■ (B) DEFINITION OF SEMIAUTOMATIC ASSAULT WEAPON

Section 921(a) of title 18, United States Code, is amended by adding at the end the following new paragraph: `(30) The term `semiautomatic assault weapon' means--

(A) any of the firearms, or copies or duplicates of the firearms in any caliber, known as-- `(i) Norinco, Mitchell, and Poly Technologies Avtomat Kalashnikovs (all models); `(ii) Action Arms Israeli Military Industries UZI and Galil; `(iii) Beretta Ar70 (SC-70); `(iv) Colt AR-15; `(v) Fabrique National FN/FAL, FN/LAR, and FNC; `(vi) SWD M-10, M-11, M-11/9, and M-12; `(vii) Steyr AUG; `(viii) INTRATEC TEC-9, TEC-DC9 and TEC-22; and `(ix) revolving cylinder shotguns, such as (or similar to) the Street Sweeper and Striker 12;

(B) a semiautomatic rifle that has an ability to accept a detachable magazine and has at least 2 of-- `(i) a folding or telescoping stock; `(ii) a pistol grip that protrudes conspicuously beneath the action of the weapon; `(iii) a bayonet mount; `(iv) a flash suppressor or threaded barrel designed to accommodate a flash suppressor; and `(v) a grenade launcher;

(C) a semiautomatic pistol that has an ability to accept a detachable magazine and has at least 2 of-- `(i) an ammunition magazine that attaches to the pistol outside of the pistol grip; `(ii) a threaded barrel capable of accepting a barrel extender, flash suppressor, forward handgrip, or silencer; `(iii) a shroud that is attached to, or partially or completely encircles, the barrel and that permits the shooter to hold the firearm with the nontrigger hand without being burned; `(iv) a manufactured weight of 50 ounces or more when the pistol is unloaded; and `(v) a semiautomatic version of an automatic firearm; and

(D) a semiautomatic shotgun that has at least 2 of-- `(i) a folding or telescoping stock; `(ii) a pistol grip that protrudes conspicuously beneath the action of the weapon; `(iii) a fixed magazine capacity in excess of 5 rounds; and `(iv) an ability to accept a detachable magazine.'.

(c) PENALTIES- (1) VIOLATION OF SECTION 922(v)- Section 924(a)(1)(B) of such title is amended by striking `or (q) of section 922' and inserting `(r), or (v) of section 922'. (2) USE OR POSSESSION DURING CRIME OF VIOLENCE OR DRUG TRAFFICKING CRIME- Section 924(c)(1) of such title is amended in the first sentence by inserting `, or semiautomatic assault weapon,' after `short-barreled shotgun,'.

(d) IDENTIFICATION MARKINGS FOR SEMIAUTOMATIC ASSAULT WEAPONS- Section 923(i) of such title is amended by adding at the end the following: `The serial number of any semiautomatic assault weapon manufactured after the date of the enactment of this sentence shall clearly show the date on which the weapon was manufactured.'.

■ SEC. 110103. BAN OF LARGE CAPACITY AMMUNITION FEEDING DEVICES.

(a) PROHIBITION- Section 922 of title 18, United States Code, as amended by section 110102(a), is amended by adding at the end the following new subsection:

(w)(1) Except as provided in paragraph (2), it shall be unlawful for a person to transfer or possess a large capacity ammunition feeding device.

`(2) Paragraph (1) shall not apply to the possession or transfer of any large capacity ammunition feeding device otherwise lawfully possessed on or before the date of the enactment of this subsection.

(3) This subsection shall not apply to--

(A) the manufacture for, transfer to, or possession by the United States or a department or agency of the United States or a State or a department, agency, or political subdivision of a State, or

a transfer to or possession by a law enforcement officer employed by such an entity for purposes of law enforcement (whether on or off duty);

(B) the transfer to a licensee under title I of the Atomic Energy Act of 1954 for purposes of establishing and maintaining an on-site physical protection system and security organization required by Federal law, or possession by an employee or contractor of such licensee on-site for such purposes or off-site for purposes of licensee-authorized training or transportation of nuclear materials;

(C) the possession, by an individual who is retired from service with a law enforcement agency and is not otherwise prohibited from receiving ammunition, of a large capacity ammunition feeding device transferred to the individual by the agency upon such retirement; or

(D) the manufacture, transfer, or possession of any large capacity ammunition feeding device by a licensed manufacturer or licensed importer for the purposes of testing or experimentation authorized by the Secretary.'

(4) If a person charged with violating paragraph (1) asserts that paragraph (1) does not apply to such person because of paragraph (2) or (3), the Government shall have the burden of proof to show that such paragraph (1) applies to such person. The lack of a serial number as described in section 923(i) of title 18, United States Code, shall be a presumption that the large capacity ammunition feeding device is not subject to the prohibition of possession in paragraph (1).'.

■ DEFINITION OF LARGE CAPACITY AMMUNITION FEEDING DEVICE

Section 921(a) of title 18, United States Code, as amended by section 110102(b), is amended by adding at the end the following new paragraph: `(31) The term `large capacity ammunition feeding device'

(A) means a magazine, belt, drum, feed strip, or similar device manufactured after the date of enactment of the Violent Crime Control and Law Enforcement Act of 1994 that has a capacity of, or that can be readily restored or converted to accept, more than 10 rounds of ammunition; but

(B) does not include an attached tubular device designed to accept, and capable of operating only with, .22 caliber rimfire ammunition.'.

(c) PENALTY- Section 924(a)(1)(B) of title 18, United States Code, as amended by section 110102(c)(1), is amended by striking `or (v)' and inserting `(v), or (w)'.

(d) IDENTIFICATION MARKINGS FOR LARGE CAPACITY AMMUNITION FEEDING DEVICES- Section 923(i) of title 18, United States Code, as amended by section 110102(d) of this Act, is amended by adding at the end the following: `A large capacity ammunition feeding device manufactured after the date of the enactment of this sentence shall be identified by a serial number that clearly shows that the device was manufactured or imported after the effective date of this subsection, and such other identification as the Secretary may by regulation prescribe.'.

■ SEC. 110105. EFFECTIVE DATE.

This subtitle and the amendments made by this subtitle-- (1) shall take effect on the date of the enactment of this Act; and (2) are repealed effective as of the date that is 10 years after that date. These laws deal with the importation of firearms as well as the assembly of firearms from imported parts. These rules remain in effect and any firearm imported into or manufactured in the U.S. today must comply with these rules. Assembly of Assault Weapons with imported parts: US Code section 922 (r) It shall be unlawful for any person to assemble from imported parts any semiautomatic rifle or any shotgun which is identical to any rifle or shotgun prohibited from importation under section 925(d)(3) of this chapter as not being particularly suitable for or readily adaptable to sporting purposes except that this subsection shall not apply to - (1) the assembly of any such rifle or shotgun for sale or distribution by a licensed manufacturer to the United States or any department or agency thereof or to any State or any department, agency, or political subdivision thereof; or (2) the assembly of any such rifle or shotgun for the purposes of testing or experimentation authorized by the Attorney General.

■ TITLE 27--ALCOHOL, TOBACCO PRODUCTS, AND FIREARMS CHAPTER II--BUREAU OF ALCOHOL, TOBACCO, FIREARMS, AND EXPLOSIVES, DEPARTMENT OF JUSTICE PART 478_COMMERCE IN FIREARMS AND AMMUNITION--

Table of Contents Subpart G_Importation Sec. 478.112 Importation by a licensed importer.

(a) No firearm, firearm barrel, or ammunition shall be imported or brought into the United States by a licensed importer (as defined in Sec. 478.11) unless the Director has authorized the importation of the firearm, firearm barrel, or ammunition.

(b)(1) An application for a permit, ATF Form 6--Part I, to import or bring a firearm, firearm barrel, or ammunition into the United States or a possession thereof under this section must be filed, in triplicate, with the Director. The application must be signed and dated and must contain the information requested on the form, including: (i) The name,

address, telephone number, and license number (including expiration date) of the importer; (ii) The country from which the firearm, firearm barrel, or ammunition is to be imported; (iii) The name and address of the foreign seller and foreign shipper; (iv) A description of the firearm, firearm barrel, or ammunition to be imported, including: (A) The name and address of the manufacturer; (B) The type (e.g., rifle, shotgun, pistol, revolver and, in the case of ammunition only, ball, wadcutter, shot, etc.); (C) The caliber, gauge, or size; (D) The model; (E) The barrel length, if a firearm or firearm barrel (in inches); (F) The overall length, if a firearm (in inches); (G) The serial number, if known; (H) Whether the firearm is new or used; (I) The quantity; (J) The unit cost of the firearm, firearm barrel, or ammunition to be imported; (v) The specific purpose of importation, including final recipient information if different from the importer; (vi) Verification that if a firearm, it will be identified as required by this part; and (vii)(A) If a firearm or ammunition imported or brought in for scientific or research purposes, a statement describing such purpose; or (B) If a firearm or ammunition for use in connection with competition or training pursuant to Chapter 401 of Title 10, U.S.C., a statement describing such intended use; or (C) If an unserviceable firearm (other than a machine gun) being imported as a curio or museum piece, a description of how it was rendered unserviceable and an explanation of why it is a curio or museum piece; or (D) If a firearm other than a surplus military firearm, of a type that does not fall within the definition of a firearm under section 5845(a) of the Internal Revenue Code of 1986, and is for sporting purposes, an explanation of why the firearm is generally recognized [[Page 59]] as particularly suitable for or readily adaptable to sporting purposes; or (E) If ammunition being imported for sporting purposes, a statement why the ammunition is particularly suitable for or readily adaptable to sporting purposes; or (F) If a firearm barrel for a handgun, an explanation why the handgun is generally recognized as particularly suitable for or readily adaptable to sporting purposes. (2)(i) If the Director approves the application, such approved application will serve as the permit to import the firearm, firearm barrel, or ammunition described therein, and importation of such firearms, firearm barrels, or ammunition may continue to be made by the licensed importer under the approved application (permit) during the period specified thereon. The Director will furnish the approved application (permit) to the applicant and retain two copies thereof for administrative use. (ii) If the Director disapproves the application, the licensed importer will be notified of the basis for the disapproval.

(c) A firearm, firearm barrel, or ammunition imported or brought into the United States or a possession thereof under the provisions of this section by a licensed importer may be released from Customs custody to the licensed importer upon showing that the importer has obtained a permit from the Director for the importation of the firearm, firearm barrel, or ammunition to be released. The importer will also submit to Customs a copy of the export license authorizing the export of the firearm, firearm barrel, or ammunition from the exporting country. If the exporting country does not require issuance of an export license, the importer must submit a certification, under penalty of perjury, to that effect. (1) In obtaining the release from Customs custody of a firearm, firearm barrel, or ammunition authorized by this section to be imported through the use of a permit, the licensed importer will prepare ATF Form 6A, in duplicate, and furnish the original ATF Form 6A to the Customs officer releasing the firearm, firearm barrel, or ammunition. The Customs officer will, after certification, forward the ATF Form 6A to the address specified on the form. (2) The ATF Form 6A must contain the information requested on the form, including: (i) The name, address, and license number of the importer; (ii) The name of the manufacturer of the firearm, firearm barrel, or ammunition; (iii) The country of manufacture; (iv) The type; (v) The model; (vi) The caliber, gauge, or size; (vii) The serial number in the case of firearms, if known; and (viii) The number of firearms, firearm barrels, or rounds of ammunition released.

(d) Within 15 days of the date of release from Customs custody, the licensed importer must: (1) Forward to the address specified on the form a copy of ATF Form 6A on which must be reported any error or discrepancy appearing on the ATF Form 6A certified by Customs and serial numbers if not previously provided on ATF Form 6A; (2) Pursuant to Sec. 478.92, place all required identification data on each imported firearm if same did not bear such identification data at the time of its release from Customs custody; and (3) Post in the records required to be maintained by the importer under subpart H of this part all required information regarding the importation. (Paragraph (b) approved by the Office of Management and Budget under control number 1512-0017; paragraphs (c) and (d) approved by the Office of Management and Budget under control number 1512-0019) [T.D. ATF-270, 53 FR 10498, Mar. 31, 1988, as amended by T.D. ATF-426, 65 FR 38198, June 20, 2000] [Code of Federal Regulations] [Title 27, Volume 2] [Revised as of April 1, 2006] From the U.S. Government Printing Office via GPO Access [CITE: 27CFR478.39] [Page 36-37]

■ TITLE 27--ALCOHOL, TOBACCO PRODUCTS, AND FIREARMS CHAPTER II--BUREAU OF ALCOHOL, TOBACCO, FIREARMS, AND EXPLOSIVES, DEPARTMENT OF JUSTICE PART 478_COMMERCE IN FIREARMS AND AMMUNITION--TABLE OF CONTENTS SUBPART C_ADMINISTRATIVE AND MISCELLANEOUS PROVISIONS SEC. 478.39 ASSEMBLY OF SEMIAUTOMATIC RIFLES OR SHOTGUNS.

(a) No person shall assemble a semiautomatic rifle or any shotgun using more than 10 of the imported parts listed in paragraph (c) of this section if the assembled firearm is prohibited from importation under section 925(d)(3) as not being particularly suitable for or readily adaptable to sporting purposes.

(b) The provisions of this section shall not apply to: (1) The assembly of such rifle or shotgun for sale or distribution by a licensed manufacturer to the United States or any department or agency thereof or to any State or any department, agency, or political subdivision thereof; or (2) The assembly of such rifle or shotgun for the purposes of testing or experimentation authorized by the Director under the provisions of Sec. 478.151; or (3) The repair of any rifle or shotgun which had been imported into or assembled in the United States prior to November 30, 1990, or the replacement of any part of such firearm.

(c) For purposes of this section, the term imported parts are: (1) Frames, receivers, receiver castings, forgings or stampings (2) Barrels (3) Barrel extensions (4) Mounting blocks (trunions) (5) Muzzle attachments (6) Bolts (7) Bolt carriers [[Page 37]] (8) Operating rods (9) Gas pistons (10) Trigger housings (11) Triggers (12) Hammers (13) Sears (14) Disconnectors (15) Buttstocks (16) Pistol grips (17) Forearms, handguards (18) Magazine bodies (19) Followers (20) Floorplates [T.D. ATF-346, 58 FR 40589, July 29, 1993] 27 CFR 478.112

(d) The Attorney General shall authorize a firearm or ammunition to be imported or brought into the United States or any possession thereof if the firearm or ammunition - (1) is being imported or brought in for scientific or research purposes, or is for use in connection with competition or training pursuant to chapter 401 of title 10; (2) is an unserviceable firearm, other than a machinegun as defined in section 5845(b) of the Internal Revenue Code of 1986 (not readily restorable to firing condition), imported or brought in as a curio or museum piece; (3) is of a type that does not fall within the definition of a firearm as defined in section 5845(a) of the Internal Revenue Code of 1986 and is generally recognized as particularly suitable for or readily adaptable to sporting purposes, excluding surplus military firearms, except in any case where the Attorney General has not authorized the importation of the firearm pursuant to this paragraph, it shall be unlawful to import any frame, receiver, or barrel of such firearm which would be prohibited if assembled; or (4) was previously taken out of the United States or a possession by the person who is bringing in the firearm or ammunition. The Attorney General shall permit the conditional importation or bringing in of a firearm or ammunition for examination and testing in connection with the making of a determination as to whether the importation or bringing in of such firearm or ammunition will be allowed under this subsection.

(e) Notwithstanding any other provision of this title, the Attorney General shall authorize the importation of, by any licensed importer, the following: (1) All rifles and shotguns listed as curios or relics by the Attorney General pursuant to section 921(a)(13), and (2) All handguns, listed as curios or relics by the Attorney General pursuant to section 921(a)(13), provided that such handguns are generally recognized as particularly suitable for or readily adaptable to sporting purposes. (f) The Attorney General shall not authorize, under subsection (d), the importation of any firearm the importation of which is prohibited by section 922(p).

■ BATF LETTER REGARDING BUILDING AK TYPE GUNS: DEPARTMENT OF THE TREASURY BUREAU OF ALCOHOL, TOBACCO AND FIREARMS WASHINGTON, D.C. 20226 AUG 13 1997 E:CE:FT:EMO 3311

Dear Mr. [   ]:

This refers to your letter of July 30, 1997, in which you ask additional questions about the number of imported parts contained in rifles based on the AK 47 that are imported into the United States.

Title 27 CFR, Section 178.39(a) states that no person shall assemble a semiautomatic rifle or any shotgun using more than 10 of the imported parts listed in paragraph (c) of this section if the assembled firearm (emphasis added) is prohibited from importation under section 925(d)(3) as not being particularly suitable for or readily adaptable to sporting purposes. Firearms based on the AK 47 design are not approved for importation with separate pistol grips, folding stocks, bayonet mounts, threaded muzzles, flash suppressors, grenade launchers, night sights or bipod mounts. Therefore, if you assemble an AK type firearm using more than 10 imported parts listed in paragraph (c), the assembled rifle must have a one piece thumb hole style stock and may not have a separate pistol grip, folding stock, bayonet mount, threaded muzzle, flash suppressor, grenade launcher, night sight or bipod mount. If you plan to assemble an AK type weapon using 10 or less of the imported parts listed in paragraph (c), the rifle is not required to have a one-piece thumbhole style stock. However such rifle many not be in a configuration that meets the definition of semiautomatic assault weapon as that term is defined in 18 U.S.C., Chapter 44, Section 921(a)(30).

2 - You also asked about marketing a parts kit containing a combination of domestic and imported parts. In order to respond to your inquiry concerning the legality of using these parts on an imported AK type rifle, it is requested that a sample of the parts kit be submitted. We trust that the foregoing has been responsive to your inquiry. If we can be of any further assistance, please contact us.

Sincerely yours,

[signed]

Edward M. Owen, Jr. Chief, Firearms Technology Branch

APPENDIX II
Military Weapons Commonly Considered "Assault Weapons"

Editor's Note: This book defines "assault weapon" as a military-styled weapon with a detachable magazine of more than 10 rounds. However, many imported military weapons are considered "assault weapons" by the general public, so we have included the following listings for many of these rifles. Note that, for certain items, prices may seem to vary from those shown elsewhere in this book due to a different grading system.

■ ARGENTINE FN MODEL 1949
Semi-automatic rifle sold to Argentina after WWII. Argentine crest on receiver. Originally, it was chambered for the 7.65x53mm Mauser cartridge and had a fixed 10 round magazine. Later, nearly all were converted for the Argentine navy. These will be marked "ARA." A new 7.62x51 Nato/.308 barrel was installed and a detachable magazine system was added. The magazines held 20 rounds and were unique to the design. Some Argentine Navy FN 1949s were imported to the U.S. in the 1990's and the magazines were shortened to 10 rounds to comply with the 1994 "Assault weapon" law. After this law expired in 2004, some unaltered 20 round magazines appeared on the market.
FN 1949 rifle, original configuration, in 7.65x53mm with fixed magazine. Very rare.

EXC.	V.G.	GOOD	FAIR	POOR
2000	1700	1200	900	700

FN 1949 Rifle, Argentine Navy Conversion to 7.62mm with one 20 round magazine. Deduct $30 for a 10 round magazine.

EXC.	V.G.	GOOD	FAIR	POOR
1000	850	750	500	400

■ AUSTRALIAN L1A1 RIFLE
This is the British version of the FN-FAL in the "inch" or Imperial pattern. Most of these rifles were semi-automatic only. This rifle was the standard service rifle for the British Army from about 1954 to 1988. The rifle was made in Lithgow, Australia, under license from FN. The configurations for the L1A1 rifle are the same as the standard FN-FAL Belgium rifle. Only a few of these rifles were imported into the U.S. They are very rare. This "inch" pattern British gun will also be found in other Commonwealth countries such as Australia, New Zealand, Canada, and India.
NOTE: Only *about* 180 Australian L1A1s were imported into the U.S. prior to 1989. These are rare and in great demand.

EXC.	V.G.	GOOD	FAIR	POOR
7500	6000	5000	—	—

■ AUSTRIAN STEYR AUG (ARMEE UNIVERSAL GEWEHR)
Produced by Steyr-Mannlicher beginning in 1978, this rifle is chambered for the 5.56x45mm cartridge. It is a bullpup design with a number of different configurations. Barrel lengths are 13.6" in submachine gun configuration, 16.3" in carbine, 19.8" in rifle, and 24.2" in a heavy barrel sniper configuration. Magazine is 30 or 42 rounds. Carry handle is an optic sight of 1.5 power. Adopted by Austrian army and still in production. Weight is 7.7 lbs. in rifle configuration. Rate of fire is about 650 rounds per minute.

▶ **Pre-1986 full-auto conversions of semi-automatic version**

EXC.	V.G.	GOOD
15000	12500	10000

■ AUSTRIAN STEYR AUG (SEMI-AUTOMATIC VERSION)
As above but in semi-automatic only. Two models, the first with green furniture and fitted with a 20" barrel. The second with black furniture and fitted with a 16" barrel.

FIRST MODEL

NIB	EXC.	V.G.	GOOD	FAIR	POOR
5000	4250	3000	—	—	—

SECOND MODEL

NIB	EXC.	V.G.	GOOD	FAIR	POOR
5500	4500	3500	—	—	—

■ BELGIAN MODEL 1949 OR SAFN 49
A gas-operated semi-automatic rifle chambered for 7x57, 7.92mm, and .30-06. It has a 23" barrel and military-type sights. The fixed magazine holds 10 rounds. The finish is blued, and the stock is walnut. This is a well-made gun that was actually designed before WWII. When the Germans were in the process of taking over Belgium, a group of FN engineers fled to England and took the plans for this rifle with them, preventing the German military from acquiring a very fine weapon. This model was introduced in 1949, after hostilities had ceased. This model was sold on contract to Egypt,

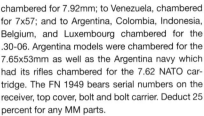

chambered for 7.92mm; to Venezuela, chambered for 7x57; and to Argentina, Colombia, Indonesia, Belgium, and Luxembourg chambered for the .30-06. Argentina models were chambered for the 7.65x53mm as well as the Argentina navy which had its rifles chambered for the 7.62 NATO cartridge. The FN 1949 bears serial numbers on the receiver, top cover, bolt and bolt carrier. Deduct 25 percent for any MM parts.

▶ **Belgium military issue. Cal. 30-06. Receiver marked "ABL".**

EXC.	V.G.	GOOD	FAIR	POOR
900	750	600	400	300

▶ **Columbian contract. Cal. 30-06. Receiver marked with Columbian crest.**

EXC.	V.G.	GOOD	FAIR	POOR
1000	850	700	450	300

▶ **Luxemborg contract. Cal. 30-06. Receiver marked "AL".**

EXC.	V.G.	GOOD	FAIR	POOR
900	750	600	400	300

▶ **Venezuelan contract. Cal. 7x57mm. Receiver marked with Venezuelan crest.**

The only FN-49 that was issued with a flash hider.

EXC.	V.G.	GOOD	FAIR	POOR
800	650	450	300	250

■ BELGIAN FN-FAL

A gas-operated, semi-automatic version of the famous FN battle rifle. This weapon has been adopted by more free world countries than any other rifle. It is chambered for the 7.62 NATO or .308 and has a 21" barrel with an integral flash suppressor. The sights are adjustable with an aperture rear, and the detachable box magazine holds 20 rounds. The stock and forearm are made of wood or a black synthetic. This model has been discontinued by the company and is no longer manufactured.

The models listed below are for the metric pattern Type 2 and Type 3 receivers, those marked "FN MATCH." The models below are for semi-automatic rifles only. FN-FAL rifles in the "inch" pattern are found in the British Commonwealth countries of Australia, India, Canada, and of course, Great Britain. These rifles are covered separately under their own country headings.

▶ **50.00–21" Rifle Model**

NIB	EXC.	V.G.	GOOD	FAIR	POOR
3500	3000	2500	2000	N/A	N/A

▶ **50.63–18" Paratrooper Model**

NIB	EXC.	V.G.	GOOD	FAIR	POOR
4000	3500	3000	2750	N/A	N/A

▶ **50.64–21" Paratrooper Model**

NIB	EXC.	V.G.	GOOD	FAIR	POOR
4000	3500	3000	2750	N/A	N/A

▶ **50.41–Synthetic Butt H-Bar**

NIB	EXC.	V.G.	GOOD	FAIR	POOR
3250	2800	2500	2000	N/A	N/A

▶ **50.42–Wood Butt H-Bar**

NIB	EXC.	V.G.	GOOD	FAIR	POOR
4000	3500	3000	2750	N/A	N/A

NOTE: There are a number of U.S. companies that built FN-FAL receivers and use military surplus parts. These rifles have only limited collector value as of yet.

▶ **Belgian FN FAL "G" Series (Type 1 Receiver)**

The first FAL to be imported to the U.S. The receivers are capable of accepting select fire parts. These rifles are subject to interpretation by the BATF as to their legal status. A list of BATF legal serial numbers is available. This information should be referenced prior to a purchase. There were 1,848 legal "G" Series FN FAL rifles imported into this country. All were "grandfathered" and remain legal to possess.

STANDARD

NIB	EXC.	V.G.	GOOD	FAIR	POOR
7500	6500	5000	3000	N/A	N/A

LIGHTWEIGHT

NIB	EXC.	V.G.	GOOD	FAIR	POOR
7500	6500	5000	3000	N/A	N/A

▶ **Belgian FN FAL–Select Fire Assault Rifle**

First produced in 1953, this 7.62x51mm select fire rifle has been used worldwide. It is fitted with a 20.8" barrel and a magazine that holds 20 rounds. It is available in several different configurations. Weight is about 9.8 lbs. Marked "FABRIQUE NATIONALE HERSTAL." Markings will also indicate many other countries made this rifle under license from FN.

PRE-1968 (RARE)

EXC.	V.G.	FAIR
18500	15000	12000

PRE-1986 FULL-AUTO CONVERSIONS OF SEMI-AUTOMATIC MODEL

EXC.	V.G.	FAIR
15000	12500	10000

■ BELGIAN FN CAL

Chambered for the 5.56x45mm cartridge and designed with a rotary bolt. It is fitted with an 18.2" barrel and has a magazine capacity of 20 or 30 rounds. Weight is about 6 lbs. With folding stock. Produced from 1966 to 1975 and is marked "fabrique nationale herstal mod cal 5.56mm" on the left side of the receiver. This rifle was not widely adopted. A rare rifle. Only about 20 of these rifles were imported into the U.S.

NIB	EXC.	V.G.	GOOD	FAIR	POOR
7000	6500	5000	3000	—	—

■ BELGIAN FN CAL-SELECT FIRE

ASSAULT RIFLE

Chambered for the 5.56x45mm cartridge and designed with a rotary bolt. It is fitted with an 18.2" barrel and has a magazine capacity of 20 or 30 rounds. Its rate of fire is 650 rounds per minute. Weight is about 6 lbs. With folding stock. Produced from 1966 to 1975 and is marked "fabrique nationale herstal mod cal 5.56mm" on the left side of the receiver. This rifle was not widely adopted.

▶ **Pre-1968 (Rare)**

EXC.	V.G.	FAIR
15000	12500	10000

■ BELGIAN FNC

A lighter-weight assault-type rifle chambered for the 5.56mm cartridge. It is a gas-operated semi-automatic with an 18" or 21" barrel. It has a 30 round box magazine and is black, with either a fixed or folding stock. This model was also discontinued by FN.

▶ **Standard**

Fixed stock, 16" or 18" barrel.

NIB	EXC.	V.G.	GOOD	FAIR	POOR
3800	3500	2750	2000	N/A	N/A

▶ **Paratrooper Model**

Folding stock, 16" or 18" barrel.

NIB	EXC.	V.G.	GOOD	FAIR	POOR
3800	3500	2750	2000	N/A	N/A

NOTE: *The above prices are for Belgian-made guns only.*

■ BELGIAN FN FNC–SELECT FIRE ASSAULT RIFLE

This model, introduced in 1979, took the place of the CAL. Chambered for the 5.56x45mm cartridge and fitted with a 17.5" barrel, it weighs about 8.4 lbs. It has a 30 round magazine capacity. Rate of fire is 700 rounds per minute. Fitted with a metal folding stock. This model will accept M16 magazines. Marked "fnc 5.56" on left side of receiver. This rifle was adopted by the Belgian, Indonesian, and Swedish militaries.

▶ **Pre-1986 full-auto conversions of semi-automatic model**

EXC.	V.G.	FAIR
7500	6000	4500

■ BELGIAN FN BAR MODEL D (DEMONTABLE)

This was the FN version of the Browning automatic rifle. It is fitted with a quick change barrel and pistol grip. It was offered in a variety of calibers from 6.5 Swedish Mauser to the 7.92x57mm Mauser. It is fitted with a 19.5" barrel and has a rate of fire of either 450 or 650 rounds per minute. Weight is about 20 lbs. Marked "fabrique nationale d'armes de guerre herstal-belgique" on left side of receiver.

FN sold about 700 Model Ds to Finland in 1940 which the Finns used during their "Winter War" with the Russians. These Finnish BARs were chambered for the 7.63x54R cartridge. Also a small number of FN guns were sold to China (2,000) and Ethiopia in the 1930s. These BARs were chambered for the 7.92x57mm Mauser cartridge. After World War II FN sold its Model 30 BAR to a number of countries around the world.

▶ **Pre-1968 (Very Rare)**

EXC.	V.G.	FAIR
37500	32500	27500

▶ **Pre-1986 manufacture with new receiver or re-weld**

EXC.	V.G.	FAIR
25000	20000	18000

■ BULGARIAN AK-47

This is an exact copy of the Russian AK-47.

EXC.	V.G.	GOOD	FAIR	POOR
700	600	500	400	300

■ BULGARIAN AKN-47

This is an exact copy of the Russian AKS.

EXC.	V.G.	GOOD	FAIR	POOR
800	700	600	500	400

■ BULGARIAN AK-47-MI

This is a copy of an AK-47 fitted with a 40mm grenade launcher.

EXC.	V.G.	GOOD	FAIR	POOR
N/A	N/A	N/A	N/A	N/A

■ BULGARIAN AK-74/AKS-74

These are copies of the Russian models. They were also exported in 5.56x45mm caliber.

EXC.	V.G.	GOOD	FAIR	POOR
N/A		N/A	N/A	N/A	N/A

■ CANADIAN C1/C1A1 (FN FAL)

Canada was one of the first countries to adopt the FN-FAL rifle. This is a semi-automatic version with 21" barrel. Twenty round box magazine. The rear sight on the C1 is a revolving disk with five different sized openings. Ranges calibrated from 200 to 600 yards; numbered 2 to 6 on the sight. The sight may be folded when not in use. Weight is about 9.5 lbs. About 1959 the C1 was modified to use a 2-piece firing pin and a plastic carry handle replaced the wooden type. Both types of rifles utilize the long prong flash hider on the muzzle. The author could find no indication that any of these were ever legally imported to the U.S. as a semi automatic. It would have to be in the same class as the FN FAL "G" series as the receiver is capable of accepting select fire parts.

For C1/C1A1 registered as NFA firearms:

▶ **Pre-1986**

EXC.	V.G.	FAIR
18500	15000	10000

■ CANADIAN C2/C2A1

This is Canada's version of the FN heavy barrel Squad Light Automatic Rifle. Select fire with a rate of fire of about 700 rounds per minute. Barrel length is 21". Magazine capacity is 30 rounds. Weight is approximately 15 lbs. Built by Long Branch Arsenal, Ontario.

▶ **Pre-1986**

EXC.	V.G.	FAIR
18500	15000	12500

■ CANADIAN C1/C1A1 (FN FAL)

Canada was one of the first countries to adopt the FN-FAL rifle. This is a semi-automatic version with 21" barrel. Twenty round box magazine. The rear sight on the C1 is a revolving disk with five different sized openings. Ranges calibrated from 200 to 600 yards; numbered 2 to 6 on the sight. The sight may be folded when not in use. Weight is about 9.5 lbs. About 1959 the C1 was modified to use a 2-piece firing pin and a plastic carry handle replaced the wooden type. Both types of rifles utilize the long prong flash hider on the muzzle. The author could find no indication that any of these were ever legally imported to the U.S. as a semi automatic. It would have to be in the same class as the FN FAL "G" series as the receiver is capable of accepting select fire parts.

For C1/C1A1 registered as NFA firearms:

▶ **Pre-1986**

EXC.	V.G.	FAIR
18500	15000	10000

■ CANADIAN C2/C2A1

This is Canada's version of the FN heavy barrel Squad Light Automatic Rifle. Select fire with a rate of fire of about 700 rounds per minute. Barrel length is 21". Magazine capacity is 30 rounds. Weight is approximately 15 lbs. Built by Long Branch Arsenal, Ontario.

▶ **Pre-1986**

EXC.	V.G.	FAIR
18500	15000	12500

■ CANADIAN C7/C8 (M16A2)

In 1985 the Canadian firm of Diemaco began producing a Canadian version of the Colt M16A2 rifle. There are differences between the Colt-built M16 and the Diemaco version. However, due to import restrictions on Class 3 weapons, no Diemaco M16s were imported into the U.S. for transferable civilian sale. Therefore, no Diemaco lowers are available to the civilian collector. There are Diemaco uppers in the U.S. that will fit on Colt lowers. The 20" rifle version is designated the C7 while the 16" carbine version is called the C8. There are a number of other Diemaco Canadian uppers that may be seen in the U.S., such as the LMG and 24" barreled versions. Values should be comparable with those of Colt uppers.

Chinese Type 56 Carbine (SKS)

A 7.62x39mm semi-automatic rifle with a 20.5" barrel and 10-shot fixed magazine. Blued with oil finished stock. The early Chinese military issue Type 56 rifles came with a blade bayonet. Later models had the spike bayonet. Price listed is for used Type 56 made for the Chinese military. Some were brought back from Viet Nam, others were imported in the late 1980s.

EXC.	V.G.	GOOD	FAIR	POOR
400	325	275	200	150

■ NORTH KOREAN TYPE 56 CARBINE (SKS)

Same overall design as the Chinese version but with high quality fit and finish. Has a gas shut off valve on the gas block. This was to allow use of a grenade launcher. Reddish-brown laminated stock. Rare.

EXC.	V.G.	GOOD	FAIR	POOR
1400	1000	800	600	300

■ CHINESE TYPE 56 RIFLE

A close copy of the AK-47 and first produced in 1958, this select fire rifle is chambered for the 7.62x39mm cartridge. It is fitted with a 16" barrel and has a magazine capacity of 30 rounds. This model has a folding bayonet hinged below the muzzle. Weight is about 8.4 lbs. Rate of fire is 600 rounds per minute. Markings on left side of receiver. Still in production. This rifle was adopted by Chinese forces and was seen in Cambodia as well.

There are a number of subvariations of the Type 56. Early guns had machined receivers with Chinese characters for selector markings, some of which are marked "m22" to designate export sales. Another style is fitted with a folding spike bayonet as well as a machined receiver. Still another style has a stamped receiver, Chinese characters for selector markings, and a folding spike bayonet. All are direct copies of the Soviet model AK-47.

Another variation of the Type 56 was the Type 56-1, which featured prominent rivets on a folding metal butt. No bayonet. Other variants of the Type 56-1 are fitted with a folding spike bayonet and folding metal buttstock. The Type 56-2 has a skeleton tubular stock which folds to the right side of the receiver with no bayonet. There is also the Type 56-C with plastic furniture, side folding butt with cheekpiece, and improved sights with no bayonet.

NOTE: *Type 56 rifles manufactured by China North Industries (NORINCO) will have stamped on the left side of the receiver the number "66" in a triangle.*

▶ **Pre-1968**

EXC.	V.G.	FAIR
32500	30000	28000

▶ **Pre-1986 conversions**

EXC.	V.G.	FAIR
15000	14000	13000

■ CHINESE TYPE 56 (AK CLONE SEMI-AUTOMATIC VERSIONS)

Imported from China in semi-automatic versions and built by Poly Tech and Norinco in different styles and configurations, some of which are listed below.

▶ **Milled Receiver—Poly Tech**

EXC.	V.G.	GOOD	FAIR	POOR
1500	1200	800	N/A	N/A

▶ **Stamped Receiver—Poly Tech**

EXC.	V.G.	GOOD	FAIR	POOR
1100	800	500	N/A	N/A

▶ **Stamped Receiver—Norinco**

EXC.	V.G.	GOOD	FAIR	POOR
950	700	450	N/A	N/A

NOTE: *For folding stock version add 20 percent.*

■ CHINESE TYPE 79

A Chinese copy of the Soviet Dragunov SVD sniper rifle.

EXC.	V.G.	GOOD	FAIR	POOR
3000	2500	1500	N/A	N/A

■ CZECHOSLOVAKIAN MODEL ZH29

Introduced in 1929, this semi-automatic rifle was designed by Emmanuel Holek of CZ at Brno. It is chambered for the 7.92x57mm cartridge and is fitted with a 21.5" barrel with aluminum cooling jacket. Fitted with a bayonet lug. The detachable box magazine has a 10- or 25 round capacity. Weight is about 10 lbs. Exported to Thailand and Ethiopia. Very rare.

EXC.	V.G.	GOOD	FAIR	POOR
13500	10500	7500	—	—

■ CZECHOSLOVAKIAN MODEL ZK420S

Chambered for the 7.92x57mm cartridge this rifle was first introduced in 1942 but did not appear in its final form until 1946. It was also offered in 7mm, .30-06, and 7.5mm Swiss. This was a gas operated semi-automatic rifle with 21" barrel and upper handguard. The detachable magazine has a 10 round capacity. Front sight is hooded. Rear sight is notched tangent with ramp. Weight is about 10 lbs. Not adopted by Czech military but tested by many countries. Built by CZ Brno in limited numbers. Very rare.

EXC.	V.G.	GOOD	FAIR	POOR
10500	9000	8000	—	—

■ CZECHOSLOVAKIAN MODEL 52

Chambered for 7.62x45 caliber, this gas operated semi-automatic rifle is fitted with a 20.5" barrel. This model has a full stock with pistol grip. Folding non-detachable bayonet. Hooded front sight and notched tangent rear sight with ramp. Detachable box magazine with 10 round capacity. Weight is about 9.7 lbs. First produced in 1952.

EXC.	V.G.	GOOD	FAIR	POOR
500	400	350	275	225

■ CZECHOSLOVAKIAN MODEL 52/57

Similar to the Model 52 except chambered for the 7.62x39 cartridge.

EXC.	V.G.	GOOD	FAIR	POOR
600	500	425	300	250

■ CZECHOSLOVAKIAN VZ58

First produced in 1959, this select fire assault rifle is chambered for the 7.62x39mm Soviet cartridge. Its appearance is similar to an AK-47 but it is an entirely different design. It is gas operated but the bolt is locked to the receiver by a vertically moving block similar to the Walther P-38 pistol. Early rifles were fitted with a plastic fixed stock while later rifles used a folding metal stock. Barrel length is 16". Rate of fire is about 800 rounds per minute. Weight is approximately 7 lbs. Production ceased in 1980. Made at CZ Brno and Povaske Strojarne. The two versions of this gun are designated the VZ58P with fixed stock and the VZ58V for metal folding stock.

▶ **Pre-1968**

EXC.	V.G.	FAIR
18000	15000	12000

▶ **Czechoslovakian VZ 58 semi-automatic (new production)**

Limited production by Ohio Ordnance Works. Built from original parts on a U.S.-made semi-automatic receiver.

EXC.	V.G.	GOOD
1500	1250	N/A

■ EAST GERMAN MPIK

A copy of the AK-47 without a cleaning rod.

EXC.	V.G.	GOOD	FAIR	POOR
N/A	N/A	N/A	N/A	N/A

■ EAST GERMAN MPIKS

A copy of the AKS without cleaning rod.

EXC.	V.G.	GOOD	FAIR	POOR
N/A	N/A	N/A	N/A	N/A

■ EAST GERMAN MPIKM

A copy of the AKM with a cleaning rod. Early models used wooden stocks while later ones used plastic. Not fitted with a muzzle compensator.

EXC.	V.G.	GOOD	FAIR	POOR
N/A	N/A	N/A	N/A	N/A

■ EAST GERMAN MPIKMS

Copy of a AKMS without shaped muzzle.

EXC.	V.G.	GOOD	FAIR	POOR
N/A	N/A	N/A	N/A	N/A

■ EAST GERMAN KKMPI69

A version of the MPiKM without the gas cylinder. Chambered for the .22 caliber Long Rifle cartridge and used as a training rifle.

EXC.	V.G.	GOOD	FAIR	POOR
N/A	N/A	N/A	N/A	N/A

■ EGYPTIAN FABRIQUE NATIONAL MODEL 1949 OR SAFN 49

A gas-operated semi-automatic rifle chambered for 7.92mm. It has a 23" barrel and military-type sights. The fixed magazine holds 10 rounds. Egyptian crest on top of receiver.

EXC.	V.G	GOOD	FAIR	POOR
800	650	450	300	250

NOTE: *Many Egyptian FN 1949s were restocked and reblued by Century Arms in the early 1990s. The new stock is a light colored wood that is stained to resemble walnut. Brass or plastic buttplate. Deduct 25 percent for a restocked rifle.*

■ EGYPTIAN HAKIM

A semi-automatic rifle chambered in 8x57mm Mauser. It has a 24 inch barrel that ends with a large recoil compensator. 10 round detachable magazine. This is a copy of the Swedish AG-42b rifle and was designed with the help of Swedish engineers. Made at the Maadi factory. Many were imported in the late 1980s.

EXC.	V.G.	GOOD	FAIR	POOR
550	450	400	300	200

■ EGYPTIAN HAKIM TRAINING RIFLE .22LR

A semi-automatic rifle chambered in .22LR that is patterned after the Hakim. Marked "Made in Italy." A few came in with the regular Hakims.

EXC.	V.G.	GOOD	FAIR	POOR
500	450	400	300	200

■ EGYPTIAN RASHID

This is a native Egyptian design; basically a scaled-down Hakim chambered in 7.62x39mm. It uses a 10 round detachable magazine. A folding bayonet is attached to the barrel, similar to the Soviet SKS.

About 8000 were made in the 1960s. Some were imported to the U.S. in the 1990s.

EXC.	V.G.	GOOD	FAIR	POOR
700	550	475	350	250

■ EGYPTIAN AKM

Maadi semi-automatic, pre-1994

A close copy of the Soviet AKM series. Chambered in 7.62x39mm. Two semi-automatic versions have been imported to the U.S. One was the first semi-automatic Kalashnikov offered on the U.S. market. These appeared in the early 1980s and were imported by Steyr.

EXC.	V.G.	GOOD	FAIR	POOR
1250	950	800	—	—

■ EGYPTIAN MAADI SEMI-AUTOMATIC, SPORTER

The second was imported after passage of the 1994 "assault weapons" law and had a thumbhole sporter type stock installed to comply with the terms of that law. The importer called these the MISR. (Maadi Industries Sporting Rifle).

EXC.	V.G.	GOOD	FAIR	POOR
600	500	400	—	—

■ FINNISH VALMET M62

Based on the third model AK-47 but with internal differences built by Valmet. SAKO also built many of these rifles. Machined receiver. Perforated plastic forend and handguard. Tube butt. Barrel length is 16.5". Magazine is 30 rounds. Rate of fire is about 650 rounds per minute. Weight is about 9 lbs. Production in Finland began in 1965. Rifles produced from 1965 to 1969 were designated "M 62 PT." PT stands for day sight. In 1969 Model 62s were produced with folding night sights. Beginning in 1972 these night sights were fitted with tritium inserts.

NOTE: *There are a number of different versions of this rifle: the M62-76–a Finnish AKM; the M62-76M plastic stock; M62-76P wood stock; M62-76T tubular steel folding stock.*

▶ Pre-1968

EXC.	V.G.	FAIR	
N/A	N/A		N/A

▶ Pre-1986 conversions of semi-automatic model

EXC.	V.G.	FAIR
12000	9500	N/A

■ FINNISH VALMET M62S

A semi-automatic version of the M62 imported for sale in the U.S. by Interarms. Offered in both 7.62x39mm and 5.56x45mm.

NIB	EXC.	V.G.	GOOD	FAIR	POOR
3000	2800	2300	900	750	500

■ FINNISH VALMET M71

A different version of the M62 with solid plastic butt and rear sight in front of chamber. Sheet metal receiver. Chambered for the 7.62x39mm and the 5.56x45mm cartridges. Weight reduced to 8 lbs.

▶ Pre-1968

EXC.	V.G.	FAIR	
N/A	N/A	N/A	N/A

▶ Pre-1986 conversions of semi-automatic version

EXC.	V.G.	FAIR
12000	9500	N/A

■ FINNISH VALMET M71S

NIB	EXC.	V.G.	GOOD	FAIR	POOR
1350	1000	850	650	450	300

■ FINNISH VALMET M76

This model has a number of fixed or folding stock options. It is fitted with a 16.3" barrel and has a magazine capacity of 15, 20, or 30 rounds. Its rate of fire is 700 rounds per minute. It is chambered for the 7.62x39mm Soviet cartridge or the 5.56x45mm cartridge. Weight is approximately 8 lbs. Marked "valmet jyvakyla m78" on the right side of the receiver. Produced from 1978 to 1986. There are a total of 10 variants of this model.

▶ Pre-1968

EXC.	V.G.	FAIR
N/A	N/A	N/A

▶ Pre-1986 conversions of semi-automatic version

EXC.	V.G.	FAIR
12000	9000	N/A

NOTE: *For rifles in 7.62x39mm caliber add a 20 percent premium. For rifles chambered for .308 caliber deduct $2,500.*

■ FINNISH MODEL 78 (SEMI-AUTOMATIC)

As above, in 7.62x51mm, 7.62x39mm, or .223 with a 24.5" heavy barrel, wood stock, and integral bipod. Semi-automatic-only version.

NIB	EXC.	V.G.	GOOD	FAIR	POOR
1750	1350	1000	850	600	300

■ FRENCH MAS 49

Introduced in 1949, this model is a 7.5x54mm gas-operated semi-automatic rifle with a 22.6" barrel and full-length walnut stock. It has a grenade launcher built into the front sight. Fitted with a 10 round magazine. No bayonet fittings. Weight is about 9 lbs.

EXC.	V.G.	GOOD	FAIR	POOR
600	500	425	275	225

■ FRENCH MAS 1949/56

This model is a modification of the Model 49. It is fitted with a 20.7" barrel. Principal modification is with NATO standard grenade launcher. A special grenade sight is also fitted. This model has provisions to fit a bayonet. Weight is about 8.5 lbs. Many were imported in the 1990's and are in unissued condition.

EXC.	V.G.	GOOD	FAIR	POOR
450	375	300	225	175

■GERMAN MODEL G 41 RIFLE(M)

First produced in 1941. Built by Mauser (code S42). Not a successful design and very few of these rifles were produced. These are extremely rare rifles today. Chambered for the 7.92mm Mauser cartridge. semi-automatic gas operated with rotating bolt. It was full stocked with a 10 round box magazine. Barrel length is 21.5" and weight is about 11 lbs. The total produced of this model is estimated at 20,000 rifles.

EXC.	V.G.	GOOD	FAIR	POOR
9500	8000	6500	4000	1800

■GERMAN MODEL G 41(W)

Similar to the above model but designed by Walther and produced by "duv" (Berlin-Lubeck Machine Factory) in 1941. This rifle was contracted for 70,000 units in 1942 and 1943. Correct examples will command a premium price.

EXC.	V.G.	GOOD	FAIR	POOR
7500	5000	4000	3000	1500

■GERMAN MODEL G 43(W) (K43)

An improved version of the G 41(W), introduced in 1943, with a modified gas system that was the more typical gas and piston design. Built by Carl Walther (code "ac"). Full stocked with full-length handguard. Wood or plastic stock. Receiver has a dovetail for telescope sight on the right side. Barrel length is 22" and magazine capacity is 10 rounds. Weight is approximately 9.5 lbs. It is estimated that some 500,000 of these rifles were produced. Used by German sharpshooters during World War II and also by the Czech army after WWII.

EXC.	V.G.	GOOD	FAIR	POOR
2000	1750	1000	800	500

■GERMAN MODEL G 43(W) (K43) SNIPER RIFLE

A G-43 or K-43 issued with a ZF-4 scope and mount.

EXC.	V.G.	GOOD	FAIR	POOR
6000	5000	4000	3000	2000

■GERMAN MODEL FG 42 (FALLSCHIRMJAGER GEWEHR)

This select fire 7.92x57mm rifle was adopted by the Luftwaffe for its airborne troops. It was designed to replace the rifle, light machine gun, and sub-machine gun. It incorporates a number of features including: straight line stock and muzzle brake, re-duced recoil mechanism, closed-bolt semi-auto-matic fire, and open-bolt full-auto fire. Rate of fire is about 750 rounds per minute. It had a mid-barrel bipod on early (1st Models, Type "E") models and front mounted barrel bipod on later (2nd Models, Type "G") models. Barrel attachment for pike-style bayonet. First Models were fitted with steel butt-stocks, sharply raked pistol grips, and 2nd Models with wooden stocks and more vertical pistol grips. The 20 round magazine is left side mounted. Fitted with a 21.5" barrel, the rifle weighs about 9.5 lbs. This breech mechanism was to be used years later by the U.S. in its M60 machine gun.

▶ Pre-1968

EXC.	V.G.	FAIR
45000	35000	25000

NOTE: *For rifles fitted with original German FG 42 scopes add between $5,000 and $10,000 depending on model. Consult an expert prior to a purchase.*

■ HUNGARIAN AKM-63

A close copy of the AKM but with plastic furniture. Fitted with a vertical grip under the forend. Weighs about 1/2 lb. less than the Russian AKM.

▶ Pre-1968

EXC.	V.G.	FAIR
18000	15000	13000

▶ Pre-1986 conversions of semi-automatic model

EXC.	V.G.	FAIR
8000	7000	600

■ HUNGARIAN AKM-63 SEMI-AUTOMATIC COPY

This semi-automatic version of the AKM-63 is in a pre-ban (1994) configuration.

EXC.	V.G.	GOOD	FAIR	POOR
1000	850	750	—	—

NOTE: *Add 20 percent for folding stock (AMD-65-style).*

■ HUNGARIAN AMD-65

This model is an AKM-63 with a 12.5" barrel, two-port muzzle brake, and a side folding metal butt. Rate of fire is about 600 rounds per minute. Weight is approximately 7 lbs.

▶ Pre-1968

EXC.	V.G.	FAIR
25000	22500	20000

▶ Pre-1986 conversion of semi-automatic version

EXC.	V.G.	FAIR
15000	13000	11000

■ HUNGARIAN NGM

This assault rifle is the Hungarian version of the AK-74 chambered for the 5.56x45mm cartridge. Fitted with a 16.25" barrel. Magazine capacity is a 30 round box type. Rate of fire is about 600 rounds per minute. Weight is approximately 7 lbs.

▶ Pre-1968

EXC.	V.G.	FAIR
N/A	N/A	N/A

■ IRAQI TABUK

This model is a copy of the Soviet AKM. An export version was built in 5.56mm.

EXC.	V.G.	GOOD	FAIR	POOR
N/A	N/A	N/A	N/A	N/A

■ ITALIAN BREDA MODEL PG

Chambered for the 7x57mm rimless cartridge, this is a gas operated self-loading rifle with an 18" barrel and 20 round detachable box maga-zine. The particular rifle was made by Beretta for Costa Rica and is marked "GOBIERNO DE COSTA RICA," with the date 1935 and Roman numerals XIII. Weight was about 11.5 lbs. Fitted for a Costa Rican Mauser bayonet. Very rare. Price listed is the author's guess only. None found on the market.

EXC.	V.G.	GOOD	FAIR	POOR
2500	2000	1500	1000	500

■ ITALIAN BERETTA MODEL BM59-SELECT FIRE ASSAULT RIFLE

This select fire rifle closely resembles the U.S. M1 Garand rifle. Chambered for the 7.62x51mm car-tridge, it is fitted with a 19" barrel and 20 round magazine. It has a rate of fire of 750 rounds per minute. Weight is about 10 lbs. Marked "p beretta bm59" on the top rear of the receiver. Produced from 1961 to 1966. This rifle did see service in the Italian army. There are a number of variations to this rifle, including the BM59 Alpini with folding stock short forearm and bipod for use by Alpine troops, and the BM59 Parachutist Rifle with 18" barrel, folding stock, and detachable muzzle brake (the Italians referred to it as a Tri-Comp).

▶ Pre-1968

EXC.	V.G.	FAIR
8500	7000	5000

▶ Pre-1986 conversions of semi-automatic version

EXC.	V.G.	FAIR
5500	4250	N/A

▶ Italian Beretta AR70/.223 Select Fire

Assault Rifle

Chambered for the 5.56x45mm cartridge, this select fire rifle was fitted with a 17.5" barrel and a 30 round magazine. Most were fitted with a solid buttstock while others were fitted with a folding stock. Weight was about 8.3 lbs. Marked "p beretta ar 70/223 made in italy" on the left side of the receiver. This rifle was not widely adopted. Produced from 1972 to 1980.

▶ **Pre-1968 (Rare)**

EXC.	V.G.	FAIR
12000	8000	8000

▶ **Pre-1986 conversions of semi-automatic version**

EXC.	V.G.	FAIR
10000	7500	5000

■ ITALIAN BERETTA SC 70 SELECT FIRE ASSAULT RIFLE

Similar to the AR 70 and chambered for the 5.56x45mm cartridge. It feeds from a 30 round magazine. The SC 70 has a folding stock and is fitted with a 17.5" barrel. Weight is about 8.8 lbs. The SC 70 short carbine also has a folding stock and is fitted with a 13.7" barrel. Weight is about 8.3 lbs. Both of these rifles are still in production and used by the Italian army since approved for service in 1990.

▶ **Pre-1968**

EXC.	V.G.	FAIR
12000	9500	8500

▶ **Pre-1986 conversions of semi-automatic version**

EXC.	V.G.	FAIR
10000	8000	6500

■ ITALIAN R-70

A .223 caliber, semi-automatic rifle with a 17.7" barrel, adjustable diopter sights, and an 8- or 30-shot magazine. Black epoxy finish with a synthetic stock. Weight is approximately 8.3 lbs.

NIB	EXC.	V.G.	GOOD	FAIR	POOR
2500	2200	1900	1500	1000	—

■ ITALIAN BM-59 STANDARD GRADE

A gas-operated semi-automatic rifle with detachable box magazine. Chambered for .308 cartridge. Walnut stock. Barrel length is 19.3" with muzzle brake. Magazine capacity is 5, 10, or 20 rounds. Weight is about 9.5 lbs.

NIB	EXC.	V.G.	GOOD	FAIR	POOR
2200	1700	1200	700	400	—

■ MEXICAN MODEL 1908 & MODEL 1915

Firearms designed by Manuel Mondragon were produced on an experimental basis first at St. Chamond Arsenal in France and later at SIG in Neuhausen, Switzerland. The latter company was responsible for the manufacture of the two known production models: the Model 1908 and 1915.

The Model 1908 Mondragon semi-automatic rifle holds the distinction of being the first self-loading rifle to be issued to any armed forces. Only about 400 of these rifles were delivered to the Mexican army in 1911 when the revolution broke out. The rifle was chambered for the 7x57mm Mauser cartridge and featured a 24.5" barrel. It has an 8 round box magazine. Weight is about 9.5 lbs. SIG had several thousand of these rifles left after the Mexicans were unable to take delivery. When WWI got under way the Swiss firm sold the remaining stocks to Germany. These rifles were called the Model 1915 and they were all identical to the Model 1908 except for the addition of a 30 round drum magazine.

EXC.	V.G.	GOOD	FAIR	POOR
7500	6000	4500	2750	1500

■ NORTH KOREAN TYPE 58

This model is a copy of the Soviet AK-47 solid receiver without the finger grooves on the forearm.

▶ **Pre-1968**

EXC.	V.G.	FAIR
20000	11000	8500

▶ **Pre-1986 manufacture with new receiver or re-weld**

EXC.	V.G.	FAIR
5500	5000	4500

■ M NORTH KOREAN TYPE 68

This is a copy of the Soviet AKM-S with lightening holes drilled into the folding butt.

EXC.	V.G.	GOOD	FAIR	POOR
N/A	N/A	N/A	N/A	N/A

■ POLISH KBKG MODEL 1960 OR PMK-DGM AND PMKM

All of these rifles are copies of AK-47 variations. Both the PMK and PMKM are sometimes equipped with grenade launchers fitted to the muzzle.

▶ **Pre-1968**

EXC.	V.G.	FAIR
30000	27500	25000

■ ROMANIAN SKS

A Romanian-manufactured version of the Russian rifle. Some were imported in the 1990s. Usually found in well-used condition.

EXC.	V.G.	GOOD	FAIR	POOR
400	350	275	200	150

■ ROMANIAN AK-47 (SEMI-AUTOMATIC VERSION)

Romanian copy of the Soviet AK-47. Current importation. Scope rail on left side of receiver. Has a SVD type stock made from laminated wood.

EXC.	V.G.	GOOD	FAIR	POOR
400	300	250	—	—

■ ROMANIAN AKM

Copy of the Soviet AKM except for a noticeable curved-front vertical foregrip formed as part of the forend.

▶ **Pre-1968**

EXC.	V.G.	FAIR
8500	8000	7500

■ ROMANIAN AKM-R

This is a compact version of the Soviet AKM with an 8" barrel and side-folding metal butt. Magazine capacity is 20 rounds. Chambered for the 7.62x39mm cartridge. Rate of fire is about 600 rounds per minute. Weight is approximately 7 lbs.

▶ **Pre-1968**

EXC.	V.G.	FAIR
25000	20000	17500

■ ROMANIAN AK-74

Similar to the Soviet rifle in 5.45x39mm. Current importation. Scope rail on left side of receiver. Has a SVD type stock made from laminated wood. Also offered in 5.56mm/.223.

EXC.	V.G.	GOOD	FAIR	POOR
400	300	250	—	—

■ SOVIET M1938 RIFLE (SVT)

A 7.62x54Rmm caliber gas-operated semi-automatic or select fire rifle with a 24" barrel with muzzle break and 10-shot magazine (15 rounds in select fire). Cleaning rod in stock. Blued with a two-piece hardwood stock extending the full-length of the rifle. Upper handguard is 3/4 length of barrel. Weight is about 8.5 lbs. Manufactured from 1938 to 1940. Approximately 150,000 of these rifles were manufactured.

EXC.	V.G.	GOOD	FAIR	POOR
2000	1700	1200	750	500

NOTE: *Add 300 percent for sniper variation with scope.*

■ SOVIET M1940 RIFLE (SVT)

An improved semi-automatic version of the M1938 with half stock and half-length slotted handguard with a sheet metal handguard and muzzle brake. Ten round magazine. Weight is about 8.5 lbs. Approximately 2,000,000 were produced.

CAUTION: *All Tokarev SVT carbines (18.5" barrel) encountered with "SA" (Finnish) markings were altered to carbine configuration by their importer and have little collector value. It is believed that few, perhaps 2,000, SVT 40 carbines were ever*

made by the USSR.

EXC.	V.G.	GOOD	FAIR	POOR
850	700	600	350	250

NOTE: *Add 300 percent for Sniper variation with scope.*

■ SOVIET SVD DRAGUNOV SNIPER RIFLE

This model, developed as a replacement for the Mosin-Nagant Model 1891/30 Sniper rifle, was introduced in 1963. It is chambered for the 7.62x54R cartridge. It is fitted with a 24.5" barrel with prong-style flash hider and has a skeleton stock with cheek rest and slotted forearm. Semi-automatic with an action closely resembling the AK series of rifles. A PSO-1 telescope sight with illuminated reticle is supplied with the rifle from the factory. This sight is fitted to each specific rifle. Magazine capacity is 10 rounds. Weight is about 9.5 lbs.

EXC.	V.G.	GOOD	FAIR	POOR
4000	3500	3000	—	—

■ SOVIET SIMONOV AVS-36

First built in Russia in 1936, this rifle is chambered for the 7.62x54R Soviet cartridge. Fitted with a 24.3" barrel with muzzle brake and a 20 round magazine. This automatic rifle has a rate of fire of 600 rounds per minute. It weighs 9.7 lbs. Production ceased in 1938.

▶ **Pre-1968**

EXC.	V.G.	FAIR
10000	9000	8000

■ SOVIET SIMONOV SKS

Introduced in 1946 this 7.62x39mm semi-automatic rifle is fitted with a 20.5" barrel and 10-shot fixed magazine. Blued with oil finished stock and half-length upper handguard. It has a folding blade-type bayonet that folds under the barrel and forearm. Weight is about 8.5 lbs. This rifle was the standard service arm for most Eastern bloc countries prior to the adoption of the AK-47. This rifle was also made in Romania, East Germany, Yugoslavia, and China. Price listed if for Russian made SKS only. See each country for other SKS pricing.

EXC.	V.G.	GOOD	FAIR	POOR
400	325	275	225	150

■ SOVIET AVTOMAT KALASHNIKOV AK-47

Designed by Mikhail Kalashnikov and first produced in 1947, the Russian AK-47 is chambered for the 7.62x39mm cartridge and operates on a closed bolt principal. Select fire. The standard model is fitted with a 16" barrel and a fixed beech or birch stock. Early rifles have no bayonet fittings. Magazine capacity is 30 rounds. Rate of fire is 700 rounds per minute. Rear sight is graduated to 800 meters. The bolt and carrier are bright steel. Weight is 9.5 lbs. Markings are located on top rear of receiver. This model was the first line rifle for Warsaw Pact. The most widely used assault rifle in the world and still in extensive use throughout the world.

▶ **Pre-1968**

EXC.	V.G.	FAIR
33000	30000	28000

▶ **Pre-1986 manufacture with new receiver or re-weld**

EXC.	V.G.	FAIR
15000	13000	11000

■ SOVIET AK-S

A variation of the AK rifle is the AK-S. Introduced in 1950, this rifle features a folding steel buttstock which rests under the receiver.

▶ **Pre-1968**

EXC.	V.G.	FAIR
33000	30000	28000

▶ **Pre-1986 manufacture with new receiver or re-weld**

EXC.	V.G.	FAIR
15000	13000	11000

■ SOVIET AKM

This variation of the AK-47, introduced in 1959, can be characterized by a small indentation on the receiver above the magazine. Pressed steel receiver with a parkerized bolt and carrier. Laminated wood furniture and plastic grips. The forend on the AKM is a beavertail-style. The rear sight is graduated to 1,000 meters. Barrel length and rate of fire are the same as the AK-47 rifle. Several other internal production changes were made as well. Model number is located on the top rear of the receiver. Weight is approximately 8.5 lbs.

▶ **Pre-1968**

EXC.	V.G.	FAIR
38000	36000	34000

▶ **Pre-1986 manufacture with new receiver or re-weld**

EXC.	V.G.	FAIR
15000	13000	11000

■ SOVIET AKM-S

In 1960 the AKM-S was introduced which featured a steel folding buttstock as seen on the AK-S. Weight is approximately 8 lbs.

▶ **Pre-1968**

EXC.	V.G.	FAIR
38000	36000	34000

▶ **Pre-1986 manufacture with new receiver or re-weld**

EXC.	V.G.	FAIR
15000	13000	11000

■ SOVIET AK-74 ASSAULT RIFLE

Similar to the AK-47 but chambered for the 5.45x39mm cartridge. Magazine capacity is 30 rounds. Barrel length is 16.35". Select fire with semi-auto, full auto, and 3-shot burst. Weight is about 8.9 lbs. Rate of fire is approximately 650 to 700 rounds per minute.

NOTE: *There are no known original Soviet transferable examples in the U.S. Prices below are for pre-1986 conversions only using AKM receiver and original parts.*

▶ **Pre-1968**

EXC.	V.G.	FAIR
N/A	N/A	N/A

▶ **Pre-1986 manufacture with new receiver or re-weld**

EXC.	V.G.	FAIR
15000	13000	11000

▶ **Soviet AK-74 (Semi-automatic only)**

Introduced in 1974, this rifle is chambered for a smaller caliber, the 5.45x39.5mm, than the original AK-47 series. It is fitted with a 16" barrel with muzzle brake and has a 30 round plastic magazine. The buttstock is wooden. Weight is approximately 8.5 lbs.

In 1974 a folding stock version was called the AKS-74, and in 1980 a reduced caliber version of the AKM-SU called the AK-74-SU was introduced. No original military AK-74s are known to exist in this country.

EXC.	V.G.	GOOD	FAIR	POOR
N/A	—	—	—	—

■ SWEDISH LJUNGMAN AG-42B

Designed by Eril Eklund and placed in service with the Swedish military in 1942—less than a year after it was designed. The rifle is a direct gas-operated design with no piston or rod. It is chambered for the 6.5mm cartridge and has a 24.5" barrel with a 10 round detachable magazine. This rifle has military-type sights and a full-length stock and handguard held on by barrel bands. Rear sight is graduated from 100 to 700 meters. There are provisions for a bayonet. There is also an Egyptian version of this rifle known as the "Hakim." The U.S. AR-15 rifles use the same type of gas system.

EXC.	V.G.	GOOD	FAIR	POOR
750	600	500	350	250

■ SWISS SIG AMT

This is a semi-automatic rifle chambered for the 7.62 NATO cartridge. Fitted with a 19" barrel and wooden buttstock and forearm. Folding bipod standard. Box magazine capacity is 5, 10, or 20 rounds. Weight is about 10 lbs. Built from 1960 to 1974.

NIB	EXC.	V.G.	GOOD	FAIR	POOR
4500	3850	3250	2500	1500	1000

■ SWISS SIG PE57
Similar to the above but chambered for the 7.5x55 Swiss cartridge.

NIB	EXC.	V.G.	GOOD	FAIR	POOR
4500	4100	3500	2700	1700	1300

■ SWISS BERN STG 51 ASSAULT RIFLE
Developed after the end of World War II; the Swiss wanted their own version of a true assault rifle. Waffenfabrik Bern was one of the companies involved in this project. The result was the Stg 51 first built in 1951. This rifle was chambered for the 7.5mm short cartridge, a special cartridge made specifically for this rifle and no longer produced. The rifle is select fire and does so in both models in closed-bolt position. A 30 round box magazine supplies the gun that has a rate of fire of about 800 rounds per minute. The barrel is 22.5" in length and is fitted with a muzzle brake/flash suppressor. A mid-barrel bipod is fitted just ahead of the forend. Weight is approximately 10.5 lbs.

A second model of this rifle was also produced with internal modifications and some small external differences. Both models were issued to the Swiss army, most likely on a trial basis. Extremely rare.

NOTE: *The first model of this rifle will interchange some parts with the German FG 42. The second model will interchange all of its parts with the German FG 42.*

▶ **Bern Stg 51 (First Model)**
PRE-1968

EXC.	V.G.	FAIR
75000+	—	—

▶ **Bern Stg 51 (Second Model)**
PRE-1968

EXC.	V.G.	FAIR
75000+	—	—

■ SWISS BERN STG 54 (STURMGEWEHR W+F 1954)
Introduced in 1954 and chambered for the 7.5mm cartridge, this assault rifle is fitted with a 28.4" barrel including muzzle brake. Weight is approximately 11 lbs. Rate of fire is about 800 rounds per minute. Select fire. Magazine capacity is 30 rounds. Fitted with a bipod. This was an experimental model and it was produced in a number of different variants. Extremely rare.

▶ **Pre-1968**
Too Rare To Price.

■ SWISS SIG STGW 57 ASSAULT RIFLE
This rifle is a select fire chambered for the 7.5x55mm Swiss cartridge. Barrel length is 23". Box magazine capacity is 24 rounds. Weight is about 12.25 lbs. Adopted by the Swiss army with about 600,000 of these rifles produced between 1957 and 1983. It is based on the German StG 45. The rifle has a pressed steel receiver, folding bipod, wood butt, barrel jacket, and carry handle. The muzzle is designed to act as a grenade launcher and compensator. As with all standard issue Swiss military rifles, this rifle will remain in service for the lifetime of the soldier.

▶ **Pre-1968**

EXC.	V.G.	FAIR
N/A	N/A	N/A

▶ **Pre-1986 manufacture with new receiver or re-weld**

EXC.	V.G.	FAIR
22000	20000	18000

■ SWISS SIG 550
This semi-automatic rifle is chambered for .223 cartridge and fitted with an 18" barrel.

NIB	EXC.	V.G.	GOOD	FAIR	POOR
9000	7000	5500	3000	—	—

■ SIG 551
▶ **Same as above but fitted with a 16" barrel.**

NIB	EXC.	V.G.	GOOD	FAIR	POOR
9500	7500	6500	4000	—	—

■ SWISS SIG SG510-4
There are actually four different versions of this rifle. This version fires the 7.62x51mm cartridge and is fitted with a 19.7" barrel. A military version, adopted by the Swiss army, is called the Stgw 57(510-1). Magazine capacity is 20 rounds. Weight is 9.3 lbs. Rate of fire is 600 rounds per minute. Produced from 1957 to 1983. Markings are on left rear of receiver.

▶ **Pre-1968 (Rare)**

EXC.	V.G.	FAIR
N/A	N/A	N/A

▶ **Pre-1986 manufacture with new receiver or re-weld**

EXC.	V.G.	FAIR
20000	18000	16000

■ SWISS SIG 530-1
This rifle is a scaled-down version of the Stgw 57 assault rifle chambered for the 5.56x45mm cartridge. Operated by a gas piston system instead of a delayed blowback operation. Receiver is pressed steel with synthetic butt and forend. Barrel is 18" in length with compensator and grenade launcher rings. Magazine capacity is 30 rounds. Weight is about 7.5 lbs. Rate of fire is 600 rounds per minute. There is also a folding stock version of this rifle.

▶ **Pre-1968**

EXC.	V.G.	FAIR
N/A	N/A	N/A

■ SWISS SIG SG540

Designed by the Swiss (SIG) and built in Switzerland, and also built in France by Manurhin beginning in 1977. This 5.56x45mm rifle is in service by a number of African and South American countries. It is fitted with an 18" barrel, 20- or 30 round magazine and has a rate of fire of 800 rounds per minute. It is fitted with a fixed stock. Its weight is 7.8 lbs. Marked "manurhin france sg54x" on right side of receiver. This rifle is still in production. There are also two other variants called the SG542 and SG543.

▶ **Pre-1968**

EXC.	V.G.	FAIR
N/A	N/A	N/A

■ U. S. M1 CARBINE

Introduced in 1941, this is a semi-automatic, gas operated carbine with a 18" barrel and a magazine capacity of 15 or 30 rounds. Half stocked with upper handguard and single barrel band. Bayonet bar located on barrel. Flip up rear sight. Later production has an adjustable sight. Chambered for the .30 U.S. Carbine cartridge. Weight is about 5.25 lbs. Widely used by U.S. military forces during World War II.

NOTE: Prices are for carbines in World War II factory original configuration. Any M1 Carbine with the earliest features such as "I" oiler cut stock, high wood, flip rear sight, and narrow barrel band will bring more than the later variations. Very few M-1 carbines survived the last sixty years with all the original parts. Carbine parts bear unique makers codes. Records were kept that state which coded parts were installed on which makers guns. The information on these codes is available from several sources, including the book listed above. It is common for "matching" carbines to be assembled using the correctly marked parts. It will be up to the buyer to decide weather a "restored" M-1 carbine has the same value as an original specimen. It is frequently impossible to tell if a gun has been re-built using the correct parts or is originally matching.

▶ **Inland**

EXC.	V.G.	GOOD	FAIR	POOR
1500	1200	600	425	350

▶ **Underwood**

Early Underwood cartouche with large square box with WRA over GHD.

EXC.	V.G.	GOOD	FAIR	POOR
1600	1250	600	425	350

▶ **S.G. Saginaw**

EXC.	V.G.	GOOD	FAIR	POOR
1800	1300	600	425	350

▶ **IBM**

EXC.	V.G.	GOOD	FAIR	POOR
1800	1100	600	425	350

▶ **Quality Hardware**

EXC.	V.G.	GOOD	FAIR	POOR
1700	1100	600	425	350

▶ **National Postal Meter**

EXC.	V.G.	GOOD	FAIR	POOR
1800	1100	600	425	350

▶ **Standard Products**

EXC.	V.G.	GOOD	FAIR	POOR
1900	1200	650	450	375

▶ **Rockola**

EXC.	V.G.	GOOD	FAIR	POOR
2000	1400	700	450	375

▶ **Winchester**

EXC.	V.G.	GOOD	FAIR	POOR
2500	1800	900	450	375

▶ **Irwin Pedersen-Rare**

EXC.	V.G.	GOOD	FAIR	POOR
4000	2200	950	650	500

■ U. S. REBUILT M1 CARBINE, ANY MANUFACTURE

Many M-1 carbines offered for sale should be considered to be rebuilt and may have mixed parts from any of the manufacturers. This would be considered a "shooter" by most collectors. This category includes any M-1 carbine that has an import marked barrel. Several thousand carbines were imported from Korea in the late 1980's. These are US. made guns that we gave them during the cold war, they were not made in Korea. Other batches of carbines have been imported from West Germany, Israel and other nations. All post 1986 imports will have an importer stamp on the barrel or receiver. The most common are Blue Sky Productions and Arlington Ordnance. There is no longer a major price difference with the import marked rifles, as this model is so much in demand. Bore condition is the main factor to consider when examining an rebuilt carbine.

EXC.	V.G.	GOOD	FAIR	POOR
700	575	450	350	N/A

■ U. S. M1 CARBINE SNIPER (T-3)

This is an M1 carbine with a M84 scope mounted with forward vertical grip. Used in Korea.

EXC.	V.G.	GOOD	FAIR	POOR
1500	1000	800	500	350

■ U.S. M1A1 PARATROOPER MODEL

The standard U.S. M1 Carbine fitted with a folding stock. Approximately 110,000 were manufactured

by Inland between 1942 and 1945. Weight is about 5.8 lbs. There are three variations of this carbine.

▶ **Variation I**

Earliest variation with flip rear sight, narrow barrel band, and high wood. These were produced in late 1942 and 1943. Carbines in original condition are very rare.

EXC.	V.G.	GOOD	FAIR	POOR
4500	3500	2250	—	—

▶ **Variation II**

Manufactured in 1944 with no bayonet lug and low wood.

EXC.	V.G.	GOOD	FAIR	POOR
3500	2500	1250	—	—

▶ **Variation III**

Manufactured in late 1944 and 1945 with bayonet lug.

EXC.	V.G.	GOOD	FAIR	POOR
3000	2400	1200	—	—

NOTE: *Original jump cases sell for between $150 and $300.*

▶U. S. M1 RIFLE (GARAND) REBUILT RIFLE, ANY MANUFACTURE

Many of the M-1 Garands seen on the market today fit into this category. Value shown is for rifles with a majority of its parts mixed/replaced. Depending on the type of rebuilding that a rifle went through, rifles could be completely disassembled with no attempt to put parts together for the same rifle. Valued mainly for shooting merits. Bore condition, gauging and overall appearance are important factors.

NOTE: *There were some M-1 Garands imported from Korea in the 1990's. These will be import stamped on the barrel. Most are Blue Sky Productions or Arlington Ordnance. These import marked rifles fit in the rebuilt category. There is no longer a major price difference with the import marked rifles, as this model is so much in demand. Bore condition is the main factor to consider when examining an imported rifle.*

EXC.	V.G.	GOOD
900	750	500

NOTE: *Rifles built by Winchester will bring a small premium.*

■ U. S. M1 RIFLE (GARAND) CMP OR DCM RIFLES

The Civilian Marksmanship Program, formerly known as Director of Civilian Marksmanship, is operated by the U.S. government to promote shooting skills. It sells surplus rifles to qualified buyers. CMP M-1 Garands are offered in several grades, currently including some rifles that were used and rebarreled by Denmark. The Danish rifles have a crown mark on the barrel. These rifles should have the correct paperwork and shipping boxes to receive the prices listed. Contact the CMP for current pricing, availability and requirements for purchase. Web site: www.odcmp.com.

EXC.	V.G.	GOOD
1000	800	600

■ U. S. M1 RIFLE (GARAND) NAVY TROPHY RIFLES

The Navy continued to use the M1 rifle as its main rifle far into the 1960s. They were modified to shoot the 7.62x51 NATO (.308 Winchester) round. This was accomplished at first with a chamber insert, and later with new replacement barrels in the NATO caliber. The Navy modified rifles can be found of any manufacture, and in any serial number range. As a general rule, Navy rifles with new barrels are worth more due to their better shooting capabilities. Paperwork and original boxes must accompany these rifles to obtain the values listed.

▶ **U.S.N. Crane Depot rebuild**

EXC.	V.G.	GOOD
1800	1000	900

▶ **AMF rebuild**

EXC.	V.G.	GOOD
1150	1000	900

▶ **H&R rebuild**

EXC.	V.G.	GOOD
1000	900	800

▶ **Springfield Armory Production**

EXC.	V.G.	GOOD
1250	1000	900

■ U. S. M1 RIFLE (GARAND) GAS TRAP SN: C. 81-52000

Values shown for original rifles. Most all were updated to gas port configuration. Look out for reproductions being offered as original rifles! Get a professional appraisal before purchasing.

EXC.	V.G.	GOOD
40000	35000	25000

▶ **Gas Trap/modified to gas port**

These rifles should have many of their early parts. Must be original modifications and not restored.

EXC.	V.G.	GOOD
5000	3500	2500

▶ **Pre-Dec. 7, 1941 gas port production sn: ca 50000-Appx. 410000**

EXC.	V.G.	GOOD	FAIR	POOR
4000	2200	1300	750	650

NOTE: *Rifles built in 1940 in excellent and original condition will bring a premium of $1,500+.*

■ U. S. M1 RIFLE (GARAND) WWII PRODUCTION SN: CA 410000-3880000

▶ **SA/GHS Cartouche**

EXC.	V.G.	GOOD	FAIR	POOR
3500	1500	900	750	500

▶ **U. S. M1 Rifle (Garand) SA/EMF Cartouche**

EXC.	V.G.	GOOD	FAIR	POOR
3200	1500	900	750	500

▶ **U. S. M1 Rifle (Garand) SA/GAW Cartouche**

EXC.	V.G.	GOOD	FAIR	POOR
3100	1500	900	750	500

▶ **U. S. M1 Rifle (Garand) SA/NFR Cartouche**

EXC.	V.G.	GOOD	FAIR	POOR
2900	1200	900	750	500

■ U. S. M1 RIFLE (GARAND) POST WWII PRODUCTION SN: C. 4200000-6099361

▶ **SA/GHS Cartouche**

EXC.	V.G.	GOOD	FAIR	POOR
2800	1200	650	500	400

▶ **National Defense Stamp**

EXC.	V.G.	GOOD	FAIR	POOR
2500	1000	650	500	400

▶ **Very Late 6000000 sn**

EXC.	V.G.	GOOD	FAIR	POOR
2500	1000	650	500	400

■ U. S. M1 RIFLE (GARAND) WINCHESTER PRODUCTION

Winchester produced around 513,000 M1 rifles during WWII. Their first contract was an educational order in 1939. This contract was for 500 rifles and the gauges and fixtures to produce the rifles. Winchester's second contract was awarded during 1939 for up to 65,000 rifles. Winchester M1's are typified by noticeable machine marks on their parts, and did not have the higher grade finish that is found on Springfield Armory production. Watch for fake barrels, and barrels marked "Winchester" which were produced in the 1960s as replacement barrels.

▶ **Winchester Educational Contract sn: 100000-100500**

EXC.	V.G.	GOOD	FAIR	POOR
10000	6000	4500	3000	2000

▶ **Winchester sn: 100501-165000**

Rifles of this serial number range were produced from Jan. 1941 until May 1942.

EXC.	V.G.	GOOD	FAIR	POOR
6500	4500	2000	1500	750

▶ **Winchester sn: 1200000-1380000**

Rifles in this serial number range were produced from May 1942 until Aug. 1943.

EXC.	V.G.	GOOD	FAIR	POOR
4500	2500	1800	1000	750

NOTE: Add a premium of $1,000 for earlier rifles.

▶ **Winchester sn: 2305850-2536493**

Rifles in this serial number range were produced from Aug. 1943 until Jan. 1945.

EXC.	V.G.	GOOD	FAIR	POOR
3000	2000	1250	900	550

NOTE: Add a premium of $500 for earlier rifles.

▶ **Winchester sn: 1601150-1640000**

Rifles in this serial number range were produced from Jan. 1945, until June 1945. These are often referred to as "Win-13's" because of the revision number of the right front receiver leg.

EXC.	V.G.	GOOD	FAIR	POOR
3500	2500	2000	1500	850

■ U. S. M1 RIFLE (GARAND) HARRINGTON & RICHARDSON PRODUCTION

Between 1953 and 1956, Harrington & Richardson produced around 428,000 M1 rifles.

EXC.	V.G.	GOOD	FAIR	POOR
1800	1200	900	500	350

■ U. S. M1 RIFLE (GARAND) INTERNATIONAL HARVESTER CORP. PRODUCTION

Between 1953 and 1956, International Harvester produced around 337,000 M1 rifles. International at several different times during their production purchased receivers from both Harrington & Richardson and Springfield Armory. Always check for Springfield Armory heat lots on the right front receiver leg.

▶ **International Harvester Production**

EXC.	V.G.	GOOD	FAIR	POOR
2200	1500	800	450	350

▶ **International Harvester/with Springfield Receiver (postage stamp)**

EXC.	V.G.	GOOD
2800	1500	900

▶ **International Harvester/with Springfield Receiver (arrow head)**

EXC.	V.G.	GOOD
2800	1500	1000

▶ **International Harvester/with Springfield Receiver (Gap letter)**

EXC.	V.G.	GOOD
2500	1300	900

▶ **International Harvester/with Harrington & Richardson Receiver**

EXC.	V.G.	GOOD
1900	1200	850

■ U. S. M1 RIFLE BRITISH GARANDS (LEND LEASE)

In 1941 and 1942, the U.S. sent a total of 38,000 M1 Garands to England under the Lend Lease program. These rifles were painted with a red band around the front of the handguard with the numerals "30" or "300" in black. The buttstock is stamped with a U.S. Ordnance cartouche and the initials "GHS" under "SA." Most known examples are found in the serial number range 3000000 to 600000. When these rifles were sold and imported back into the U.S., they were stamped with either London or Birmingham proof stamps.

EXC.	V.G.	GOOD	FAIR	POOR
2250	2000	1500	1000	750

■ M1 GARAND CUTAWAY
Used by factories and military armorers to facilitate training.

EXC.	V.G.	GOOD	FAIR	POOR
3000	2500	1000	600	500

NOTE: *For examples with documentation add 300 percent.*

■ YUGOSLAVIAN MODEL 59
This is an exact copy of the Russian SKS made under licence in Yugoslavia by Zastava. Only the markings are different.

EXC.	V.G.	GOOD	FAIR	POOR
350	250	150	125	100

■ YUGOSLAVIAN MODEL 59/66
This is a Yugoslavian copy of the Soviet SKS rifle. The major difference between the two is a gas shut-off valve on the gas cylinder and an integral grenade launcher fitted to the barrel. Recently imported by the thousands.

EXC.	V.G.	GOOD	FAIR	POOR
300	200	150	125	100

■ YUGOSLAVIAN MODEL 64
This is a Yugoslavian copy of the Soviet AK-47, but with a 19.7" barrel with built-in grenade launcher sights that pivots on the barrel.

▶ Pre-1968t

EXC.	V.G.	FAIR
16000	14000	12000

NOTE: *Add 20 percent for folding stock.*

■ YUGOSLAVIAN ZASTAVA M70B1
This Yugoslavian copy of the AK-47 rifle was first produced in 1974. It is chambered for the 7.62x39mm cartridge and is fitted with a 16.2"

barrel. Its rate of fire is 650 rounds per minute. Weight is about 8 lbs. This model features a folding grenade sight behind the front sight. When raised, it cuts off the gas supply to the cylinder redirecting it to the launcher. This is the standard Yugoslav service rifle. Still in production.

▶ Pre-1968

EXC.	V.G.	FAIR
N/A	N/A	N/A

▶ M70B1 (Semi-automatic version)

EXC.	V.G.	GOOD	FAIR	POOR
2350	2150	1850	900	500

■ YUGOSLAVIAN M76 SNIPING RIFLE
This is a copy of a Soviet AKM with a 21.5" barrel and wooden butt. The rifle is fitted with iron sights and a telescope mount. Semi-automatic operation. Chambered for the 8x57mm cartridge. Weight is about 9.5 lbs. Prices listed below are for rifles with correct matching military scope.

EXC.	V.G.	GOOD	FAIR	POOR
2500	2000	1500	—	—

NOTE: *For rifles without scope deduct $1,500. For rifles with commercial scopes but marked M76B deduct $1,000. For rifles in .308 caliber without scope deduct 70 percent.*

■ YUGOSLAVIAN M77B1 (SEMI-AUTOMATIC)
Copy of the Soviet AKM with a fixed wooden butt, straight 20 round magazine, and 16.4" barrel. Weight is about 8.5 lbs. Prices listed are for semi-automatic version.

EXC.	V.G.	GOOD	FAIR	POOR
2250	1650	1100	800	300

■ YUGOSLAVIAN M77 B1 ASSAULT RIFLE
Copy of the Soviet AKM with a fixed wooden butt, straight 20 round magazine, and 16.4" barrel. Rate of fire is about 700 rounds per minute. There are examples in this country chambered for .308 and .223. Weight is about 8.5 lbs.

NOTE: *For rifles chambered for .223 add 75 percent premium.*

▶ Pre-1968

EXC.	V.G.	FAIR
N/A	N/A	N/A